29.95

In
Royal
Service

EDITED BY DUFF HART-DAVIS

In Royal Service

The Letters and Journals of
Sir Alan Lascelles 1920–1936
Volume II

HAMISH HAMILTON
London

HAMISH HAMILTON LTD

Published by the Penguin Group
27 Wrights Lane, London W8 5TZ, England
Viking Penguin Inc, 40 West 23rd Street, New York, New York 10010, USA
Penguin Books Australia Ltd, Ringwood, Victoria, Australia
Penguin Books Canada Ltd, 2801 John Street, Markham, Ontario, Canada L3R 1B4
Penguin Books (NZ) Ltd, 182–190 Wairau Road, Auckland 10, New Zealand

Penguin Books Ltd, Registered Offices: Harmondsworth, Middlesex, England

First published in Great Britain 1989 by
Hamish Hamilton Ltd

Introduction copyright © 1989 by Duff Hart-Davis

1 3 5 7 9 10 8 6 4 2

British Library Cataloguing in Publication Data
Lascelles, *Sir* Alan, *1887–1981*
In Royal Service: Lascelles diaries 2.
1. Great Britain. Social life, ca 1901–1920
Correspondence, diaries, etc.
I. Title   II. Hart-Davis, Duff
941.082′3
ISBN 0-241-12562-6

Photoset by Rowland Phototypesetting Ltd
Bury St Edmunds, Suffolk
Printed by Butler and Tanner Ltd
Frome, Somerset

CONTENTS

ACKNOWLEDGEMENTS

Once again, I am greatly indebted to Lavinia Hankinson and Caroline Erskine, who encouraged me to edit this second volume of their father's papers and helped most generously in preparing the book for publication.

I am grateful to Sir Michael Thomas, Bt., and Lieutenant Colonel the Lord Wigram for permission to quote from their fathers' letters; and to Janet Adam Smith, the Earl of Bessborough, Tana Fletcher, daughter of Tommy's great friend Bunt Goschen, William Fong, Sir Edward Ford, John Grigg and Charles Ritchie for helping collect material.

I should particularly like to thank Elizabeth Bennett, Librarian of the Archives Centre at Churchill College Cambridge, where the Lascelles papers are now housed, and her assistant, Lesley James, for their efficient and cheerful help. I am also indebted for prompt assistance to George F. Henderson, of Queen's University Archives, Kingston, Canada.

The letters from the Prince of Wales are Crown Copyright.

LIST OF
ILLUSTRATIONS

LIST OF ILLUSTRATIONS

Tommy as best man at the wedding of Bunt Goschen and Vivienne de Watteville, 1930. The bridesmaid is Jean Meynell, Bunt's niece.

Lord Bessborough, Governor General of Canada, lays the foundation stone of the new armoury of the Victoria Rifles of Canada in Montreal, June 1933. *(Keystone Collection)*

In his element: Tommy on the Bonaventure river in Canada.

The King is dead: the body of George V lies in state in the chapel at Sandringham, January 1936. *(Popperfoto)*

The former King Edward VIII leaves Windsor Castle after making his Abdication broadcast, December 1936. *(Keystone Collection)*

INTRODUCTION

A selection from the early letters and diaries of Sir Alan Lascelles, published as *End of an Era*, described his life to the age of thirty-three. Now his autobiographical writings take up the story in December 1920, when he became Assistant Private Secretary to the Prince of Wales.

Born in 1887, a nephew of the fifth Earl of Harewood, and known throughout his life as 'Tommy', the author was educated at Marlborough, which he hated, and at Trinity College, Oxford, which he loved; but although endowed with striking good looks, incisive intelligence and a prodigious memory – to say nothing of his distinguished pedigree, wide reading and love of classical music – he had great difficulty finding a career that suited him.

Having twice failed the Foreign Office exam, he half-heartedly became a stockbroker, but soon left the City to travel through South America. When the outbreak of war in 1914 caught him far from home, he hurried back to enlist in the Bedfordshire Yeomanry, and spent most of the next four years in Flanders and France. That terrible experience marked him deeply: one after another his closest friends were killed in the mass slaughter, while he – the most patriotic of men – was condemned by the fact that he was in the cavalry to wait helplessly in reserve. Even so, he was wounded and won the Military Cross.

The Armistice left him still with no clear idea of what he wanted to do, so he signed on as ADC to his brother-in-law Lord Lloyd, who was then Governor of Bombay, and went out to India in March 1919. By then Tommy was thirty-one. For several seasons before the war he had swum unhooked through the giddy whirlpool of London society; his last intention in going to India (he told his father) was to look for a wife. Nevertheless, he found an admirable one there, in

ix

the form of Joan Thesiger, eldest daughter of the Viceroy, Lord Chelmsford, and the couple were married with great pomp in Delhi on 16 March 1920.

Returning to England that summer after a honeymoon in Kashmir, they went to live at No. 6 Seville Street, a house left to Tommy by his uncle and godfather, A. G. C. Liddell. Until his marriage he had been relatively poor, for the Harewood riches had escaped his branch of the family: his great uncle, the second and last Marquis of Clanricarde, who might have presented him with a fortune, in 1916 left almost all his money (some £2.5 million) to Tommy's cousin Harry, Viscount Lascelles. When Tommy got married, however, Harry magnanimously gave him £30,000 (worth perhaps £400,000 at 1988 values), remarking that 'it ought to provide biscuits and margarine if not bread and butter.'

Financial security was welcome, but what Tommy needed above all was a career. To his rescue, on 12 November 1920, came Letty Elcho,[1] one of his closest friends, who brought the news that the Prince of Wales was looking for an assistant private secretary. Within a few days Tommy had clinched the job, and at the beginning of December he set out with the highest hopes to work for the man in whose hands, he felt certain, the future of the Empire lay.

From the start the two got on extremely well. As initial common ground, they shared a passion for horses, and the Prince, who at twenty-seven was nearly seven years the younger, was still going all-out in point-to-point races and the hunting-field, which Tommy by then had more or less given up. Quickly adapting to the royal routine, the new recruit made himself invaluable, not least as a writer of the Prince's speeches.

Tommy looked every inch a courtier. His aristocratic lineage showed in his finely-chiselled features; he was always immaculately turned out, and throughout the period covered by this book he retained an extraordinarily youthful figure: at thirty, forty and even at fifty, he was scarcely less spare and erect that he had been at eighteen. Although 6′ 1″ tall, he weighed no more than ten stone.

For eight years he served Edward at home and abroad, three times travelling with him on long trips overseas – to America and Canada in 1924, to Canada again in 1927, and to East Africa in 1928. As he himself put it, he gave the eight best years of his own life to the job of

---

[1] Lady Violet Manners, eldest daughter of the eighth Duke of Rutland, had in 1911 married Hugo Charteris, later Lord Elcho, who was killed on active service in Egypt in 1916.

trying to make the Prince fit to be King; but gradually he began to despair of accomplishing the task, and in January 1929, when he saw that it was impossible, he resigned.

After two years living at home in the country, he became Secretary to the Earl of Bessborough, Governor-General of Canada; and, when he returned to England late in 1935, he once again, by a strange twist of fate, found himself in royal employment, first as Assistant Private Secretary to George V, and then, after the old King's death in January 1936, to the man of whom he had come to despair, Edward VIII.

In retrospect, Tommy's career seems curiously devoid of motivation: never sure what he wanted to do, he lurched from one opportunity to the next, frequently telling friends that he had had enough of being a private secretary, yet always signing on again in the same capacity. The clue to his career – apparently so aimless – surely lies in his sense of duty, his patriotism, and his regard for the institution of monarchy. Even after his show-down with the Prince of Wales, he devoted the last seventeen years of his working life to royal service.

It could be said that Tommy was the wrong person for the Prince of Wales: that his moral outlook was too severe, his idea of duty too rigid, his code of conduct too unbending, for him to be compatible with such a high-spirited employer. Yet it could equally be said that he was exactly the *right* person for the Prince, and that someone of precisely his calibre, with his powerful intellect and high principles, was needed to shape the future King for his role. Indeed, contemporaries often remarked that, of all the Prince's staff, Tommy had by far the best influence on him; and one has the impression that, if anyone could have made Edward fit to reign, it would have been he.

Although Tommy did not keep a journal during most of the years covered by this book, he sent home vivid descriptions of his travels with the Prince through Africa, America and Canada in letters to family and friends. He wrote with exceptional fluency and precision, hardly ever crossing out a word, and still less often wasting one.

All through his life he acknowledged that the first duty of a private secretary was 'to hold his tongue and his pen', and never while he was in royal service did he dream of making public anything about his work. All the same, he was at heart a writer, prevented from publishing in his own lifetime as much by a deep natural reticence as by the confidential nature of his employment; and in old age, when he looked through his own papers, he added several notes which made it clear that he hoped his view of the Prince of Wales would sometime see the light of day.

In a fascinating sidelight on history, this volume traces the progress of Tommy's disillusionment with 'the most spectacular, the most discussed personality with whom I shall ever be in intimate association.' It also gives graphic glimpses of America, Canada and East Africa in the 1920s; and Tommy's long memorandum of advice to John Buchan, the incoming Governor-General of Canada in 1935, on how to treat Canadians, is a vintage slice of social and political observation.

LONDON
1920–1923

It has been truly said that, although Edward VIII failed as King, he succeeded triumphantly as Prince of Wales. His grand tours of the Empire – Canada in 1919, Australia and New Zealand in 1920, India in 1921–22, and South Africa in 1925 – were all reckoned to have done immense good by showing far-flung peoples how handsome and high-spirited and full of energy was the heir to the British Throne. With his wonderful gift of talking easily to everyone he met, the Prince captured the imagination of distant lands on a scale impossible by any other means before the days of television. Even in India, in 1921–22, when nationalist stirrings led by Mahatma Gandhi sparked off riots in many areas, he scored no small personal success.

At home, the story was the same; and although the dashing young Edward made an odd contrast with his father, the stern and crusty George V, the truth was that between them King and Prince formed an unusually effective royal double act, the first upholding the dignity of the Crown in a traditional fashion which appealed to older subjects, and the second able to communicate with young people, as well as with social classes other than the aristocracy, in a way denied to his father.

It was thus in a period of exceptional royal success that Tommy made his bow to the Prince of Wales at St. James's Palace on 29 November 1920. 'He won me completely,' he wrote in his diary. 'He is the most attractive man I have ever met.'

Members of the family were delighted by his appointment, not least his father-in-law, Lord Chelmsford (still Viceroy), who wrote to Joan from Delhi on 16 December:

My darling Joan, I was immensely interested to hear of Tommy's new adventure. May it prosper! As also your strong financial

1

position – £2,000 a year, I understand. It seems to me that you and Tommy will have probably to give a leg up to your old parents when they return to obscurity!

Tonight we have our first dance in the new ballroom, a great room which Buckingham Palace might envy, and which Tommy's Prince even does not possess.

My best to Tommy, and all best wishes to him in his new job.

Your loving father.

At the beginning of December 1920 Tommy began work as Assistant Private Secretary in York House, the part of St James's Palace which for the past year the Prince had been using as both home and office. As it happened, he found the place in uproar, for the accredited photographer on the tour of Australia and New Zealand earlier that year had stolen a copy of the unofficial diary – packed with scurrilous anecdotes – kept by the Prince's cousin Lord Louis Mountbatten, and had tried to sell it to an American journalist. Now, at the last possible moment, detectives tracked him down to Kettners restaurant in Soho, where a deal was about to be struck.

As the dust from this fracas settled, Tommy fitted himself into a hand-picked team. First among them was Sir Godfrey Thomas,[1] the Private Secretary, whom the Prince had lured away from the fertile recruiting ground of the Foreign Office a year earlier. Then thirty-one, having recently succeeded to his father's baronetcy, dark and good-looking – a bit like the film-star Cary Grant – Thomas usually wore a troubled air, as if he had just been slightly done down; he was much liked and respected, if found by some to be a shade dull.

Tommy got on well with him from the start, and in due course became a close friend; he also formed an excellent relationship with one of the equerries, Captain the Hon. Piers Legh[2] (known as Joey) of the Grenadier Guards. An early riser, a dogged operator, and very slow spoken, Legh was the butt of many jokes: Tommy used to rag him mercilessly, but at the same time was very fond of him. So was he of Rear-Admiral Sir Lionel Halsey,[3] an experienced naval officer and a much older man (then 48) appointed at the direct instigation of the King, and known to all as 'the Old Salt'. Another good friend was

[1] 1889–1968, he had succeeded his father as the tenth baronet in 1919.
[2] 1890–1955.
[3] 1872–1949. He had been third Sea Lord 1917–18 and had commanded the Australian Navy 1918–20.

2

Lieutenant-Colonel Edward Grigg, also a Grenadier, a classical scholar and journalist whom the Prince had taken on as Military Secretary. Finally, there was Colonel (honorary Brigadier-General) G. F. Trotter,[1] always known simply as 'G.', Assistant Comptroller of the Prince's household. Yet another Grenadier, he had lost his right arm in the Boer War, but served again with distinction in the First World War. When the Prince himself, in his memoirs, re-marked that he had 'learned from G. Trotter that life should be lived to the full,' he hinted at the easy relationship that existed between them, even though Trotter was more than twenty years the elder.

These men were Tommy's immediate colleagues; but just at the end of the Mall, in Buckingham Palace, loomed the Olympian figures of Lord Stamfordham,[2] Private Secretary to the King, who had been in royal service for forty years, and his assistant, Clive Wigram,[3] distinguished by his rasping voice, old-fashioned courtesy and irrepressible penchant for sporting metaphors. As Tommy soon found, Wigram was doing his best to introduce a more realistic attitude to the Press, and in general to eliminate some of the more archaic practices by which the Monarchy was still encumbered.

Into this strange new world Tommy plunged with gusto, and his surviving remarks about his employer all reflect the highest admir-ation. To him, at that date, the Prince of Wales was a hero – an inspiring and brilliant leader, the main hope for the future of the Empire. It is perhaps a small indication of the esteem in which the Prince was generally held that, when a metallurgist claimed to have discovered a chemical means of manufacturing gold, it was not to any leading scientific institution, but to York House, that he was directed. For a few days Tommy and his colleagues thought they had in their hands a means of gaining economic control of the whole world – but needless to say the inventor proved a charlatan.

It must have taken Tommy a few months to learn the rudiments of his new job; all the same, it seems strange that he did not travel with the Prince on his tour of India in 1921–22 – for his own year with the Lloyds in Bombay would surely have made him a particularly useful adviser. Perhaps the fact that Joan was pregnant with their first child

[1] 1871–1945. Mentioned in despatches in both the Boer War and the First World War, he had commanded the British Military Mission to the United States 1917–18.

[2] Rt. Hon Arthur John Bigge, 1849–1931, had begun his royal service in 1880; and had been created first Baron Stamfordham in 1911.

[3] 1873–1960, Knighted 1931, created first Baron Wigram, 1935.

contributed to the decision that he should stay at home. Yet the fact that he did by no means cut him off from news of what happened as the tour progressed. His own excellence as a correspondent, combined with the fact that he was now at one of the seats of power in London, encouraged colleagues to send back intimate gossip about particular triumphs and disasters.

Thus in December 1921 Halsey wrote from the Prince of Wales's Camp in Nepal: 'I *must* tell you that George Lloyd [still Governor of Bombay] and your sister [Blanche] were quite splendid, and he was perfectly wonderful with HRH.' When Tommy and Joan's first child, John Frederick, was born on 11 January 1922, news of the event immediately reached the Prince's party. 'My dear Tommy,' wrote Halsey from aboard RJMS *Dufferin en route* from Rangoon to Madras, the very next day, 'This is not going to be a real letter, as I hear everyone has been writing to you, but only a line to say how very delighted I am to hear of the safe arrival of Tommy Mark 2.' The other royal news which sped to the Far East was that Princess Mary, only daughter of the King and Queen, had become engaged to Viscount Lascelles, Tommy's cousin. 'I suppose you are now about to be a member of the Royal Family as a cousin-in-law of Princess Mary,' wrote Halsey. 'We shall have to treat you with terrible respect. No more "Old Chap".'

From Joey Legh came the news that the Prince was 'doing far too much in the way of exercise . . . Probably through sheer exhaustion he becomes fractious and unreasonable at times, and as no one [else] seemed willing, I undertook the unpleasant task of telling him off properly the other night. I must say, he took it in good part.'

Relations among the entourage were harmonious until February; but then, with the recruitment of an outsider, things became less comfortable. The newcomer was Captain Edward Dudley Metcalfe, always known as 'Fruity', one of the Indian army ADCs, whom the Prince retained to look after his horses. 'In my opinion Metcalfe is not *at all* a good thing for HRH,' wrote Halsey from Lahore. 'He is an excellent fellow, always cheery and full of fun, but far, far too weak and hopelessly irresponsible. He is a *wild, wild* Irishman . . . a bad judge of men and other matters.' So began an association which caused the Prince many difficulties over the next few years.

As the royal tourists sweated in the Raj, Tommy helped run the office in York House, living in London and making occasional visits to Sutton Waldron, the family home in Dorset now occupied only by his father. With him – the Hon. Frederick Canning Lascelles, younger brother of the fifth Earl of Harewood – Tommy had a good but never close relationship: F.C.L. had nothing like the intellectual capacity with which nature had endowed his son, and the two were united principally by their passion for hunting and fishing. In letters to other members of the family Tommy habitually referred to his father by the affectionate but faintly-mocking formula of 'The Honble F.', 'The Honourable Frederick', or 'the Old Man'. With his heavy, neatly-trimmed beard, his antique clothes, his habit of banging doors and giving vent to loud utterances, the Honble. Frederick was a real old Tory squire, uninhibitedly philistine and jingoistic. Among his sayings which Tommy treasured were, 'Wagner? I could make as good music as Wagner by slamming my bedroom door,' and 'God made a great mistake when he created foreigners: I've always thought that Frenchmen were pigs and Germans were swine.'

Colleagues apart, Tommy's principal correspondents, now as always, were his sister Helen Maclagan, whom he and other members of the family addressed as 'Whelk', and whose husband Eric was rising through the ranks at the Victoria and Albert Museum to become its Director; Letty Benson (Letty Elcho, now married again, to Guy Benson); and the journalist and author John Gore, with whom he exchanged letters for more than sixty years.

For Tommy and Joan, the great event of 1922 was the arrival of their first child, a son, on 11 January. Tommy wrote to his sister Blanche on 6 February:

'My dear B., Many thanks for your telegram. Joan has been extremely well ever since the event, and is now beginning to resume normal life. The child is enormous – over 11 lbs. He is to be christened John Fredk. next Friday.

I'm afraid HRH is extremely despondent and indignant at the results of his tour – exaggeratedly so, many of us think, though it is almost impossible to gauge here the importance of the rebuffs he has had. Probably, in spite of such schooling as he has had from people who have seen India, he has never yet grasped the immense abyss which separates an Indian from a Dominion tour; with his intense, and on the whole healthy contempt for Convention, I doubt if he has been able to take in the fact that in India individual charm and personality count for practically nothing, and the halo of impersonal Tradition for almost everything. I was afraid when he started that he was going too much as Edward P. and not enough as the King's Son. Which, obviously, is a *fatal* frame of mind, and would naturally result in disappointment even in a perfectly loyal and contented India.

As the *Nation* said last week in a first-rate article on 'The Prince's Progress', if royalty is to go down in India, it must go down hot and strong. The natural result is that he resents the partial triumphs of Gandhi as *personal* insults to himself, and is ashamed of them as the first *personal* failures in an otherwise triumphant progress through the world. He will not see that even if it isn't roses, roses all the way, his tour may be doing more good than harm in India; and that in England and the Empire people admire him all the more just because he has not flinched from a palpably unpleasant job, and is coming through it with his flag still flying, if bespattered.

If George sees him off at Karachi, as I suppose he will, I think he would be doing a great service by rubbing this in, even at the risk of over-estimating such good as the tour may have done. It is so essential that he should not get into his blessed little head that he is never to be asked to take on a job which will involve his sailing in rough waters. And if he rails, as he does, at the futility of sending him to India and not allowing him to mix with the people, and wander alone through every blasted bazaar, G. might try and explain to him that the Indian people don't *want* this in a King's son – if only because of the caste problem, of which he don't appear to have grasped even the elements.   Love, T.

To Helen

18 February 1922   *St James's Palace*

My dear Whelk, Many thanks for your letter and enclosure for Joan. I believe she is shortly sending a photograph of John F. We made the christening the occasion for a great gathering of aunts – Peg, Maud, Polly and Daws, B. Wayland and Lady Gore, who, arriving ten minutes late, was too oppressed in spirit to enter the church and sat on the steps till it was all over.

A few days after it, I was really touched to get a charming letter from Harry,[1] saying that, though it was no business of his, he hoped

---

[1] Tommy's cousin Harry, Viscount Lascelles. News of his engagement provoked much ribald comment in London society, for Princess Mary, though only twenty-four, was reputed to be unmarriageable, and Lascelles, who was nearly forty, was said to have proposed to her for a bet in his club. In 1929 he succeeded his father as sixth Earl of Harewood, and in 1934 the King created Mary the Princess Royal.

very much that I was entering the boy for a house at Eton; that, if financial considerations stood in the way, he would like to be allowed to obviate them, as, for all he knew, he might share George Fox's fate and have rows of daughters, in which case it would be a great pity that any son of Eddie's[1] or mine should not have an Eton education.

Beyond mutual exchange of congratulations on his family event and mine, we have not met for months; and I thought it particularly nice of him to have thought of such a thing just now, when he has hardly time to turn round. (Incidentally, can one conceive of his father ever having done this to any of his brothers, let alone a cousin?) And I like his frankness in saying, in so many words, 'I shall do my best to have a son myself; but if I don't succeed, yours is the heir of the house' – so many men would feel a false shame in ever alluding to the possibility.[2]

As it happened, I had always determined (*pace* your natural Wykehamist prejudices, and Lord Chelmsford's) that any son of mine should at least have a chance of going to Eton, knowing what I missed (though I retrieved it largely at Oxford) by not going there myself. And two days after John F. was born, I wrote, on the advice of Jasper Ridley[3] and several other Etonians, to a man called Sheepshanks,[4] who, it seems generally agreed, is about the best of the housemasters. He is a nephew of my brother-in-law Dick S., so I hoped that, although I am handicapped by not being an O.E., he would stretch a point in my favour. At first he wrote to say that he had no possible vacancy till 1936; but shortly afterwards wrote again to say that on reconsideration he hoped to be able to squeeze the boy in in 1935. So I trust it may be all right; though I shall of course run him for a scholarship, if he shows any signs of getting one. I don't see why he shouldn't, as I got two, and his grandfather is a fellow of All Souls.

The approaching wedding, as you will see from the newspapers, now completely fills the bill. People have lost their heads over it in an

---

[1] Tommy's cousin Edward Lascelles (1881–1935), second son of the fifth Earl of Harewood.

[2] In due course Harry fathered two sons, of whom the elder became the seventh Earl of Harewood in 1947.

    Although Tommy was fond of his cousin, he loathed Harry's father, the fifth Earl, of whom he once wrote, 'There is no living creature that I know that I have a more profound contempt for than that bloated, scurfy, snarling little nobleman.'

[3] 1887–1951, son of the first Viscount Ridley and a close friend of Tommy's at Oxford.

[4] A. C. Sheepshanks, Eton housemaster 1922–38.

extraordinary way. Ham [Lord Desart, his uncle] told me that an obscure Lady XY – some remote Sligo relation, whose name I forget – had written to Peg [Lady Desart] an almost peremptory letter asking her to have four tickets for the Abbey sent to such and such an address as soon as possible; as if it was a cinema-show, and poor old Peg the lady in the box-office. And I believe Harry has, quite rightly, returned a number of wedding-presents from dim connections he has never met in his life. Blood may be thicker than water; but it wasn't thick enough for them to send their oblations to you and me, who are just as much Lascelleses, though we weren't nationally married.

Among the many problems confronting the Dean of Westminster, one of the most urgent has been the provision of suitable sanitary accommodation for the many old gentlemen who will feel the strain of a long wait. He has solved it by rigging up a neat latrine – where? In the Poets' Corner. I suggest that for the future the Corner should be re-named with the letters e and t omitted. Joan and I are chaperoning Irene [Lawley, his cousin] to the ceremony; Aunt C.[1] and the Honble. Frederick, who, with all the older generation, have got to go to a 'breakfast' at Buck House, go hand-in-hand in a separate motor.

20 February 1922   We dined with the Harewoods on the 18th, to meet the King and Queen and Princess Mary; they had the gold plate out, which I had never seen before, and, as you can imagine, a most excellent and quite short dinner. Their Majesties were in most genial mood, and stayed till 11 pm, which, I believe, is unusually late for them. The Queen was quite splendid, with gorgeous emeralds, and Aunt F.[2] looked quite lovely, and was very nice and kind – insisted on Joan going and sitting down in the back drawing-room while we had to stand about. We both took kindly to Cousin Mary, whom we'd never met before – she's very fresh and jolly, and wrinkles up her nose when she smiles; and from what I could see of her and Harry at dinner, they seem the best of friends.

To Blanche Tommy added:
They seem to be making a proper botch over the wedding *bandobast* [an Indian word meaning ceremony or festivity], first in their

---

[1] Lady Constance Lascelles, sister of Tommy's father, had married the third Baron Wenlock in 1872. Although constantly cracking jokes about her deafness, her silver ear-trumpet and the inscrutable oils and water-colours which poured from her brush, Tommy was devoted to her, easily his favourite aunt.

[2] Florence, Countess of Harewood, the bridegroom's mother.

quarrel with the Dean of Westminster over the Pauline convention
about does [an Edwardian expression for ladies] not going to church
bareheaded; and secondly over the invitations. Even the Hon. Fredk.
has dug out his naval uniform from under the stairs, and was
surprised by Maud the other day mending his sword with glue. He is
going to stay with Aunt C. for it.

The Church and State quarrel is very amusing. I found poor old
Stamfordham one evening in hot and desperate conflict with the
Dean (who is an ass) as to how many or how few square inches of lace
a woman must wear on her head to satisfy St. Paul. It is a wonderful
instance of the Church clinging to the letter of the law long after it is
dead – which, so far as I recollect, is exactly what its Founder
enjoined them not to do. St. Paul wrote for hot-blooded Levantines
in the first century, when, no doubt, young men could not be trusted
in church with unveiled females. But, really, in the twentieth century, there can be no risk of us making indecent advances, even in the
spirit, to our cousins and aunts collected in Westminster Abbey, just
because they happen not to have their bonnets on – and at 11 o'clock
on a February morning, too, when even Scatters Wilson[1] couldn't
feel carnal.

The result, as you will have seen, is that morning clothes have
suddenly been substituted for low-necks, to the fury of the many
women who have already bespoke expensive wedding-garments of
the latter order, and to the great joy of every milliner in Mayfair. The
devil fly away with them all, as Carlyle used to say.

The wedding, held in Westminster Abbey at noon on 28 February
1922, was the social event of the year, not merely for the families
involved, but for the entire nation. A special Wedding Supplement,
brought out by *The Times* on the morning, immediately sold out, even
though the paper's normal print-run had been almost doubled, and
copies (which had been distributed free) were said to have changed
hands at up to £1 apiece. On 1 March every London newspaper
reported the event exhaustively: *The Times* devoted six pages to its
coverage, including one whole page to the dresses worn by leading
ladies, and thought it worth recording that a single aeroplane flew
over the Abbey during the service.

Apprehensions had been raised by a gale which raged all night,
but the morning of 28 February came out fine, with warm sunshine

[1] Sir Matthew ('Scatters') Wilson, a notorious Edwardian rake, claimed to have
caused more divorces than any other man in London.

to temper the breeze. Public enthusiasm was immense: the crowds lining the Mall were fifteen-deep, and the entire staff of the 22,000-acre Harewood estate came south to swell the throng. Seventeen royal guests were among the congregation. The bride wore a gown of striped silver lamé; Joan Lascelles chose 'a Handley-Seymour gown of periwinkle blue crepe romain', and Tommy's beloved Aunt Constance 'a draped gown of silver-grey velvet'. After a wedding breakfast in Buckingham Palace, and sundry appearances on the balcony there, the couple left for their honeymoon by Royal Train from Paddington Station.

With his employer, Tommy was soon on easy terms; and it quickly became clear that he had a particular facility for drafting the Prince's speeches. He would have the bones of them typed out on rectangular cards, of a size that fitted easily into a breast-pocket, with one complete sentence or idea on each line. People began to remark on the excellence of the speeches the Prince was making – and, although in the short term the arrangement worked well, it proved in the end rather dangerous, for it led many people to overestimate the Prince's intellectual capabilities. Not that things always went smoothly: there was one notable fiasco in November 1922, when, required to produce an address for the dedication of a memorial to the sons and relations of members of the two Houses of Parliament, Tommy 'somewhat rashly' (as he later reported) sent his draft to the playwright J. M. Barrie. Instead of commenting on it, Barrie sent back a draft of his own which was ludicrously high-flown and inappropriate ('To the new recruits to Immortal Death, I dedicate this monument. This mighty heart still beats through the grey shades; not the abhorred shears themselves shall stop that throbbing . . .'). The Prince would not look at this rubbish, and Tommy had to break it to Barrie that his offering had been rejected.

One subject on which Tommy was able to pronounce with authority was that of the Prince's riding: having himself hunted furiously when young, and ridden in steeplechases, he knew the risks better than anyone else on the staff. Internal evidence suggests that this undated memorandum, drafted for Godfrey Thomas, was written early in 1922, by which date the Prince's numerous accidents had given rise to much public and private concern:

So much nonsense – due partly to ignorance and partly to sentiment – has been talked and written about the question of the Prince riding in 'chases that it is difficult to see the thing straight.

The first point to be clear about is that the 'agitation' has nothing to do with hunting. Nobody suggests that the Prince should give up hunting. The only question raised is, 'Should he or should he not give up riding in point-to-points and steeplechases?'

You can look at it from two distinct points of view – the personal and the public. Take the first, the personal. Obviously the Prince loves riding races and gets a tremendous amount of fun out of them. Also, most of us who work for him are fond of anything to do with a horse and share his keenness; when he won the Pytchley light-weight race – probably the most satisfactory race of all for an amateur to win – we were all as pleased as if we had won it ourselves. But it is not all jam for us: nowadays, when the Prince rides a race, we spend a pretty jumpy afternoon till we get the telegram announcing the result. Obviously, too, the Prince's own family, and most of his personal friends, go through just the same anxiety.

That is about all there is to be said on the personal side. Now take the public side . . .

It might be said that the Public has no business to feel anything at all, and that the matter is no concern of theirs; but you cannot argue that nowadays – indeed, you never could at any time since there have been Princes of Wales. Both for the Prince's sake, and for the Public's sake, one is simply bound to consider Public Opinion and give it a fair hearing.

From the purely commercial point of view, the Public has a right to have a say in the matter. The Public has, for centuries, sunk a good deal of money in the Prince of Wales as an institution, and an appreciable amount in this particular Prince – e.g. on his Dominion tours, and countless local expenses. Consequently, the hard-headed Public – one can't altogether blame it – expects some sort of return for its money in future. When you get down to bed-rock, you have to admit that, in the long run, the Prince of Wales's title, his estates, his income and his many little privileges all depend on Public goodwill. You can't afford to alienate that goodwill.

From conversations, from the Prince's letters, and from what one reads in the Press, there can be no doubt that the great majority of all classes hope, for one reason or another, that the Prince will give up riding races. They have got various lines of attack:

1. The Prince's physical safety. For sentimental reasons, as well as for the commercial reasons alluded to above, they obviously don't want the Prince to break his neck. Equally, they don't want him to go on concussing his brain or breaking more bones, partly because they like him, and partly because they think each successive accident may

11

render him less fit to do the job which (they maintain) nobody else but he can do – i.e., be King.

Some people and one or two newspapers ridicule this idea, and say it is mere 'molly-coddling'. But one can't dismiss it like that – steeplechasing is easily the most risky sport we have got now, and it's no use pretending otherwise. Of our own contemporaries who have died violent deaths (apart from in the war), quite two-thirds have died as a result of racing falls, and there are any number of good fellows who are more or less permanent crocks from the same reason. So it is simply not true to say that there isn't a certain amount of risk.

'The percentage of casualties is very small,' some people say. The percentage of Princes of Wales is 1,000 times smaller. 'Even if he were to break his neck,' they say, 'he has three brothers to succeed him.' That is absolute bunkum. If there is one thing more than another which is quite final about the Public's estimate of the Prince, it is that he is irreplaceable and has no substitute.

It comes to this, then: the Prince does run avoidable risks by riding races. Is he justified in taking these risks?

The general opinion is that it is not his job to take them. If, for example, Harry Brown (who is booked to ride the favourite in the Grand National) were to go off winter-sporting and break his collar-bone a week before the race, the Public (except such bookies as had laid the favourite too heavily) would be justly indignant and would say, 'What the hell does he go winter-sporting for when he has contracted to do the other job? His business is to keep himself fit for the Big Race.'[1] That is very much what the British Public (except the Bolshies, who, again, have laid the favourite) feel about the Prince of Wales.

2. Another line of attack is that, apart from its risks, riding is too much of a whole-time job for the Prince of Wales: that it takes up more than its fair share of his physical energy, of his mind and of his time, leaving him very little of these three things to use in his ordinary life. There may be something in this. It is certainly true that nearly everybody who has been fond of riding races finds he has to give it up when he starts to do a regular job in life; and conversely, that nearly all those who consistently ride races are precious little use

---

[1] The oustanding amateur rider of his day, who often coached the Prince of Wales, Harry Atherton Brown came second in the Grand National of 1921 on his own horse, the 9-1 favourite The Bore, having fallen over the final fence, broken his collar-bone and gallantly remounted. In 1922 his mount, the favourite Southampton, fell at the first fence.

at anything else, besides developing rapidly into the most crashing bores.

3. Thirdly, it is maintained that, through no fault of his own, the Prince is damaging something which belongs to him even less than his own life and limbs – namely the position of the Prince of Wales, of which he is only a life-time trustee. The Prince's falls are becoming a joke all over the world, particularly in America. They are a regular subject for caricaturists and comedians in two continents, with the inevitable result that the general public abroad, having ceased to be amused by them, is bored by them, and, by implication, with the Prince.

The goodness or badness of the Prince's horsemanship has nothing whatever to do with it. We, who know him, know perfectly well that he is now every bit as good across country as two-thirds of our friends who ride races. But you cannot convince the world of that. What you have got to remember is that the world – particularly the foreign world – cannot discriminate between a genuine fall and a 'voluntary'. When the world reads, 'Prince Has Another Fall,' it only thinks – and always will think, 'He's fallen off again. Why can't he learn to sit tight before he starts riding in public?' Consequently, the name of the Prince of Wales is getting everywhere a sort of panto-mime association.

At first this was largely discounted by the fact that people genu-inely admired the Prince's pluck on a horse and his ability to come up smiling. But this admiration – largely because of the idiotic stuff written in the Press – seems to have worn itself out. Moreover, people are disgusted by the horrible photographs of the Prince which any Press-photographer can always secure at a race-meeting.

4. People who do understand sport in general and racing in particular have said that the Prince's continued participation in steeplechases is doing no good to the sport as a whole. His presence in a race does not make for good racing, and is a severe strain on other riders. The 'other side' of any fence is always a bit of a problem; it must be a perfect nightmare if you approach it with the possibility of landing in the small of the Heir Apparent's back.

It is not clear whether or not Tommy made any definite rec-ommendation. But the Prince went on riding, and eased off only when a serious fall in the winter of 1924 put him in bed, with the after-effects of concussion, for nearly a month.

The closeness of the friendship between Tommy and his master –

as well as the extent to which the Prince relied on the help of his staff – is evident in two letters written from Scotland in the autumn of 1922:

Prince of Wales to A.L.

14 September 1922   *Balmoral Castle*

My dear Tommy, Thanks for your note and the letters. I'll fix up with Borthwick the artist to come up here one day. I've got off the St. Andrew's Ball on 28th on the plea of 'Court Mourning'[1] (that's a good one, isn't it?) but its *the King's orders* I must obey!!!!!!!! I've written the Admiral and told him so I suppose he'll advise St. Andrew's and I'll fix up to come south that night, Thurs. 28th.

It's bloody cold and wet up here and I'm very bored, but I'll have some fun on the hill if only the weather will improve and it's not for long. But I do miss all my riding terribly and am praying that all this walking and climbing won't make it impossible for me to get into my boots again!!!!

Tell G. that the St. Andrew's Ball is off and that I'll be back early morning on 29th. Please send everything you have to.   Yours, E.P.

PS You know those engagement date-boards in my sitting room, white cardboard with two months on each. Well could you please fill in any engagements that aren't down, to bring them up to date, and send them to me *as soon as you can*. Write in pencil. I enclose three letters from ex-Servicemen and re unemployment. I don't know what one can do about them and it all. Perhaps you would see that man Gregsten if you thought it could help the men.

Prince of Wales to A.L.

19 September 1922   *Balmoral Castle*

My dear Tommy, I am afraid I haven't written for a day or two and now I've got quite a bunch of stuff to send down though it's mostly balls and I am only commenting on the letters you are likely to show me.

---

[1] For the Duchess of Albany.

1. *Broadcasting message to boy scouts on 7 Oct.* I've talked to old Stamfordham and *made* him say he 'approved', as I personally think it is [an] admirable scheme though you simply must make it quite clear to Marconi Co. that it is a special occasion and that I am not going to make a habit of it!! But what a hopeless hour 9 pm is as it bitches one's evening. Can't they make it 8 or even 7.30? Try it on the Chief Scout though I suppose you'll have to make it 9 o'clock if they insist. But have a try as it makes such a difference doesn't it.

2. *Amateur Menagerie Club.* Tell Tyrwhitt Drake I can't possibly see his animals at Crystal Palace on Sat. 30th.

3. *Stourbridge War Memorial.* I am ashamed to say I don't know what part of the country this city is in but you can easily get out of it under our war memorial ruling. Only regiments of which I am Colonel-in-Chief or more suitable answer in this case; places where I own property. But you know what to say and anyway I'm not going to do it. I've shown the Mayor's letter to the young Duke of York, who also says NO and I shouldn't think my other two brothers *want* to go and I don't suppose they can. But if it's an important place – I mean in an industrial area – it might be as well for Harry to do it. You better tell them to communicate with him.

4. *Wilkin, who wants to rejoin RAF.* Send letter to Air Ministry though I can't recommend him as I don't know him.

I hope all this is coherent. I haven't done so much writing work for a long time and it's very good for me and I open *everything* that comes to me and so am getting a pretty good insight of all the drudgery and toiling that you and Godfrey do for me and for which I may not appear grateful. But I am I can assure [you] particularly after seeing all the stuff myself. I am only sorry for any delays but I don't get back from the hill till dinner-time often, and then am sleepy and tired. But it's no effort really, as I say it's d-d good for me. Very wild weather still.   Yours, E.P.

To Letty Benson

27 December 1923   *St. James's Palace*

Dear Letty, Christmas without your Flaming Handkerchief would be like Paradise without Michael's Flaming Sword. Early each December my nose starts itching for it, with a craving no other handkerchief can assuage. This morning's post brought relief, which I was beginning to fear might not be coming. I don't know what I should have said to my Nose if it had been delayed another twenty-four hours.

Has Conrad [Russell] ever told you of the song which, when he was dining as a freshman with the Master of Balliol, another freshman sang at the request of the Master's wife, to 'give them a little music after dinner'? The chap, who was a shy, inoffensive-looking sort of man, sat down at the piano, struck three chords, and burst into the following:

'Jolly Nose, the red rubies which garnish thy tip
    Were quarried in mines of Canary . . .'

I forget the rest, but those two lines are pretty good, aren't they?

I don't believe there is a Jeremy in Dickens, though I'm not sure. But the Lord remembered DANIEL, you know, so it wouldn't do for you to forget it. 'Dan Benson' is a very fair name. Peggoty *père* was Daniel, wasn't he?[1] Conrad always calls his cows after Shakespeare heroines. I told him I was doing the same by my daughter,[2] to which he wrote, 'A very good plan, but I shouldn't choose Mouldy or Bullcalf.' (See Henry IV Part 2). Yours, Tommy.

---

[1] In fact Daniel Peggoty was the brother of Clara, David Copperfield's nurse.
[2] Tommy's daughter Lavinia had been born on 27 June 1923.

AMERICA AND CANADA
1924

In the summer of 1924 the Prince of Wales went on vacation to the
United States and Canada. His aim was to watch the international
polo matches between Great Britain and America, which were to be
played on Long Island, 'to see something more of the country,'[1] and
then to visit the ranch in Alberta which he had bought on impulse
during his travels the year before. The trip of 1924 was thus a private
visit, rather than an official tour; even so, the Prince was inevitably
seen as an ambassador of his country.

From a purely social point of view, the exercise was an immense
success. The visitors were entertained in grand style by the mil-
lionaires of New York; everywhere people flocked to see the royal
tourist, and newspaper coverage of 'the indefatigable vacationist' (as
the *New York Times* called him) was itself indefatigable. Yet the
extravagant Press reports, which played up the Prince's taste for
all-night parties, jazz and dancing, so alarmed Buckingham Palace
that they led in the end to a rebuke from King George V, who felt
outraged by the effrontery of the US editors in 'daring to portray his
eldest son so flippantly.'

The main responsibility for trying to keep the American journalists under control, and for covering up the Prince's worst excesses,
fell on Tommy; and there is little doubt that, but for his efforts, things
would have become a good deal worse. That he carried out a difficult
job with no mean skill is confirmed by a note from Sir Esmé Howard,
the British Ambassador in Washington:

I feel that Lascelles was the best influence and must have been
responsible for a good deal that was done in the last week. He had a

---

[1] The remarks here attributed to the Prince are taken from his memoirs, *A King's
Story*, published in 1951.

most unenviable position, I should think, but acted always with the greatest tact and good nature. My own feeling is that it is due chiefly to him that the visit proved a success rather than the reverse, and I think it was very much of a toss-up at one time. I noticed a distinct improvement in the tone of the Press when Lascelles began to receive the reporters.

To Joan

23 August 1924   *RMS Berengaria*

My Darling, Just got on board. All most palatial – my cabin quite as big as my dining-room in Oxford Square, with a vast bathroom and enough cupboards for all your clothes and mine. She's a wonderful ship – as long as a street – and apparently full to the brim. Diana and the Duchess[1] came down in our train, looking very film-starish, and were seen off by a most revolting crowd of impresarios etc. Weather looks better – anyhow a ship this size can't be much worried by any weather.

God bless you always, my darling. I do wish you were here.

All my love, T.

23 August 1924   *RMS Berengaria*
                                                    Off Cherbourg

Darling, This is the last chance I shall get of writing to you for nearly a week, so I'll send it to Ardgowan.[2] HRH said at tea, 'Now, if we were in that Newhaven to Dieppe boat, we should all be bloody sick.' Which is perfectly true, for it is really pretty rough, but this vast ship has only got the very faintest roll on, and I don't notice it at all.

Had a hectic time so far answering all the letters and wires before we get to Cherbourg, interviewing the Captain, and the Purser, and journalists, and Diana Cooper, who is playing up well, and in spite of tempting offers refuses to undertake to send daily wireless messages to American papers.

[1] Diana Cooper, accompanied by her husband, Duff, and her mother, the Duchess of Rutland, was on her way to the revival in New York of *The Miracle*, the play in which she had starred with immense success the year before.
[2] The house belonging to the Shaw Stewarts on the Firth of Clyde, at which the Lascelles family several times stayed in the autumn.

HRH rather peevish after a late night, but after a tough struggle and failure by G. Trotter, I have induced him to promise to go to church at 10.30 tomorrow, which will be excellent propaganda.

My darling, I am beginning to miss you dreadfully, and shall much more when I have time to think about it. However, I gather there's not much danger of our staying away later than 23 October, which is a comfort. I wish you could see my nice cabin – it's got a practically full-length sofa in it, and room for all my luggage without crowding. It's a great joy to have a place where one can sit and read in security and peace!

Bless you always, and give my love to Lady Alice [Shaw-Stewart]. T.

27 August 1924   *RMS Berengaria*

My darling, Offham[1] seems a hundred years away, yet it is only a week today that I was getting into the 5.20 for the last time. I'm never very happy at sea, though I'm bound to say that so far as physical comforts go, this trip could hardly be beaten. The food is delicious, you don't realise you are at sea, even when it is blowing quite hard, and my state-room is as good a bed-sitting room as you could find in any hotel. Moreover, the passengers have really behaved very well, and worried none of us; considering that five out of six are Yankees, they've been surprisingly oblivious of HRH, and have scarcely worried him at all. But there are nearly a dozen Press men on board, and these are a decided thorn in my flesh. At the beginning I promised them that if they wouldn't bother the Prince and spy on him, I would see them all in my cabin every day, at eleven and seven, to answer any questions they liked to ask – within reason.

They've kept their side of the bargain very fairly well, though one of them got pretty tight last night and annoyed him by trying to stalk him round the decks; but mine is no light job, because one must think about every word one says to the brutes, and to say nothing that could be twisted or perverted. I've seen most of their messages every day – the poor wretches have to radio at least 500 words daily – and so far there's been very little I couldn't pass; but, of course, there's no knowing what lies they may print once they get to New York.

HRH, D. Boyle [an equerry] and I naturally foregather in the gymnasium about eight, to do exercises and throw a medicine-ball about, which is very good for one. The rest of the day passes much as

[1] Offham House, Lewes, Sussex, where the family had spent part of the summer.

other days on board ship – deck-walks, reading, and practising for the tug of war, which is to come off in the deck-sports this afternoon. Our team consists of L. Mountbatten,[1] Duff (the Hurlingham secretary), Duff Cooper, T. Bouch (late Master of the Belvoir), Chilton (Embassy), Boyle, HRH and myself. We are very light, but Mountbatten, who understands tugs of war, has trained us scientifically. Personally, I hope we shall be knocked out in the first round, as it is most exhausting. I play a good deal of Mah Jongg with Duff C. and Diana, and sometimes J. Norton or Boyle; and chess with Duff or Bouch. Beyond these, and the Chiltons, we hardly know anybody on board. Chilton used to be with Sir Edward[2] in Berlin, and she is a nice woman, American, though one would never guess it.

There is a vast ballroom, where HRH dances himself into a muck-sweat every night, but is generally reduced to pulp fairly early, when I am released from my role of guarding his table in the 'Palm-Court' while he and G. foot it with the damsels, and can then adjourn to Bridge, Jongg or bed.

This morning we went all round the ship with the Captain – exhausting, but very interesting. It is an astonishing p'ace, and the kitchens and store-rooms were great fun. There was one electric machine for squeezing oranges with which I could have played for hours.

Duff and Diana are my chief companions – both in good form. J. Norton is certainly a marvel of prettiness, and less tiresome than I thought, but not my line of goods at all; nor is Edwina, though they are both agreeable enough when we meet, which isn't often. I suppose I ought to be enjoying myself and thinking myself very lucky; but it's all rather wearisome, and I would gladly swap the whole of the American part of this trip for just four delicious days with you at Ardgowan, such as we had last year.

That's a rotten book, *The Two Strange Men*, but Mason's *House of the Arrow* is a first-class thriller. HRH is devouring *Ordeal*[3], which I gave him, at his usual rate of reading – about 7½ pages a day; but he seems to be enjoying it.

---

[1] Lord Louis Mountbatten, then aged twenty-four, had married Edwina Ashley in 1922. Duff Cooper was then a budding politician of thirty-four, and Tommy Bouch an elderly admirer of Diana's. Sir Henry Chilton (1877–1954) was about to take up his job as Envoy Extraordinary and Minister Plenipotentiary at Washington.

[2] Sir Edward Goschen (1847–1924) was the father of Tommy's great friend George Gerard Goschen, known as Bunt, and had been Ambassador in Berlin 1908–14.

[3] A melodramatic novel by the Australian Dale Collins (1897–1956).

Thursday   Well, we were, to my great relief, soundly beaten in tug of war by eight large Americans, who quickly pulled us over the line as if we weren't there at all.[1] It was terribly sticky all yesterday – regular Bombay weather – as we were on top of the Gulf Stream. Today it is a bit better, but still pretty warm. The Prince and I went all round the engine-rooms before luncheon, and when we came out even my leather sock-suspenders were wringing wet. The engines were worth seeing, though machinery means little to me, except as a spectacle, which this certainly was. The thermometer is hardly ever below 120 degrees down there, in spite of every kind of modern ventilating device. The men do four hours on and eight off.

We shall get in about luncheon-time tomorrow, and our party gets straight off at Quarantine, into a private yacht, which Oscar Solbert[2] has produced. This will take us straight to a landing-place on Long Island not far from Woodside.[3] We spend most of Saturday in the train, going down to Washington and back to lunch with Coolidge.[4]

God bless you, my darling, and have fun in Scotland. I feel terribly homesick for it.   All my love, T.

30 August 1924   *Woodside*
                                                        Syosset
                                                        Long Island

My Darling, I've been in bed all day, but hope to be up tomorrow. I started a cold in the *Berengaria* (those big ships are devilish draughty), which might not have been a bad one, but a couple of hours in the engine-room with HRH turned it into a real corker. I was to have gone to Washington with him today, but all yesterday afternoon I felt so increasingly feverish that by dinner-time I thought it wiser to borrow a thermometer, as I began to see visions of malaria, which a long day in the train might have made serious. My temperature was over 103, so I went straight to bed, and Solbert produced a doctor, an intelligent man, who said he didn't think there was much wrong

---

[1] In his memoirs *Old Men Forget* Duff Cooper recorded: 'They pulled us over so easily that they must have thought for a moment, as they lay on their backs, that the rope had broken.'

[2] Major Oscar Solbert, US Army, an equerry to the President of the United States, who acted as ADC to the Prince during his tour.

[3] The home on Long Island of Mr and Mrs James A. Burden, who had lent the house to the Prince for his visit.

[4] Calvin Coolidge, President of the United States 1923–28.

beyond a feverish cold and a congested liver (due to ship life); and he seems to have been about right, for after a sweaty night my temperature has dropped to 99, and apart from a bad head I feel quite different. I am rather glad to get out of Washington, which would have involved ten very hot hours in the train with what looked like being a most resentful and irritated Prince, and only about three in Washington, including luncheon. So, old G. being very lame as a result of a violent hack on the ankle from a fellow-dancer on the ship, I was quite glad to let D. Boyle go and do the job.[1]

We got clear of the *Berengaria* very fairly well, though a few hours before we got in Esmé Howard[2] alarmed us by sending a radio message that he thought it would be better after all if HRH consented to give five minutes to the boatload of Press representatives who were coming out to the ship at Quarantine. This was a complete reversal of policy. But as we are more or less bound to follow the Ambassador's advice on a question of that sort, we gave in. I daresay he was right, and that HRH, having given them this 'interview', will have a better chance of being left in peace till he leaves Long Island. It wasn't much of an 'interview'; they came round him like a pack of hounds, and fired off simultaneous questions, of which he only attempted to answer about a tenth. He then handed them a typed message I had prepared, and we escaped on to the yacht which Solbert and Co. had provided for us.[3]

The journey in the yacht lasted about 1½ hours, and took us right through the heart of New York – past the skyscrapers and under Brooklyn Bridge. The group of skyscrapers at the end of Manhattan – i.e. New York proper – is perfectly lovely. On a rather hazy afternoon, like yesterday, they stand up out of the sea like a vast medieval monastery; even when one is right under them, they are beautiful, but, from a distance, I think they are, next to the Taj, the greatest architectural performance I've yet seen.

Except for an occasional hoot of welcome from some small steamer that recognised us, nobody took any notice of us; eventually we disembarked at a private landing-stage on the far side of the Island, and motored over here, about twenty miles, I suppose. It is not

[1] If Tommy's concern about his health sounds excessive, it should be remembered that he had suffered repeatedly from malaria in India.

[2] 1863–1939, Ambassador to the United States 1924–28, became the first Baron Howard of Penrith in 1930.

[3] The gathering of reporters and photographers was the largest that had ever greeted a ship in New York.

beautiful country – the nearest parallel I can think of is the Bourne-mouth–Christchurch coast – studded with countless big houses, some of them monstrous imitations of a Loire château, others quite successful copies of English Queen Anne and Georgian. I have seen little of Woodside, beyond the hall and my own room, but it is certainly one of the latter: a really nice 'country house' feeling about it, with good furniture (though a bit jumbled) and jolly chintzes. Of the cooking I can say little save that they make the best bread-and-milk I've ever eaten.[1]

We were received by the son and daughter-in-law of our host, James A. Burden, who is in Europe; a typical *Nash*'s magazine couple, just back from their honeymoon, he tall and good-looking in the high-cheekboned style; and she a very pretty, soft-haired, oval-faced little thing, who, though she can't be more than twenty, took charge of the Prince and gave him tea with a quiet self-possession for which I gave her full marks. With them were the Roger Winthrops, who are officially our hosts – i.e., she runs the house, and he looks after us generally, though they actually live in their own place half a mile away.

Uncle Ivor seems to have got himself properly disliked.[2] To begin with, he let the British polo team in for staying with a certain Louis Fleischmann, whom nobody here will know, and who has been blackballed for all the clubs (perhaps Uncle I. has a fellow-feeling for him on that score). W[imborne] then, having encouraged the team to bring out their wives, turns up with one of the worst of his women, whom he expects to stay in the house. The team, and their wives, couldn't stand this, and eventually sent W. an ultimatum that they or the woman must leave the house. W. then withdrew in a huff, with the lady, and has apparently left Long Island, which is laughing discreetly.

Meanwhile, our polo prospects seem very dismal – 40–1 against the British team seems to be the sort of odds. I don't think there's a hope of our winning a match, and I shall be relieved if we are beaten by less than ten goals each time.

The minute it is dark here, the 'katy dids' – a sort of cricket – all

---

[1] Warm bread-and-milk, with a little brown sugar, was Tommy's lifelong diet whenever he felt ill or over-tired.

[2] Ivor Guest, first Lord Wimborne (1873–1939), was Joan's mother's brother. He had provided some of the ponies for the English team, but his presence seems to have been highly corrosive, and reports of dissension in the British camp were soon leaked to the American papers.

start chirping. As there are mosquito-doors, it is quite easy to imagine oneself back at Ganeshkhind.[1] It is pretty hot, too.

Monday I am very much better today. My doc has given me a capital tonic. However, I didn't attempt to go out all day, but sat about and did the letters and saw journalists and explored the books in this nice house till tea-time. Then, when it was slightly cooler, Boyle and I motored over to a neighbouring millionaire, one Clarence McKay, who is giving a big party for us one night soon. He has got a house full of wonderful things, including the famous Wilton armour and some marvellous tapestry, but this evening we got no further than his real-tennis court, a beautiful building, to which is attached a squash court and the most complete bathing outfit imaginable, with a professional masseur always in attendance. I didn't feel equal to more than a mild knock-up, which made me sweat profusely and did me a lot of good. Then I went and had a bath, while Boyle played with the pro, 'Punch' Fairs, ex-champion of the world. You've probably never heard of him, but he is to tennis what Donoghue is to racing or J. H. Taylor to golf, and a bit more besides. So I was proud to meet him, and am looking forward to his giving me one half thirty and beating me six-love, which he does to anybody who comes along, with great good nature. A dear little man, and a great artist. His backhand shot is the most perfect thing I know in any game.

After my bath, and while my clothes were drying in the electric drying-room, a typical stage valet, six feet and a half high, and full of reminiscences of the English peerage (he was born at Amesbury – all the servants in Long Island are English) plied me with pre-war whiskey. There is certainly no dearth of the very best alcoholic liquor in this part of the USA.

Our host, who had been to the races, where Epinard was beat by a neck, then came in and urged us to come back twice a day, or oftener, so long as we were in Long Island. A kind little man, type of Sid Green, vastly rich, and works like a black at his job, which is the big International Cable Company of New York. In the intervals, he takes moors in Scotland and wins the amateur squash racquets championship of America.

Mrs Solbert came over to see Oscar S. for a few minutes yesterday, looking very well and pretty. She sent you her best love and wished you were here. But, honestly, I don't believe you would be very much

[1] In Kashmir, where they had stayed on honeymoon.

amused, at present. It is too hot and sticky to enjoy anything really – though they say that this is an unusual year, as people always do when one goes abroad – except the bathing, which certainly looks jolly. But Long Island seems to be run almost entirely in the interests of men, and apart from dancing, which can't be much fun in this weather, women don't seem to get much of a show. The country is dreary to a degree – like the suburbs of Bournemouth – and there is an atmosphere of over-population and over-civilisation, over-everything. I am quite prepared to be amused for ten days or so, if it gets cool enough to appreciate the unusual joys of private golf links and real-tennis court. But I shall be glad when we're in the train for Canada and open spaces.

Goodbye, my blessed – perhaps there will be a letter from you the day after tomorrow. The days are beginning to slide by now, and the next six weeks will go like lightning. All love, T.

3 September 1924 *Woodside*

My Darling, The weather broke yesterday, and now, after some heavy rain, it is deliciously cool and fresh. Last night we all went to a dinner and dance given by the Roger Winthrops – quite amusing for a bit. The lights kept going out, so most of it happened by dim candle-light. Emboldened by this, I twice took the floor with Betty Gilbert, who dances beautifully, and stayed on it, you'll be glad to hear, for quite a long time.[1] Tonight we all went to a stag party given by the American Polo Association for the two teams at the Piping Rock Club. HRH only told me this afternoon that he had been let in for a short speech, but I managed to produce something tolerably amusing, which seemed to go down well.

I sat between two famous veterans, Harry Whitney and Devereux Milburn – the latter a splendid man whom I liked a lot; though he was too much of a gentleman to say so, it was pretty clear he thinks that our team haven't an earthly chance of winning one match. Nor do they themselves; both Geoff Hornby and V. Lockett, whom I saw afterwards, had quite reconciled themselves to a crashing defeat. For this, Lockett chiefly blamed Wimborne. Lord, how they all hate him. Most of them, English or American, won't speak to him at all. He was at the dinner, looking very dissipated, but he has such a

[1] Tommy's experiences during the First World War seem to have left him with a horror of dancing. Before it, at constant parties in high society, he had taken to the floor with the greatest enthusiasm; but the references in these letters from America show that some form of rehabilitation had become necessary.

25

hippopotamus-hide that I don't believe he realises in any way that he is at all unpopular.

When the speeches were over, they turned on their famous Will Rogers, a comedian of the patter-type. His stunt is just to stand up and make a rambling, extempore speech about current topics; tonight he went on for over half an hour, and I think it was one of the funniest things I've ever listened to – mostly about HRH, who adored it, with a wonderful passage about Fruity [Metcalfe]. He said a lot of witty things, and a lot of very nice ones, both about the English race in general and HRH in particular.

4 September 1924   I was too sleepy to finish this last night, and am now – midday – sitting peacefully under a tree in the garden on the most lovely morning imaginable. Last night I met the Master of the Meadowbrook Hounds, whose kennels are just across the road here. They have started cub-hunting, and I daresay somebody will lend me a horse one morning. Of course, it is a funny sort of hunting here at the best of times – to me it looks about as practicable as Wimbledon Common; but I believe they have got some open bits where there are genuine wild foxes. Just now the ground is as hard as a brick, and I don't expect they go out of a walk; still, I always like seeing a new pack of hounds.

How I wish you were here on this delicious day, a perfect English June day. HRH is being very sweet to me, though as he is either at polo or at his own friends' parties most hours of the twenty-four, I see little of him. He is frightfully pleased with the effect of my speechlet last night, and it certainly did go down wonderfully. I was completely stuck for an anecdote to put in it (the Yanks love anecdotes, you know) till just before dinner I remembered a silly little story I cut out of the *Daily Herald* months ago and dropped into a drawer at York House, thinking it might come in useful some day. It came in very appropriately, and they loved it.

Goodbye, my darling Joanna. Kiss the babies, and give my love to the Mels.[1] It's funny to think of you all still at Offham. God bless you,
T.

9 September 1924   *Woodside*

My darling, This is at 3.30 a.m., after several hours of energetic dancing with a series of beautiful creatures, most of whose names I

---

[1] His sister Daisy and her husband Melville Balfour.

have already forgotten. None of them showed any reluctance about dancing with me, and those whose opinion I asked thought we were getting along quite nicely. So I feel I must be improving, which will be good news to you. I hope it's not merely the effect of Long Island air – which has been like champagne the last few days – and that when I get back to London I shall not lose the nimbleness of foot which I have certainly got now. It was quite a good party, given by some people called Ambrose Clark. I knew hardly anybody, barring some old trouts (wives of polo players etc.) whom I found I could trot round to their own satisfaction and with comparative comfort to myself. However, Kermit Roosevelt (Theodore's younger son) then took me in hand and introduced me to some very pretty pieces, with whom I made play energetically. The only English woman I danced with was Lady Airlie[1]; she is staying quite close to this place. Most of the men at these parties (which are ultra-respectable) get quite fairly tight as the evening goes on, which everybody, including the women, seem to take quite as a matter of course. There is always liquor in abundance and great variety.

I had an amusing day's cub-hunting with the Meadowbrook Hounds last week, on a wonderful brown Irish horse which would jump any obstacle ever built. In the course of the morning we encountered several large posts-and-rails, which he flicked over without causing me a moment's anxiety. It is rather like hunting in a series of big parks all joining on to each other, but is quite fun for a few hours. I am going out again Thursday with HRH.

Bless you always, my darling, and kiss the babies. T.

11 September 1924   *Woodside*

My darling, We look like being here another week, as, though it is usually fine otherwise, there is always torrential rain on the mornings fixed for the polo matches. HRH having repeatedly announced that his sole object in coming to USA was to see these matches, he can't very well leave till they are over.

Uncle Ivor is again the talk of the town. Last week our Ambassador (Sir Esmé Howard, a very delightful man) gave a big dinner for the two polo teams and their wives, HRH and all of us, and everybody connected with the polo world. He didn't ask Wimborne – deliberately – and when W. heard of the party, he flew into a passion

---

[1] Mabell, Countess of Airlie (1866–1956), the lifelong friend of Queen Mary, had been widowed in 1900. She became a great admirer of Tommy's.

and vowed that not one of his ponies should play in the matches. I believe he has been persuaded to think better of this, under great pressure, but it has quite done for him here, and I don't think he has been asked to one of the parties on Long Island. The Ambassador having done this, HRH obviously can't have him here, which is a great relief to both G. and me.

I am doing pretty well with the Press, who are my chief preoccupation. Every morning and evening a deputation waits on me and asks me a string of foolish questions; and next day the 'genial British captain' has about a column and a half of twaddle on the front page. I talk the purest balderdash to them, but my theory is that if only I give them a sufficient quantity of harmless rot, it will divert their attention from HRH, and, so far, it has worked very well. But I tremble to think of what Balmoral may think of my 'copy', if it ever reaches there.[1] I am keeping every single Press cutting about the visit; the pile is already nearly a foot high, but some of them are very amusing.

Goodnight, my darling. I do love you, and wish daily you were here, because you would enjoy so much of it. Kiss J.F. and Lavinia. I would have sent them postcards, but haven't seen a shop since I left England. Bless you, my sweet pretty. T.

12 September 1924   *Woodside*

I was driven to New York by my friend Betty Babcock. We had quite an interesting day, though exhausting. She is such a darling – a childhood friend of Alice Astor, but not very rich herself, and a nice, direct mind, with a good dry humour. Rides well, and adores her husband Richard, so you needn't worry. Two young daughters, about three and one, I think; tall, and quite a pretty little head, with hair plastered over the ears – I forget the right name for the style. She motored me in through the thick of the New York traffic, which is terrifying, and after Schmidt (shopping) took me to the Natural History Museum, a marvellous place, with fascinating models and reconstructions. Then we drove round the town a bit and picked up her husband and brother for luncheon. In the afternoon, Richard Babcock took me 'down town' (the City) where we saw the Stock Exchange, which naturally amused me,[2] called on one or two friends in offices nearby, looked at the big buildings, the Grand Central

---

[1] Tommy's apprehension was not misplaced. American Press reports *had* reached Balmoral, where they had thrown the King into a rage.

[2] Tommy had worked at the Stock Exchange in London.

Railway Station, the new Cunard offices (just like a Palladian cathedral), and so back to tea at the Racquet Club, where Mrs B. picked us up and drove us home.

American architecture is certainly pretty good. Nearly all the buildings I saw – especially the Central Station – were magnificent, and some of the new streets are very impressive. Many of the older ones are ruined by the overhead railways; these are to be pulled down shortly. But heaven knows what would happen to that town if ever it were subjected to an air-raid, or even a mild earthquake. The Flat-Iron building, which is the oldest of the skyscrapers, sways two feet each way in a gale of wind! Yet they don't seem the least worried about it.

Though I've taken things easily lately, and only been to one party since I last wrote, yet I'm beginning to long for peace and quiet; everybody else on this Island of Revelry, male and female, is quite exhausted and living on nerves or alcohol. The Prince is tireless, but even he is feeling the strain a bit.

Tomorrow being fixed for the first polo match, it is now obviously blowing up for more rain. I am beginning to think we shall be here till Xmas![1] I do wish I always felt as well and energetic in London as I do here – it would be so much more fun for you. I suppose it is the climate, but I seem to have twice as much staying-power now as I have had any time since 1914; and when I feel bobbish like this, I never get that black disgust of my fellow-creatures, even when I am mildly bored. Let's hope it will be permanent; anyhow, I give you a written guarantee, here and now, that I am quite prepared to dance with you in any public place in England in the future! Not that I have really learnt to dance, but I do seem able to get round the room without exciting suspicion and alarm.   Bless you, T.

To the Hon. F. C. Lascelles

15 September 1924   *Woodside*

My dear father, On the second [day out hunting] we didn't do much but had to negotiate a number of the largest posts-and-rails I've ever

---

[1] In fact, after three postponements, the first polo international took place, before a crowd of 35,000, on 13 September, and resulted in a runaway victory for the Americans, who won 16-3. According to *The Times*, 'Outplayed both individually and collectively, the British polo team sustained the most overwhelming defeat in the history of the international matches.'

had to ride at – usually in cold blood. There are no gates, and one must either jump these things or go miles round. I was riding an Irish horse, lent me by a man called Ladew, who hunts with the Pytchley, and, although horses are schooled to go faster at timber than I like, he was an extremely fine performer, and negotiated everything without a rap. The ground is as hard as iron, and, as I have not attempted to ride over any fences for nearly two years, I was none too happy till I realised what an exceptional jumper he must be. There was little grief, and, in a large field, very few horses ever touched a rail; they school them most elaborately, I believe, and anything that is not first-class at timber is at once drafted. There are no other obstacles save an occasional stone wall.

The first polo match was a better game than the score suggests. Lewis Lacey [of England: an Anglo-Argentine] was the best man on the field, in spite of his injuries, and if even one of our other three had been able to hit the ball more than fifty yards, we might have put up a fight. As it was, we more than held the Americans in the last two chukkas, and, if they draft Kirkwood, who is a sick man and quite useless, there is just a faint chance that the second game might be more even, though nobody, even Lacey himself, has the faintest hope of our winning.

The Americans played magnificently, both individually and together. There seemed little to choose between the ponies, and I don't grudge them their victory. They are all good fellows, especially Devereux Milburn, who is a very fine sportsman, and completely free from any sort of conceit.[1]   Your loving Tommy.

To Joan

21 September 1924   *Woodside*

My darling, Our train 'pulls out', as they say here, at 10 p.m., and by morning we shall be in Canada. Now that it is all over, I am very sad

---

[1] The second polo match was played on 16 September and, although it was a better game than the first, the Americans again won easily, 14-5. Because of the repeated postponements, and the fact that the Americans were in an unassailable position, the third match was called off. By then, however, the disorder in the British ranks had become common knowledge, especially after Major Hurndall – dropped from the team without warning or consultation – made a statement to the Press saying that their chances had been wrecked by changes of plan and bad management. Recording the sudden departure of Lord Wimborne from New York, *The Times* came so far into the open as to remark: 'Lord Wimborne has sailed to attend to his private affairs, and there is complete harmony in the team.'

at going away – people have been so kind and good, and so many of them are such dears. If ever you and I can get over here, we can find half a dozen people who would really like to put us up for as long as we like. In fact, the Roger Winthrops, when I said goodbye to them this afternoon, extracted a quarter-promise out of me that both of us and the children would come and spend next May with them! We certainly might do much worse, given time and money, than spend a week or two here, a few days in Washington, and a fortnight camping up in the hills, which is the programme they proposed.

The Winthrops are a nice, middle-aged couple with a delicious house and a genius for amusing their guests. You would like them, and a good many more of the Long Islanders; they are all rich, of course, but one only resents their riches in about a third of them. The rest have such good manners and good taste that they can carry it off. So you can feel safe that I have played John the Baptist successfully and that if ever you want to come out here, you will be given a wonderful time. But I do wish it didn't take a week to get here.

Having danced Long Island to a standstill (they were all stone cold at the end of last week, and I don't think there's been a single party since the second polo match), HRH, whose vitality is quite unimpaired, decided to do a few days' serious stunting in New York. I was delighted because, apart from the fact that the things he wanted to see were all interesting, something of the kind was badly needed to correct the growing impression through all the American papers that he never did anything else beyond dance till dawn and play polo.

So we carried it out, though it was of course quite outside the scope of his visit as originally planned, and I daresay there will be a row. However, it went off so well, and has so completely changed the whole tone of the Press, that I don't regret it. At the time, it was pretty tricky, because all his little visits to various institutions – the big telephone exchange, the Natural History Museum, a baseball match, newspaper offices – had to be organised more or less on the spur of the moment and quite secretly. If anybody had known in advance where he was going, such crowds would have collected as to make it impossible. As it was, the fact that he was in any one place always got about with astonishing rapidity – he is terribly easily recognised – and we often had to cut his stay there short so as to escape before the street became quite impassable. It was always a most friendly and affectionate crowd, but a great nuisance.

New York is a marvellous place, and I get more and more fascinated by those great towering buildings. Most of them are

31

positively beautiful, and none of them are anything like so offensive as, say, Queen Anne's Mansions. I have never seen it at night, which I regret, as they say it is astonishing.

One day we organised an informal tea-party, to which seven or eight of the biggest newspaper men and editors were invited to meet him; they all came, and it was amusing to see how every one of them, even the two Hearst editors, who have been anti-British for years, succumbed to him completely after five minutes' talk. It did a lot of good, that little party, and since it happened there's hardly been an unkind word written, even in the Sunday rags, which are notoriously filthy and scandalous.

On the same day I got out, through one of the Press agencies, a sort of appreciation of the serious side of his life in England, which the Ambassador and I concocted jointly. It read very well, and so far as I can see, none of the papers has hinted that it was in any way inspired by any of our people. The principal item in it was the announcement of his intention to do a really serious tour through the industrial parts of America at the first opportunity. He is very keen on this, and I believe he'll try to do it in 1926.

The result of all this, from my point of view, has been five very strenuous days, in which I have not had much time to amuse myself, and have done little beyond go to a few quiet dinners and play Bridge – higher points than I like, but so far I'm a few dollars up. However, I put in a morning's cub-hunting yesterday, which was quite amusing and gave me a chance to say goodbye to a lot of people en bloc.

Tonight, in the train, I am going to tackle HRH seriously on the question of fixing a date for sailing. I am extremely well, but, though I hate the train, I shan't be sorry to sit in it for four days with nothing to do but look out of the window. I don't think HRH will allow us to sit still on the Ranch for very long! Still, we ought to get a week there.

Bless you again, my darling, and give my love to J.F. and Lavinia.

Your T.

24 September 1924   *Canadian National Railways*
Private Car 'Balmoral'

My darling, It is hopeless trying to write with pen and ink as the train rocks so, and I am only a moderate performer on the typewriter [which he used, nevertheless]. We have been steaming all day through endless forests of pine and birch – quite flat and very monotonous; no life at all save an occasional small lumber-camp or railway-town. I think I dislike a train even more than a ship, though this one is the last word in luxury. My stateroom has a large double-bed and a very adequate shower-bath; there are three or four sitting rooms, and a radio and a gramophone. The Prince's car at the rear of the train has an observation platform, which will be fun when there is anything to look at. It has been the most glorious day, typical Indian summer with a delicious nip in the air, and I resent wasting it in this stuffy place – in spite of all its splendour, it is almost impossible to get any of the windows to open.

I don't really like travelling. However, I am going to get plenty of it in the next month, for he has now decided to spend only four days on the Ranch. We get there tomorrow evening, and on Tuesday afternoon start off across the Rockies for Jasper Park – a sort of Gulmarg,[1] which I believe is very lovely. One night there, and on to Vancouver, twenty-four hours of train, where I shall get my first sight of the Pacific, like stout Cortez. There, thank God, we take root for two whole nights, and then go on five hours in a boat to the island of Victoria. Thirty-two hours there, and then back over the Rockies to Banff, another Gulmarg. Halt for one day, and then thirty-six hours' train back to Winnipeg, where we put in one day.

From there he wants to nip down to Chicago, see the stock-yards, go on to Detroit, see the Ford works, and up to Toronto. This part of the trip, as it involves another excursion into USA, has to be approved by the Ambassador at Washington, and as I only wrote to him today, we shan't get his answer till the end of the week. You must treat it as a secret until you see it mentioned in the Press. I hope he says Yes, as not only would Chicago and Detroit be very interesting, but coming back by that route would really mean less train and avoid the dreary monotony of this journey. It would also be damned good propaganda with the great American Public.

Assuming that little detour comes off, we shall fetch up at Toronto for breakfast on 15 October, leave there at 1 a.m. that night, and make Ottawa early on the 16th. There we stay two or perhaps three nights with the Byngs at Government House, and then go to Montreal for two nights. I believe there is most amusing hunting there, and they will probably fix up a day for us. Next, we go back to USA to hunt with the Myopia Club, a plan already approved by the Ambassador and by Balmoral. After that the web again becomes

---

[1] A village high in the Himalayas, near Srinagar, which they had visited on honeymoon.

tangled so much that I can't go into details. But it looks quite certain that we shall sail from New York either in the *Olympic* on 25 October or in the *Aquitania* on the 29th. I hope the former, though *qua* ship there is nothing to choose between them.

It is a very good tour, and I am very lucky to be able to do it in these circumstances. Still, I do wish we were going to have a few more days vegetating at the Ranch, as I have seldom in my life worked harder than in the last three weeks.[1]

25 September 1924   Last night after dinner the whole sky was ablaze with northern lights – first time I have ever seen them. We made Winnipeg after breakfast and halted till luncheon. Squash racquets at the local club, the Prince taking on relays of Winnipegians, whom he exhausted in turn, while I played six games with Fruity, and won four of them. We are all the better for a good sweat.

Today the country is quite different. We have left the forests of Ontario, and have been going all day through the corn-lands of Manitoba – acres of wheat, now being harvested, interspersed with clumps of birch, rather jolly little white farms, and countless small meres from which duck and teal get up. All dead flat, and I, who can't do with plains, am thirsting for our first glimpse of the Rockies, which won't come till tomorrow evening. We shall, *d.v.*, reach the Ranch by 10 p.m.

We are quite a happy party, and old Fruity is not bad value in a Buntian way.[2] But he is a damned nuisance, and has just got into a mess which may involve us in trouble of really serious dimensions. There is just a hope that nothing may come of it, but it has worried us all and cost me many cipher telegrams and midnight letters. Damned old fool – but it is impossible to be really angry with him, and, though the incident might do the Prince very serious harm, we

---

[1] Tommy consulted Admiral Halsey by telegram about the possibility of going back to America, and from Badanloch, in Sutherland, where he had gone on holiday, the Admiral wrote back on 21 September:

I've sent you a cable strongly advising that our Foreign Office should be consulted before a definite decision is made to return to the US I think if they are not so consulted Ramsay MacDonald [the Prime Minister] and [W.G.] Tyrrell [Assistant Under-Secretary at the Foreign Office] will get their backs up badly and the King will be furious. The polo accounts in the English Press read very badly indeed, and Wimborne seems to have made himself singularly unpopular, even in the USA.

[2] Though constantly condemning Bunt Goschen for his incompetence, Tommy was deeply devoted to him.

have all rocked with laughter over it. I'll tell you all about it some day.[1]

26 September 1924   We are now fairly in the boundless prairies, and very dreary they are – unlimited vistas of brown grass, with nothing but occasional swarms of duck to enliven them. Last night our engine broke a rod, so we are three hours late and shan't make High River (station for the Ranch) till long after dark. However, the Prince has already decided to sleep in the train tonight and motor out (twenty-five miles over very bad roads) tomorrow early: a much better plan.

Last night, just as we were going to bed, came a voluminous telegram from the Ambassador at Washington. Code telegrams always frighten us to death, and when we found the first word was 'Confidential', we all had to have a glass of old brandy, as we felt sure it was something terrible about *l'affaire* Fruity. It took G. and me one-and-a-half hours to decode it, and it was all about nothing at all, written in the style of a *Times* leader, and could perfectly well have been expressed in two sentences, telegraphically. He is always sending us these Lord Chesterfield letters in code, and the Prince has made me write privately to Billy Chilton, the second-in-command at Washington, and a very good chap, to say that neither our hearts nor our tempers can stand the strain. When he gets the tangled-web telegram I sent him yesterday, I shudder to think of the mass of stuff the old man will launch over the wires. It is really the fault of that ass Jock Balfour (one of Nina's tiresome sons) who is the attaché there responsible for encyphering, and ought to see that the taxpayer's money isn't squandered in this way.

One result of this trip is that I have made friends with the Prince in a way I never could have done at home. He really is the most wonderful travelling companion, and we have the greatest fun together. And I am finding out that he is a much bigger character than I ever suspected. From the idiotic Press dope that has appeared during the last three weeks you might think he had done nothing but jazz and ride and flirt from the moment he set foot in America. Don't

---

[1] Metcalfe had visited a house of ill repute, but, finding himself unable to pay, was chased from the premises by the lady who had been entertaining him, minus his trousers, which she had stolen. After the tour Tommy one evening incautiously denounced Fruity as a bounder to his neighbour at dinner, not realising that she was a close friend of Lady Alexandra Curzon (known as 'Baba'), who was unofficially engaged to Metcalfe. Next day Metcalfe called at his house uninvited, while he was dressing for dinner, and knocked him down in the drawing-room. The two men made up their quarrel in April 1925, though Tommy insisted that his remarks had been justified.

believe it. He certainly enjoyed himself to the top of his bent, sat up late, and did everything with that super-energy which is merely natural to him, but makes him appear rather profligate to the ordinarily-constituted man; though any hint that he did anything whatever, either on Long Island or in New York, of which he need be the least ashamed, is utterly false.

Until one has seen it, it is impossible to believe the way American newspaper men will twist quite meaningless incidents into a 'story'. For instance, they came out with columns, one morning soon after we got there, about HRH being 'lost', and I have no doubt the *Daily Mirror* has reproduced it. All that happened was that he dined at a perfectly respectable Long Island house belonging to a very nice New York banker (where I subsequently dined myself, both with him and on my own) who took him on to a dance. The only people to whom he was 'lost' were the sleuths of the Press – everybody else in the island knew perfectly well where he was. Similarly, they made a tremendous song out of a perfectly ordinary loony-letter, which they twisted into a threat on his life.

All the surface-chat in the papers gives a totally wrong impression of the visit. Underneath, he has in his own little way done as much good to the British Empire as the Baldwin debt-settlement. Arthur Page (son of Ambassador Page,[1] and the real editor of the Letters – a most delightful and amusing man) came round to Woodside on our only quiet evening and smoked pipes with Oscar Solbert and me till 1 a.m. The Prince had spent some time in his printing-works (Doubleday Page, where the father used to work) the day before. They employ a number of Irish, most of whom are rabidly Sinn Fein and anti-British. The Prince had a talk with one of the worst of them, and, the next morning, he was heard to admit that possibly, in some of the rows between England and Ireland, Ireland had not always been right – which tickled Page immensely. As most of the propaganda against us in the USA starts from disgruntled Irishmen, the incident is more significant than it may sound.

Another notorious Sinn Feiner, who for years has done everything in his power to hurt us, and is now Mayor of one of the Long Island districts, astonished everybody by mobilising the whole of his town council and taking them off in motors to watch the Prince play in a practice game of polo twenty miles away – the result of ten minutes' talk with him at a garden-party. But his greatest triumph, perhaps,

[1] Walter Hines Page (1855–1918) was US Ambassador in London from 1913.

was at a private tea-party we organised, in considerable fear and trembling, at the house of one Arthur Woods in New York (he was the head police-boss in New York – the Basil Thomson[1] of America – and now controls the distribution of the vast funds of the Rockefeller Institute – a very powerful and staunch friend of England). We got Woods to ask to meet the Prince about eight of the big newspaper bosses, including Hearst's[2] two ablest and most vitriolic editors, who have done us infinite harm since the war. It was rather a risk – first, they might have refused to come, which would have been a distinct snub to the Prince, and one out of which they could have made some spicy headlines; and second, the party might have been a floater, if he had made a bad impression on them; also, we hadn't consulted the diplomatic people, who would certainly have vetoed the idea.

So I went there in a muck sweat, feeling rather like Guy Fawkes, or an author on a first night. As far as I could see – and all the others agreed – it was a howling success; they all turned up, though Brisbane, the most dangerous and important of the lot, was late, and I began to think he was deliberately cutting it. The Prince was in his best form, and talked to one after another of them, or, what was more important, set them talking, on every sort of subject. Two of them talked to me, both before and after the interview (I don't think they had any idea who I was), and they had certainly fallen for him completely. But the most satisfactory proof of the thing having accomplished some good was that, from that evening on, the Press quite obviously dropped its former stunt of giving exaggerated publicity to his amusements, expensive tastes, uselessness etc., and began to say something about his job in life, and the way he was doing it. No mention of the tea-party ever appeared in the Press, so far as we could discover, which was significant, because I know that the house was under observation by the reporters, who must have spotted everybody who entered or left it, and who described in full detail every other item of our afternoon in New York.

If they will only give him a fair chance, when, in two or three years'

---

[1] Sir Basil Thomson (1861–1939), son of the Archbishop of York, and an Old Etonian, was called to the bar and for a while acted as the Prime Minister of Tonga. He crowned a career in the prison service by becoming Assistant Commissioner of the Metropolitan Police 1913–19 and Director of Intelligence 1919–21.

[2] William Randolph Hearst (1863–1951), newspaper magnate and pioneer of sensational journalism, who had vigorously opposed America's entry into the First World War and the League of Nations.

time, he comes over to do his self-conceived tour of the big industrial cities, he may change the whole current of American opinion towards us, and the debt, and a hundred other things.

You might show the first three sheets of this letter to J. Gore, your father, Helen and the Mels (nobody else), if you think it would amuse them. Impress on them that it is all obviously private. I probably shan't have time to write to any of them, and it is no use sitting down to write a lot of short letters on this sort of trip.

I haven't the faintest idea what is going on in England, as it is too much of an undertaking to wade through *The Times* when it is over a week old, and the radio news, which we get on the train, only tells one that Lord Long[1] is dying, which we all thought he had got safely over a year ago, or how the billiards championship is going. Talking of billiards, I suppose Bunt has not shown any signs of refunding the £3 I lent him for his passage-money?

It is grey and cold outside now, and if the ranch is in country like this, I really shan't be sorry to move on. G. tells me it is only one degree more attractive.

I have got very fond of old G. – he is such a gallant old thing, and so cheerful and unruffled. But I really do believe that trying to live at the Prince's pace, as he has now been doing for over a year, will kill him before long. He looks perfectly ghastly some mornings, after a night's dancing, though he is much too game to admit it or even allow himself to be bad-tempered. I notice that he keeps himself going on large quantities of the strongest black coffee he can get, which is a bad sign. After all he is fifty-three, and there are few men of any age who can compete with the Prince's inexhaustible vitality. I shall be really relieved on his account when we get safe home, and he can disappear to the Tweed for a bit.

It seems a long way off still, and I'm afraid there's not much hope of hitting England before the last few days of October. However, I'm quite sure it is all doing me a lot of good, and I feel younger than I ever have since the war, and more interested in my fellow-creatures.

Have fun and keep happy, my pretty, and kiss the infants for me.

Bless you always, T.

---

[1] The first Viscount Long, former Secretary of State for the Colonies and First Lord of the Admiralty, finally expired on the day Tommy was writing, 26 September 1924.

29 September 1924

E.P. Ranch
Pekisko
Alberta

My darling, Nothing could have been more melancholy than our arrival here; HRH with a roaring cold and very depressed, leaden skies and bitter sleet storms. The drive out from High River was the chilliest I've ever had, and we got here to find all the fires smoking and the one living-room practically uninhabitable. It seemed a very depressing place, and I began to wonder how we could endure five days of it. But, three hours after we got here, the sky cleared and since then we have had the most flawless, golden weather, with blazing sun and air like wine.

The Ranch consists of the homestead – a large wooden bungalow in which we all live – and three or four barns and cattle-sheds, all thrown down by the side of the little Pekisko river, which winds through a narrow belt of trees and scrub from the Rockies, bounding the whole horizon some thirty miles to the west. There are two low ranges of hills on each side of the river, and between them lies a vast, undulating plain, broken only by occasional bluffs, set with stunted trees. It is not really beautiful country, save for the wonderful line of the mountains, but the space and the cleanness of it make one love it.

31 September 1924   We are off this afternoon, and I must finish this before luncheon, as a sale of the surplus cattle is being held here at 2.30, to which all the countryside is flocking. I got up early for a final go at the fish, and had a delightful hour, catching seven, weighing, I suppose, about 6 lbs altogether. They are very lively, and it is a most amusing little river to fish, full of cunning holes and unexpected pools. G. and I have had capital sport with them and although I don't really regret leaving the Ranch as a whole, I do regret the river.

Yesterday we had an alfresco luncheon for about a dozen 'old timers', as they call them – old ranchers who have been out here since Alberta was first opened up; splendid old boys, mostly Scotch, all looking twenty years younger than they really are. It was a very cheerful meal, and they walked into the whisky with great gusto.

I must say, it is all being far more fun than I expected, and I am frightfully well, and winning quite a lot of money at poker.

All love, T.

To the Hon. F. C. Lascelles

2 October 1924   *Jasper Park Lodge*
Alberta

My dear Father, We had five pleasant days on the Ranch, mostly beautiful weather – warm and still, and wonderful air. It is a very good ranch, as ranches go, but I'm bound to say that if I hadn't been a fisherman, and if it hadn't been fine, I should have found precious little to do there. As it was, I used to go down to the river as soon as I had done my work – letters and telegrams arrived continuously by telephone, motor and even aeroplane – and G. Trotter and I between us caught a lot of fish.

It is a beautiful little river, like a small Highland salmon river, with lots of straightforward pools varied by deep holes and crannies made by fallen tree-trunks, which make for tricky fishing. The trout are the indigenous rainbow, supplemented by a lot they turned down some years ago, and there are plenty of them – too many, in fact. They don't run big – our best was a few ounces over 1 lb – but they are extremely lively; twice a fish I had hooked threw himself right up the bank, for which I was grateful, as, owing to it being rough wading, with a lot of scrambling through thick brushwood between pools, I couldn't be bothered with a landing-net. Though they are unsophisticated, they take some catching, as the water is clear as gin and one is usually fishing in strong sunlight; also, one must use large flies – they won't look at anything smaller than one of your biggest Tangbole flies.

HRH spent most of his time stacking corn and hay – hard labour which don't appeal to me unless there is nothing better to do; but we rode round the country once or twice, and one afternoon had quite an amusing shoot after duck, prairie-chicken and partridge – the last having been imported from Hungary a good many years ago by the local ranchers.

Yesterday there was a sale of cattle and sheep, which all the countryside attended; in spite of having previously consumed liberal supplies of whisky in the house, they showed no enthusiasm in the ring. Prices were disappointing, not, I gather, because the stock wasn't all that it should be, but because there is very little spare cash in these parts.

We boarded our luxurious train again last night, and today have been climbing through the Rockies. The scenery so far has been nothing wonderful, and, even if the mountains have snow on their tops, is certainly no better than that provided by the Highland Railway. This place is a new summer resort recently opened up by the Canadian National Railways, and we are stopping off for a few hours simply to oblige them and give them a bit of an advertisement, which they badly need, as no wise Canadian ever travels on any line except the Canadian Pacific Railway.

There is nothing whatever to do, and we are very thankful we are not spending the night here, as originally planned, but going back to the train, and on to Vancouver, as soon as we have had dinner. It has certainly been a capital trip so far, though, between work and play, I've scarcely had time to sit down for a month. I feel very much better for it, and have enjoyed it all immensely. I'm glad, too, to have met some of the right sort of Yankees; most of their polo-players and their friends are as good sportsmen as one could find anywhere, and, I am sorry to say, infinitely more agreeable than the majority of the polo crowd from England.   Your loving Tommy.

To Joan

10 October 1924   *Private Car 'Balmoral'*
                                                  near Brandon
                                                  Manitoba

My darling, We shall now sail from New York in the *Olympic* early in the morning of the 25th. This should get us to Southampton on the 31st, in time to reach London for dinner. If you ring up York House the day before, somebody there will be able to tell you the exact times. You are not to come to any station to meet me, but to wait for me in the drawing-room at Oxford Square, whither I shall come with all possible speed – probably straight from Victoria, as I expect Godfrey [Thomas] will come down to Southampton and I can hand over everything to him in the train. I have, by the way, told him I mean to take a fortnight's leave early in November.

It is very thrilling to think we shall, *d.v.*, actually be arriving in London this day three weeks. I am beginning to get very homesick, and your nice letters make me more so. It's a good job that circumstances have made the Prince finally choose the *Olympic* – partly because it is high time he travelled on a White Star boat, and also because she is, I think, the only transatlantic liner with a squash court, which will be a great boon to all of us.

I don't think I have written since the Ranch, but time goes so quick in this hustling life that I can't remember. I had a delicious morning's fishing there the last day before breakfast, and we left that afternoon. Since then we have been through the Rockies by two different routes – disappointing, I thought, though the weather was not suitable for mountain scenery. Anyway, one mountain always looks much the same as another from a train, and I get very bored winding endlessly through narrow gorges, with a grey river on one side and the eternal cliffs of pine and rock on the other.

Vancouver is a very fair spot, where we had a good game of golf and quite an amusing party at the Country Club, at which I danced hard till 3 a.m. One of the party has to be out of bed at a fairly respectable hour next morning, and as the Prince and G. never by any chance come home before 6, and so are not visible till high noon (and not much use to anybody then), I am compelled to keep comparatively early hours.

Victoria, on the other hand (on Vancouver Island, five hours by boat), is one of the world's really jolly places, and very beautiful. Our entry into the port in a perfect autumn sunset was the best thing of its kind I have seen since Rio[1] – a marvellous bay, dotted with little islands, and the whole horizon ringed with blue hills, with Mount Baker – as fine a snow-peak as there is anywhere in the Himalayas – rearing himself up behind you. The town, too, is a nice clean little place, with quite good Government buildings. They say that all the year round they get continuous weeks of what the English weather ought to be; only, where we get just one sample of the perfect autumn or spring day, they get a whole consignment. The Prince, who had been there in 1919, told me he was going to show me the most beautiful golf-links in the world, and he is probably about right: I certainly never expect to see a better. I warn you that, if ever England becomes impossible, I shall go and live in Vancouver Island. There isn't much to do there, except farm and enjoy life, and the society, consisting largely of axed navy and army officers, is not very exciting, perhaps, but harmless, and not 'colonial'. But there is an atmosphere about the whole place which made me feel that it would at a pinch be the only possible substitute if one could not live at home.

The Lieutenant Governor of British Columbia lives there, and gave us a curious but quite amusing dance. His hobby is working lime-light – a curious taste I have never come across before. So, after we had been peacefully dancing for a short time, all the electrics were

[1] Which he had visited, and described with lyrical enthusiasm, in 1914.

suddenly switched off, and our only illumination till about 2.30 came from rays of every shade in the rainbow which the old boy played on us from a balcony. I felt as if I was one of the male beauty chorus at the Gaiety. Luckily, however, the Lieutenant Governor's other hobby is old brandy, and as the evening wore on he became so rascally drunk that he could no longer manipulate the apparatus, and was propped quietly against a pillar in the hall till it was time for the Prince to say goodbye; when, having assured HRH he was 'as full as a bloody goat' (which was undeniable), he fell flat on his face on the floor, crushing a china vessel to powder. It was a very funny scene, and the old man wrote a most amusing and quite unrepentant letter next day, sending us two bottles of his special brandy for our journey. He was really a very nice old man, drunk or sober.

Yesterday at Calgary we hoped to get a game of golf *en passant*, but as there had been a heavy fall of snow, it was impossible. We are now approaching Winnipeg, where we spend a couple of days; no snow here, but it looks cold and grey. Then Chicago and Detroit and Toronto and Ottawa.

You might try to get the Joeys – nobody else – to dine on 1 November, the night after we get back; I shall have lots of gossip for them both. If you like, we will go and dine at Claridge's, and dance on the Sunday or Monday.

Goodbye, my pretty. Lots of love, T.

16 October 1924 *Private Car 'Balmoral'*
between Toronto and Ottawa

My darling, This letter may not get very far at present, for the country we are going through now is so lovely in its autumn plumage that I have to keep looking out of the window: the first time it has been worth doing it since we entered Canada, except occasionally in the Rockies.

Goodness, the life we have been leading lately, both work and play. Chicago, stunting all day amid very friendly but very rough crowds, who nearly pulled us to bits in their enthusiasm, and a marvellous party till 3.30 a.m. Detroit by luncheon time, and more stunting till dinner, followed by another wild party which ended in young Ford taking us all on board his yacht and sailing us across the lake to join our train at Windsor, Ontario, at about 3. It was a terribly pink-eyed party which turned out on the platform at Toronto at 9 to receive the greetings of the Lieutenant Governor of Ontario. We then jumped straight into motors and drove about twenty miles to a meet of the Toronto hounds, which, on a day like July, we pursued all day over a trappy country.

By dinner time I had come to the conclusion that I must have a comparatively early bed, as I have got to be on my toes in Ottawa, where we have a big dinner and reception tonight, a ball tomorrow and a jazz party on Saturday. So, after dining with the Lieutenant Governor, I retired to the hotel and was asleep by 1.30, while the others went to three parties in succession, getting back at 7. They, of course, can sleep most of the day, which I can never get a chance to do even in the train. However, I have no ground for complaint, as I can always leave any party whenever I like; but I really do enjoy most of them a lot, and am beginning to pine if I don't get my nightly jazz. That will make you smile – or possibly rather sad. I am afraid I have done you out of a lot of fun that way, my pretty, and I really am sorry about it, and will do my best to make amends. But it was the only one of my post-war complexes which you haven't been able to overcome; I don't really know what has overcome it now. Probably it was the feeling that if one is thrown into the water, one must sink or learn to swim, and I really should have been completely lost if I hadn't danced on this trip.

Then there's no doubt to my mind – and G. and the other experts confirm this – the music and the general level of dancing are far better on this continent than in London. The bands are certainly marvellous – they made me want to dance in a way I have never felt anywhere else – and one hardly ever strikes a partner who isn't superb. Not that I can claim much experience of London dancers, as yet, but I am afraid the criticism about the bands is true enough. However, there are some tunes I shall always be able to dance to – 'Driftwood', 'Lazy' and 'So This is Venice'. You had better get them for the gramophone. When I take you out dancing for the first time, I shall have to wait till they play one of these, to give my feet assurance. But I think I must be able to do it fairly well now – of course they all tell one one dances like an angel – because I never seem to touch either my partner's feet or other couples' ribs, which after all is the main test. I only wish my golf had progressed as rapidly, though I believe I have now acquired the interlocking grip, which certainly makes one far less wild. All love, T.

18 October 1924   *Government House*
                                                                          Ottawa

My darling, It is pleasant to be back in the familiar Government House atmosphere – it is all reminiscent of India – and to feel the

sheltering arms of Government round one again, after the unpro-
tected life of hotels and trains. It is a nice place, too; Old Byng[1] is a
dear, whom I've always revered since Cambrai, and she, though a
queer, dominating creature, is interesting, and is being very gracious
to me. Their senior ADC, Tommy Erskine (Old Mother Mar and
Kellie's second son), is a very nice boy, so with him and Pat about, it
is all very friendly.

A formal Government House dinner and reception for the old stiffs
the first night, and a ball for Young Things last night. I behaved very
badly, I fear, and danced continuously for two hours with the same
young woman, whose married name I can't for the life of me
recollect, but who I know was a Miss Mulvey when they were all out
here in 1919, when Joey made an impression on her.

I have now got to the stage when I can't endure being asked more
than three or four times in one night, 1. Do you like America
/Canada? 2. Is the Prince enjoying himself? 3. Are you a brother of
Viscount Las-celles? – so if I find a doe who suits my step and who
works off these three preliminary questions fairly early, I damn well
stick to her. Incidentally, I must have asked fully twenty young
Americans and Canadians to lunch with us in Oxford Square when
they come to London, as they are all going to do in the next few
months. I hope to God I shall remember them, and that they won't
all come the same day. They are all pretty, all good dancers, mostly
married, one or two single, and one or two divorced. We shall have to
'give them a rush', as they say over here, which means taking them
out to dance somewhere. By the way, G. said at luncheon yesterday
that his first act when we got back would be to have me made an
honorary member of the Embassy Club, and I agreed. I am coming
on, aren't I?

No, you are *not* to come to the station to meet me; I love you too
much, my sweet pretty, to say how-d'ye-do to you on a Victoria
platform after being away ten weeks. Just you wait for me in Oxford
Square, and I promise you I'll be there within quarter of an hour of
our train arriving.

Your letter has suffered at the expense of one I had to write to
HM the Queen – only the third I have managed to bring off in the
whole tour, but a damn good one to finish up with. Now it's time to
dress for dinner. God bless you, my Joanna – it's wonderful to think I
shall be back with you in a fortnight.   All love, T.

[1] First Viscount Byng (1862–1935) served with distinction in the First World
War and was Governor-General of Canada 1921–26. He married Marie Evelyn
Moreton, author of two novels.

A day or two later, in Montreal, the newspapers seized on a minor incident which Tommy himself did not mention. Under the headline CAPT. LASCELLES DASHES FOR TRAIN–NEARLY MISSES ROYAL CAR AS HE STOPS TO SPEAK IN MONTREAL, the United Press agency reported:

Montreal, Monday. Every office boy within four miles radius of the Turbot yards of the Canadian National Railways must have been playing hookey this morning when the Prince of Wales spent fifteen minutes just outside the city limits, for every covered freight car within sighting distance was swarming with boys, while the more venturesome fellows climbed the telegraph and electric light poles to get a glimpse of the popular visitor.

Captain Lascelles, his Private Secretary, stepped from the royal train to say a few words to the newspapermen, who were herded at a respectful distance. He spoke of the wonderful welcome to the Prince everywhere in the United States. 'He got a wonderfully hearty send-off yesterday,' continued Captain Lascelles, and glancing over his shoulder he saw that the royal train was pulling out of the yards, so the sentence was never finished. Captain Lascelles took one spring toward the train and with a hoist from an obliging official he was landed safely in the royal coach.

The SS *Olympic* docked in Southampton on 31 October 1924. Tommy's admiration for the Prince was, if anything, enhanced, and there was as yet no sign of the disillusionment which set in later. On his part, the Prince was delighted with the way things had gone, and sent Tommy a characteristically generous note of thanks:

Prince of Wales to A.L.

November 1924   *St. James's Palace*

My dear Tommy, Thanks so much for your letter which I've been meaning to answer every day but I've been so rushed – I quite understand and think it very nice of you and a good compromise so that neither of us need feel beaten!! We don't either of us propose to die just yet awhile still I hope it'll be me first!!

I hope you are enjoying a very well-earned rest-up or *va*-cation though it's too cold to enjoy anything really!! I do want to thank you for all your help and work in America but you must know I'm very grateful, and that kind of thing is so hard to say and still worse to write – I can only hope you enjoyed some of the two months we were over there, and I believe you did, and I'm glad.

I'm working very hard and I hate it and can't settle down though that isn't surprising. I've got a slight chill or rather had one last night and feel very limp today and not in shape for a public dinner this evening or a long day of *arterial roads*! tomorrow but I'll be all right. Best of luck.   Yours, E.P.

In 1925, when the Prince toured South Africa, Tommy stayed in London, and from the accounts coming back it soon became clear that he had escaped an exhausting and difficult trip. The distances travelled were enormous, the heat and dust formidable, and many of the people dour to a degree. The Prince himself told Tommy that he found the Boers 'a sticky, slow, dull, narrow-minded and unattractive race,' who hated the English, and that it went against the grain to be nice to them.

In spite of these problems he was in his best fettle. 'HRH has been in the most marvellous form ever since he left England, just like he used to be in the old days – full of fun and rags with everyone,' wrote Halsey. The Admiral attributed this striking improvement to the fact that the Prince had, for the time being, got rid of Fruity Metcalfe. 'His present frame of mind started as we left England,' he wrote from on board HMS *Repulse* on 27 April. 'To my mind the change entirely took place after saying goodbye to Fruity.'

Two weeks later Joey Legh wrote from South Africa:

'Many thanks for your two letters, which amused me enormously. In fact I showed them both to HRH, who was mightily tickled by them . . . I am further to add that HRH considers you a bounder for not having written to him, and I understand he is addressing a letter to you in these terms.'

So he was, in his own hand:

Prince of Wales to A.L.

7 May 1925   *Union of South Africa*
                                                                                          On Tour

Tommy – why in hell haven't you written me at all? You've written Joey twice though – I laughed a lot. Till I get a letter, none from me though I'm sorry you were laid up again after I left. Too bad.

Life not so good just now and v. strenuous and irritating but it'll improve perhaps. Here's hoping to God it will!

Now please write to me quickly and I don't want pompous or official news – some dope to make me laugh. I'm glad there's no more chance of you or Fruity putting up a show in the ring at the Albert Hall!   Best wishes from E.P.

'V. strenuous and irritating' was evidently a fair description of the party's existence. 'Constant long motor drives in appalling dust,' Joey reported, 'stopping at these small dorps every day, every day the same.' According to Admiral Dudley North, 'the dances and evening entertainments so far have been dreadful. There simply isn't a nice-looking woman in the whole of the Union.' The Prince, he said, had to talk to all the old Dutch farmers every time they stopped, 'and masses of old and zeppelin-shaped women.' HRH had excelled himself and captured the old Dutchmen's hearts, 'but it is, as I said, the most rotten tour we have ever done.'

In Joey Legh's words, the Prince really had been 'absolutely marvellous', but by the middle of July he was writing: 'Thank God we have nearly finished with sunny South Africa. I can tell you we've had a pretty fair bellyful.' Nevertheless, as they set out for home on 3 August, Halsey reported, 'It is marvellous how Boer and Briton have come together in the last three months entirely to do honour to HRH.'

At the end of a long letter written in mid-tour, the Prince wrote: 'The others have shown me your priceless letters, and they cheered us up.' So perhaps Tommy felt that, although he had been lucky enough to escape the privations of the trip, he had played a small supporting role in helping make it a success.

CANADA
1927

In the autumn of 1927, together with his brother Prince George, Duke of Kent, the Prince of Wales travelled to Canada, where, at the invitation of the Canadian Govenment, he took part in the Diamond Jubilee of the Confederation. As he himself remarked in his memoirs, the trip brought him 'for the first time into intimate contact' with the political leader destined to oppose him at the time of his Abdication – Stanley Baldwin, who travelled with the royal party.[1]

The Prime Minister's decision to visit Canada at that point caused intense debate. To Lord Eustace Percy it was 'the most eccentric act of his whole public life,' for the Cabinet was deeply divided as a result of the Geneva Conference, which had been called to settle the disposition of cruisers, destroyers and submarines among the nations, but had ended inconclusively. Percy believed that Baldwin went to Canada mainly in an attempt to spend some time with the Prince of Wales and influence him for the better. Others, including Baldwin's son, thought he went simply because he had been invited by the Canadian Government.

Either way, the Prince was by no means at ease in the company of the Prime Minister, and later remarked waspishly in his memoirs: 'As I studied Mr. Baldwin, I thought I detected traces of the arrogance that some Englishmen display when travelling abroad. The deeper we penetrated the North American continent, the more he became the embodiment of old John Bull himself. In my hour of Sovereignty I was to rediscover that side of him.'

Evidently it did not occur to the Prince that Baldwin disapproved of his conduct. 'Life seemed pretty good to me in 1927,' he later wrote

---

[1] Stanley Baldwin (1867–1947) was Prime Minister three times – 1923–24, 1924–29, and 1935–37 – and in 1937 was created first Earl Baldwin of Bewdley.

blithely. Nor did he realise that by then his irresponsibility, immaturity and lack of any real sense of duty had driven even the loyal Captain Lascelles to the point of mutiny. In the words of the Prince's biographer, Frances Donaldson,

> Baldwin was quite quickly given an example of the kind of behaviour that had upset so many people. The Prime Minister, his wife and son who had travelled with him were invited to dine at Government House, where the Prince of Wales and Prince George were staying. Arriving punctually for dinner, they passed on their way into the house the two brothers dressed in shorts and shirts and going out to play a game of squash. The whole party was then kept waiting until, the game being over, the princes had had time to dress for dinner.[1]

It may have been this incident that made Tommy react with uncharacteristic lack of restraint. The Prince stayed at Government House, Ottawa, from 2 to 5 August. On the 2nd Tommy wrote to Joan telling her that things were 'bad internally', and that he was considering resignation; and on the 3rd or 4th he arranged a private meeting with Baldwin, which he later described:

> I felt in such despair about him that I sought a secret colloquy with Stanley Baldwin one evening at Government House, Ottawa, and in his little sitting room at the end of the passage on the first floor (which I have never since been able to enter without a reminiscent qualm) I told him directly that, in my considered opinion, the Heir Apparent, in his unbridled pursuit of wine and women, and whatever selfish whim occupied him at the moment, was rapidly going to the devil, and unless he mended his ways, would soon become no fit wearer of the British Crown.
>
> I expected to get my head bitten off; but Baldwin heard me to the end, and, after a pause, said he agreed with every word I had said. I went on, 'You know, sometimes when I sit in York House waiting to get the result of some point-to-point in which he is riding, I can't help thinking that the best thing that could happen to him, and to the country, would be for him to break his neck.'
>
> 'God forgive me,' said Stanley Baldwin, 'I have often thought the same.' Then he undertook to talk straightly to the Prince at an early

---

[1] *Edward VIII*, p. 135.

opportunity; but he never did, until October 1936 – too late, too late.

Galvanised by this conversation, Tommy wrote to Joan on the night of the 4th saying that he had definitely decided to resign: he said that he would 'strike at once', discussed the possibility of leaving their London house and going to live at Sutton Waldron, and asked her to send him a cable simply saying 'I agree.'

To Joan, who was pregnant with her third child, this letter came as an awful shock. Writing back, she protested strongly, calling Tommy's news 'a complete bombshell', and she feared that some sudden scandal might have thrown him off the rails. In fact there had been no scandal: rather, his malaise came from the realisation that, no matter how hard he tried, he could never make the Prince fit to be King.

Unfortunately the letters of 2 and 4 August have been lost, so that Tommy's disillusionment is not articulated as clearly as it might be; but, in the documents that survive, his struggle with his own conscience is vividly documented.

To Joan

30 July 1927   *SS Empress of Australia*

My darling, It now seems pretty certain we shall sail from Quebec in the *Empress of Scotland* on 7 September. That gets us to London on the 13th or 14th. We have had a very dreary and depressing voyage – cold, grey days and choppy seas, which were bad enough to send me to bed prematurely and have made me feel chronically ill. Today we are more or less sheltered, in the Gulf of St. Lawrence, and there has been a thick fog more or less all day, which involves reduced speed and incessant hooting. There were icebergs about in the morning, but I didn't see any.

In the circumstances, nobody has been very sociable, and everybody inclined to be bored. Angus McDonnell[1] is the bright spot of the whole shipload – a very cheerful and amusing soul, who has been everywhere and done everything without losing the outlook of five-and-twenty.

---

[1] Colonel the Hon. Angus McDonnell (1881–1966), was then Conservative Member of Parliament for Dartford. He had served with distinction in the First World War and become an officer in the Canadian General Reserve.

The Baldwin party do not contribute much. I am frankly disappointed in him; he is very agreeable – almost ultra-agreeable – and bonhomous, but I have never met a man in a big position with less inspiration in him. George Lloyd has more electricity in one finger than Stanley Baldwin has in his whole system. In the analogy game, his dish is unquestionably cold mutton, without mint sauce. I like cold mutton, as you know, and often eat it from choice, but all the same, it is cold mutton. Mrs. Baldwin is warm mutton. The children are more interesting; Mrs. Monro is a nice little thing, dances well and plays the piano, and Windham is a curious dreamy creature. I am not sure yet if he is an outrageous young prig or something of a humourist. He hated both Eton and Cambridge, which is a bad sign, though not necessarily a conclusive one.[1]

I can quite understand now how inevitably impatient men like Winston or F.E. [Smith] must get with Stanley Baldwin. But his very impeccability will probably make him proof against their wiles in the long run. Parsifal he is, though a very plain and unromantic knight.

Last night was the first relief in a terribly dull week. We danced a bit, and then a curious woman called Miss Jeanne Gordon[2] was suddenly produced by G. (who invariably knows everybody in a ship before the anchor is dry) and, in the empty ballroom, everybody else having gone to bed, she burst into a series of operatic extracts in the most glorious mezzo-soprano imaginable, accompanied by first-rate acting. She sang, and acted, all the Carmen songs quite perfectly, and other arias out of obscure operas like *Lucrezia Borgia*, which were new to me, and the *Samson and Delilah* song, which I don't like, but which certainly shows up a voice like that wonderfully well. It appears she is a Canadian who is quite well known at the Metropolitan Opera House in New York, and Mr. T. Burke,[3] the famous tenor, who is also on board, and in charge of her, says she will probably appear at Covent Garden next summer.

Till she starts singing, you would write her off as a rather blatant bar-maid; but once she is off, she becomes a great artist. Some of her low notes set one humming all over, just as old Kirkby Lunn used to do.[4] Mr. Burke has not condescended to sing yet, but there is a ship's concert tonight, at which HRH intends to make him give tongue.

[1] 1904–76, Stanley Baldwin's second son, succeeded his elder brother as third Earl Baldwin in 1958. He and Tommy became great friends.
[2] 1884–1952. She had made her operatic début in 1918, and in 1924 was principal contralto at the Metropolitan Opera House in New York.
[3] 1890–1969, an Englishman specialising in Verdi and Puccini.
[4] Louise Kirkby Lunn (1873–1930), the English mezzo-soprano.

We have had no further trouble about USA, and he has been quite cheerful and good, accepting my drafts for his speeches without much demur. We shall get five days on the Ranch, and four at Victoria, BC, where my favourite golf links is. This is better than I hoped.

I'm afraid, from the Marconigrams, you must have had bad weather for Goodwood, but it can't have been worse than this eternal slatey sea. God, how I hate it. I would sooner be a blind man than a sailor. Goodbye, my darling, and God bless you. T.

[The two missing letters, announcing Tommy's intention of resigning, were written on 2 and 4 August.]

6 August 1927   *Government House*
                                                   Toronto

My darling, This has been a shattering week, but after tomorrow, which will be the worst day of all – a ninety-mile drive to Niagara, with this idiotic ceremony at the end of it – the official part of the tour really ends.

I am too beat to write, and must go to bed, as it is now 1 a.m. and we start again at 8.30. It worries me to think of all the unkind things I seem to have said to you lately. Will you forgive me? My darling, I don't really mind about anything in life so long as you are fairly happy, but I don't seem to have put it into practice very well.

Goodnight, T.

9 August 1927   *Canadian Pacific*
                                                   Royal Train

My darling, Our official programme finished, thank God, on Sunday night, after a shattering day with the Yanks at Fort Erie. We left Government House, Toronto, at 8.45 on a grilling morning, and, just to put us in a good temper for the day's proceedings, went to an enormous open-air service of ex-servicemen, lasting forty minutes, where the Prince had to read the lesson, in the teeth of a heavy barrage of photographers and movie-men, standing a few yards in front of him. Then, the whole of our party, the Baldwin party, and every conceivable official in Canada, got into a string of motors about a mile long and started off hell-for-leather for Niagara, ninety miles away.

After a hurried lunch in a small hotel overlooking the Falls, where we had also to change into top hats etc., we were whirled off again to Fort Erie, twenty-two miles further, which is the Canadian end of the new Peace Bridge, whose formal dedication was the object of the expedition. In the middle of the bridge was a tape, surmounted by Union Jacks, Stars-and-Stripes, and a couple of stuffed seagulls whose *raison d'être* puzzled me till I realised that they were deputising for doves, emblems of Peace. (This Peace, by the way, is nothing to do with 1918, but that which has subsisted precariously between Canada and the USA since the latter tried to invade the former in 1812, and got it in the neck.)

To this barrier, the Prince and the Canadian Cabinet advanced from one side, and the Vice-President of the United States from the other[1] – the latter, as it happened, looking at that moment none too peaceful, since we had kept him waiting nearly two hours, and his police officials had scared him to rights with warnings that there was a damned good chance of a bomb being thrown at him during the day by the champions of those two ice-cream merchants who are due to be electrocuted tomorrow and whose names escape me.[2]

However, after a due amount of nose-rubbing, the tape was ceremoniously cut, and we drove on to a grandstand erected on the American side, entirely surrounded by an enormous concourse of people, kept at a most respectful distance, as good democrats should be, by serried ranks of troops and barbed-wire entanglements ten feet high. To emphasise the fact that we king-ridden Britons had really reached the land of the brave and the free, quantities of policemen, armed to the teeth, did a ceaseless ladies'-chain through the crowd all the time the ceremony was in progress.

The ball was opened, for some obscure reason, by the Chief Rabbi, who invoked Jehovah at considerable length by the medium of very loud loud-speakers. I was reminded of Joshua doing his trumpet-stunt round the walls of Jericho. The walls of Buffalo, however, within which we were now standing, remained firm, a tribute to the grand qualities of American workmanship. After the Rabbi, every-one else had a go, all saying what a capital thing peace was, and all obviously acutely conscious of Geneva. Our party kept themselves

[1] Charles Gates Dawes (1865–1951) was Vice-President of the United States 1925–29, and in 1925 had received the Nobel peace prize.

[2] Nicola Sacco (1891–1927) and Bartolomeo Vanzetti (1888–1927) were two Italian-born radicals who had been convicted, in 1921, of the murder of a pay-roll guard in Manitoba. The judge and jury were widely thought to have been prejudiced against the defendants because of their foreign origin and political activities. Protests against their conviction poured in from all over the world, and the controversy rumbled on for six years; but in the end both men went to the electric chair, amid demonstrations, on 10 August 1927.

rigorously to pre-arranged platitudes, which sounded like a set of texts stolen from the walls of an infant school; but Vice-President Dawes wasn't going to let a chance like this slip, not he, and when his turn came – he was the last on the programme, doubtless by design – he blew out his chest and his cheeks and let fly about armaments and cruisers and mutual give-and-take till we began to wonder whether the American fleet mightn't suddenly sail up the river and blow us and the peace and the bridge and the Rabbi into a thousand fragments.

When at last he ended, we were hustled back into our sun-baked motors, and treated to a drive like nothing except the chariot-race in *Ben Hur,* back to Niagara, which, by comparison, seemed a very peaceful little waterfall when we got there. Our forty large Cadillac cars had by this time got all out of their official order, their drivers were determined to regain their allotted stations in the procession or die, and the police had released the normal Sunday traffic along a very popular road. The result beat anything I have ever seen for good healthy excitement: I don't think you would have survived ten minutes of it.

It was now nearly six, and the pitiless sun was getting low. Though I have never been through such a day since the early part of the Retreat in 1918, the next five hours were really quite pleasant. Some two miles from Niagara Falls we were improbably transferred into little yellow tram-cars. Like Alice through the Looking Glass, I was long past wondering at any sudden change, and should have made no demur if we had been asked to do the next stage of the journey on ostriches. The tram-cars proved, too, to be very friendly, for they contained not only arm-chairs, but tea and iced ginger-ale and whiskey; moreover they took us straight to the very brink of the Horseshoe Falls, and to look down into that amazing crater, with the sun making a dozen different rainbows in the mist of spray, is worth a good deal of tribulation. Even better, perhaps, are the rapids, along which, for a distance of more than ten miles, our little cars then took us: mile after mile of roaring, boiling water, like no river one has ever seen.

The final stage, after cordial farewells to the Americans under the most appropriate shadow of Brock's monument (he was the general who thrashed them in 1812[1]), began when we embarked on a river

[1] Major-General Sir Isaac Brock (1769–1812) had taken command of British troops in Canada in 1806, when hostilities between Great Britain and the United States were threatening. In 1812, soon after forcing the American General Hull to surrender, he was killed at the battle of Queenstown Height.

steamer, which took us, in the cool of the evening, back to Toronto. By 11 p.m. we were safe in our train, and two hours later it pulled out for the west, and is still pulling tirelessly in the same direction. I don't think I have ever before been so tired as I was that night.

The rest of the trip seems just a mottled blur of crowded streets, garden-parties and interminable public meals. It has gone well enough, and the Prime Minister has had a real *succès*, and made some very fine speeches. Nobody alive could have captured the Canadians so completely as he has done. He seems to thrive on it, and looks infinitely better than when we started. The Willingdons[1] asked after you. They too have had a great success out here, and one hears nothing but praise of them from all sides.

We get to the Ranch tomorrow evening, and I am already itching for the cool of Thursday morning, when I shall get up before breakfast and catch some trout. It is too hot in this train to write more. I think sadly of the Ridgeway garden, where I daresay you are sitting today. It seems very far away. There are masses of amusing flowers out all along the line, and I long to get out and do some botanising.　　　　　　　　　　　　　　　　　Bless you. T.

11 August 1927　　　　　　　　　　　　　　　　　　　*E.P. Ranch*
　　　　　　　　　　　　　　　　　　　　　　　　　　　Pekisko
　　　　　　　　　　　　　　　　　　　　　　　　　　　Alberta

My darling, My God, the relief of being safe in this blessed spot for five whole days and nights. I had a bad jolt when we de-trained at Calgary yesterday, for the Lieutenant Governor of Alberta got hold of the Prince and induced him to say he would go off to Edmonton, another one-horse town one hundred miles off, and do stunts there the day after tomorrow. I had already, on his instructions, told the Mayor and everybody else connected with the place that he couldn't possibly fit in a visit there, but he is so utterly bored here that he clutched even at that extremely unattractive straw to get him away from it into the whirl of crowds and cities again, and I'm damned if he didn't say he would do it. I looked so mutinous when he tackled me (especially since, at the very moment he was talking to the

---

[1] The first Marquis of Willingdon (1866–1941) was then Governor-General of Canada. From 1913–19 he had been Governor of Bombay, preceding Tommy's brother-in-law George Lloyd in the post, and Governor of Madras from 1919–24. He thus knew both Tommy and Joan, whose father Lord Chelmsford had become Viceroy of India in 1916. Tommy could not bear Lady Willingdon, describing her as 'a bad, bossing woman who makes herself a nuisance wherever she goes.'

Lieutenant Governor, I was once more explaining personally to the Edmonton Mayor what I had told him in several letters – that we couldn't possibly go) that he said hurriedly there would be no need for me to go too. To which I have held him, so that either G. or Joey, who are both thoroughly happy here also, will have to pack up again tomorrow and go off again till Sunday, when they all come back here for one night only. The wretched Prince George is being dragged off too, so I shall have a lovely two days here, practically alone.

I feel a little mean about it, but after all it is their job and not mine to do the actual ADC-work, and neither of them will hear of my going. Angus McDonnell (at HRH's urgent invitation!) is coming to stay this Sunday, which will be fun, though HRH will hardly see him at all.

We were made to stop in Calgary and play golf yesterday, when I had the satisfaction of beating Prince George by seven and five, so didn't arrive till 8 p.m., pretty dead. None the less, as it is blazing weather, and fishing not likely to be any use except at dawn and sunset, I borrowed the faithful Burt's alarm-watch, set it at 5 a.m., and woke feeling incredibly well. After some tea from a thermos, and a ham sandwich, I started off before 5.30. You know my theory that life is only worth living at isolated moments set in the flat plain of hum-drummery. There has not been one such moment, even a little one, since we left England, but the next three hours practically made up for all.

I was walking straight for the Rockies, forty miles away, with a red sun just rising over the foothills at my back, through the clearest possible dawn to a really fine day. Early August is still high summer in Alberta, and the prairie for miles was ablaze with a mass of flowers – clusters of trailing dog-roses, great clumps of Golden Rod and Michaelmas daisies, and golden acres of a great yellow Marguerite with a velvety brown centre, which they call Brown-eyed Susan, and a dozen varieties all new to me. Kites overhead, and little birds still busy with their broods scolding me from the bushes, and a drenching dew under foot.

The river was mine, at any point I liked to choose for forty miles, for the others were all in bed; so I walked for no more than half an hour and then started to fish home, the river slightly coloured from an overnight thunderstorm in the mountains, but otherwise in perfect order. By 6.15 I had hooked my first fish, and by 8.30 had filled my bag so full I could carry no more, though I had put back as many as I kept. They were all (twenty-five) about Loch-na-Bo size, averaging about half a pound, save one beauty of one-and-a-quarter, which is a monster for this river; all rainbows and all very lively. It was great fun.

G. and Joey went off right upstream after breakfast (too late in this weather), and I am taking the Admiral out after tea. The royal brothers are haymaking; but they were so impressed by my catch that they announced their intention of coming out with me tomorrow!

12 August 1927   They gave instructions to be called at six, but the united efforts of the whole house failed to stir them till nine, so they got no fishing.

I am hoping for a telegram from you before we leave here. My mind is quite unchanged, [here Tommy obliterated a few words by scrawling 'applepieapplepieapplepie' closely over them] though of course I will wait if you want me to. But it is difficult to applepie-applepieapplepie one is really in sympathy with applepieapplepie-applepie ninety-five per cent of him, and that is disheartening.

The Admiral leaves tomorrow, to my great regret; he has been extremely good and efficient throughout, and has gone up immensely in my estimation.[1]

I am missing you, my darling, more than I ever have before, and think of you a great deal. What fun it would be to bring John and Lavinia here for a whole summer. Never forget that, for me, any storms we have had are nothing but thunderstorms, and I love you more now than ever I did. T.

Joan Lascelles to A.L.

13 August 1927   *Holton Park*
                                                           Wheatley
                                                             Oxon.

My darling, I found your letter of the 2nd when I got here yesterday. Darling, I am sorry you are so depressed about the whole thing. I

[1] Halsey had fallen out with the Prince, and next day, 13 August, wrote Tommy a letter heavy with disappointment: 'I was genuinely sorry to part company yesterday, and I have loved working with you at what I call a very uphill job . . . As I daresay you already know, I have very definitely made up my mind to gracefully retire the moment I can get wind of someone who can succeed me.' The Admiral added that he was not looking forward 'to joining the ranks of the unemployed', but that 'anything is better than feeling one is the fifth wheel of a coach.' In the event, he settled down and continued to work for the Prince.

thought you were bottling something up when we were at The Ridgeway, and I suppose you were worrying about it all, and you were very naughty not to tell me how you were feeling – I think I can guess what you are feeling about it all, as from the little I know about him I can see where the despairing part lies. I don't quite know how much his personality matters in the job. It matters more on a trip like this than it does in the office in London. It seems to me that you have to decide whether, as a job, it is sufficiently worth doing, sufficiently interesting and congenial for the personality of the chief not to weigh tremendously – especially the first. If you think it is, the disappointment as regards his character is less important, and of course makes the whole thing more of a duty and less of a pleasure. In fact it becomes more of a business proposition.

Of course, if the whole thing is intolerable to you, you must chuck it. My own opinion about the job is and has been for a long time the following – that it is quite a sound, honest (!) one (well paid, though with no great prospects of increase, but still sufficient), the work easily got at, congenial surroundings and people to work with (that is, not cads, excepting for our late acquaintance, Fruity) and that you are a sufficiently good influence to make it worthwhile.

I have no illusions about, and not much respect for, your Chief, but if you think it is all worth working for as an institution, and part of the country – then I think it's worth while. Only then I think, as I said, you must look upon it more or less as you would upon a business firm. If on the other hand the whole thing is utterly uncongenial, and you feel it to be of no great importance to the country in general how it is run, and of no great importance whether it is a success or not – you must chuck it and do something you feel to be more worth while. I can't say anything more about it till I have talked to you.

I hope Vancouver was a change and a rest. It is nice to think you will be back this day month, but it feels a long way off. Goodbye, my darling. I do love you, and liked your writing and saying you wished you had me to talk to, as it made me feel of some use after all! Bless you, my darling, and don't get too depressed.   All my love, J.

With her letter Joan enclosed notes from the children. Lavinia, aged four, wrote: 'Are you quite well and having a nice time? We are having nice rides on the donkey. Please write us some letters. I have fallen off Woggie twice, and John has once. We sing "Frère Jacques" by ourselves. It is a French song. Love from Lavinia.'

Life was less simple for her parents, both of whom by then were in a fever of doubt and worry.

59

Joan Lascelles to A.L.

16 August 1927   *Holton Park*

My darling, I am sending you a cable saying 'Please wait my letter 16th', as I want you to read this carefully and think it over. To begin with, your letter of the fourth came as a complete bombshell to me, your letter of the second having only said that you were thinking it over and that you meant to do nothing in a hurry. I imagined that you were going to wait and talk it all over with me when you got home.

First, I want to impress on you that I am quite ready to trust you to do the right thing in any big thing that affects us both, and our lives; that I am ready to give up things and follow you into the wilderness, as you express it, if need be – that I should never try and urge you to go on with a job which keeps you awake at night or is inconsistent with your self-respect. I want you to believe that.

Now, *second*, I do feel very strongly that you have no right to take any big step that affects us both without first talking to and consulting with me (I had always thought that one of the essentials of being happily married, and I am a little upset that you shouldn't feel it equally strongly). One can't discuss a thing like this in letters – I must hear and understand all about it from you, and you must hear my arguments for and against. You must remember that you have never so much as dropped a hint to me that this was all going on in your mind, and I must confess that your reasons for not saying anything to me – if you *have* decided that this trip was to be a final test – were a little far-fetched. It was unfair not to give me any warning or chance of thinking it over, and I was not likely to try to prejudice you one way or the other if you had told me that you wanted to keep an open mind about it during the trip. Darling, I feel you haven't quite trusted me, anyhow in a way you are asking me to trust you, and it is *essential* if we are to be happy together.

Now, as regards the whole thing, I am quite prepared to believe you may be right in chucking your job, and that you have good and sound reasons for doing so, and am ready to agree with you that it is right – but I do implore you not to do or say anything till we've had a chance of talking about it, for the following – I think – perfectly sound reasons:

1. That I have a right to know all about it and approve *before* you hand in your resignation.
2. That though you say you have thought about it from my point

of view, and that it is an awkward time for me to have to make changes, I don't think you have sufficiently thought about all it means. For the next six months all I ask is to be allowed to stay quietly in my own house, and I think I have a right to ask it. You suggest letting, and parting with the servants. Short of dire necessity, I could not face it. You cannot expect me, two months before a baby, to come back and collect a new household, with all the bothers and difficulties it involves, for the sake of going to Sutton for two months (I don't think it would do either of us any good to sit there doing nothing, and I personally should not be happy with nothing to do, and unable to play golf or motor, or do any of the things that make life possible there for a *holiday*. You know how much I love being there – so you must see my point.) We have got a particularly good lot of servants, who are nice and quite fond of us, and it seems to me quite pointless to break up our whole life and arrangements without due consideration.

3. Without being mercenary, what are we going to live on till you get another job, and what plans have you got for the future? I am practically bound to stay in our own house for the next six months (short of a great deal of bother and inconvenience), and we shall have a good deal of extra expense in the spring with the new baby. John ought to start a school then – which he badly needs – and I had really planned some classes for him this autumn, which I think he also needs and which would be extremely good for him – and I think they would both be better for London, and doing things with other children, after a summer alone in the country – which is another reason that I am against Sutton (though I admit this last is a minor point, but just worth mentioning).

My real point is that if you have a wife and children, and a house, you cannot quite suddenly change your whole life – as if you were unmarried – till you have thought what you are going to do for them instead – which brings me to

4. What plans have you got for the future? It is true, as you say, that we have a certain amount of capital behind us, but not enough to live on and send John to school without something else, and as we *do* know that we shall have a certain amount of unavoidable expenses in the next six months, it seems wrong to chuck away a definite income till we have talked it over – and there again, in this matter I think I have a right to ask you to wait and talk to me about it all before resigning.

5. What reason are you going to give everybody for chucking at a moment's notice? You must either say straight out what you think of

the Prince, and that he's a hopeless rotter, or whatever it may be, which I don't imagine you would want to do – or you must have some other reason, in the way of a job. I don't think it can do either of you any good to make it look as if there were some fearful scandal – either for him from the point of view of the country, or people in general, or you from your own.

6. I think it is very hard on Godfrey and the whole *ménage* not to give them plenty of time to find someone else. You yourself have often said it's not an easy job to find anyone to fill suitably. You went to it with your eyes open, and have been there long enough to know the good and bad of it, and it seems it is only in the last few months you have become really restless about it. Therefore I do feel that if possible you should say that you are going to leave at the end of the year. As you seem to feel so strongly about another whole winter there, I don't suggest that you should even try to go on till Easter. After all, in all contracts of service, some decent interval is given in the way of notice of a change. You have worked there successfully, and more or less happily, for nearly seven years, and I think it is wrong to make such a big change in a frantic hurry (1) to yourself, (2) to the Prince and your colleagues, (3) to me and the children.

I take it you are leaving entirely on general grounds and not owing to any personal incident between you and the Prince which makes it impossible to stay on a day longer. Therefore I feel you might try and put up with another two or three months, even if slightly tiresome and unpleasant, for everybody's sake.

I am not trying to persuade you to give up the idea of leaving, only am asking you not to do it in such a frantic hurry and before I have had a chance of hearing what you have to say. You have often asked me to sleep on a thing, and I ask you to do the same, and to talk it over with me when you are away from the whole entourage. My only argument for your present job is that you are practically the only good influence, and the only one in the whole show with any vision. But if you despair of even that being any good to him, or the country, why, then you must go. (I don't agree with your argument about being a courtier – it's not what is known as a courtier's job, and I think you're slightly morbid about that. It's just as bad to funk royalty, as royalty, as to suck up to it.)

But I'm not going to attempt to persuade you to stay on against your happiness. You speak of its not making for *my* happiness, but it doesn't make any difference to me whether you work in an office in York House or anywhere else in London – so long as you are happy. It's not much good our thinking of living in the country, as you have said yourself that we couldn't ever afford it, even as done by the Meads – and they haven't got any sons.

Change – do anything you like, but not in this headlong fashion, and give us a month or two's grace to talk it over *together* and think what we are going to do next. After all, lots of people have to carry on with far more uncongenial jobs for the sake of their families, and I'm not asking you to do it for ever, but only for another month or two.

I have talked it over with Helen (in strictest secrecy – she won't even tell Eric) and she agrees with me that I am right in asking you to wait, and that no man has any right to take such a step without fairly consulting his wife – anyhow if it's a decent marriage. You can't accuse Helen of being anything that isn't fair-minded and wise, and she isn't likely to want you to do anything, any more than I do, that isn't consistent with your self-respect – and she feels as strongly as I do that you ought to wait till you get home. I had to talk to someone. I felt so worried and upset by the suddenness of it all, and afraid of seeming selfish from my point of view. Luckily she was here. I shan't mention it to anyone else.

Please think this all over carefully. You have put your hand to the plough, and even you can't leave it in the middle of the field, but must anyhow get to the end of the furrow, even if you aren't going to do the whole field.

I shall try to put the whole thing out of my mind till you come back, and do hope and pray that you will give me a chance of hearing more about it before you decide definitely or anyhow say anything.

I thought you had something on your mind in the summer – but you wouldn't tell me. I feel unhappy and sad that you have shut me out so completely from your thoughts and feelings, and that you can take such a step without doing more than write a letter about it – which after all can tell one nothing.

My darling – I see no real happiness for us in the future, wherever we are, whatever we do, if you can't tell me more of what you are feeling and thinking. You said you had felt lonely lately, but how can you expect me to be any good if you won't tell me anything? I don't want to reproach you, as I know you're probably very worried over the whole business, but anyhow let me share it with you – and that's why I ask you to wait.   All my love, J.

Luckily for Joan, Tommy had in any case held his hand. Before this powerful appeal reached him, but perhaps spurred by some form of thought-transference, he wrote again:

To Joan

18 August 1927   *Hotel Vancouver*
                                                        Vancouver
                                                  British Columbia

My darling, About my letter from Ottawa: I feel I may have tried to
rush you into what is, after all, a big decision. I don't want to do that,
and if you have any qualms at all, and would like me to wait till we
have talked it over together, I will certainly do so. You have only to
telegraph 'Please wait' to me, and I will say nothing till we get back.
By the way, if you telegraph, it is perhaps safer to put 'Lascelles, care
of Royal Train CPR'

We got here this morning and have had a very busy day in hot,
stuffy weather. The Premier of this province, British Columbia, died
today, which has complicated things and involved me in a lot of
hectic telephoning and alterations. Must stop. God bless you, my
darling. I would give so much to be able to talk to you, if only for an
hour.   All love. T.

21 August 1927   *Empress Hotel*
                                                     Victoria, BC

My darling, I was cheered a lot by your letter of the 4th, which I got
yesterday, a few hours before your telegram from Escrick [Park, the
Wenlocks' home in Yorkshire]. I shall wait for your letter of the 16th,
but, apart from that, other things make me inclined to do nothing till
we get back. 'There is no better solvent of a strained situation than
clean and impartial ridicule' – and old Joey and I have had so many
secret laughs about the whole business that I feel less bitter and
disheartened than I did. Also, the Prince, to give the devil his due,
has played up well lately, and got off two speeches at Vancouver and
Victoria, which I had put a lot of work into, so well that I forgave him
a lot. And, damn him, he is so affectionate to me, that I find it terribly
hard to nourish vipers in my weak bosom. I am rather ashamed of
this, but I fear I am ridiculously forgiving to people who do like
me.

But the chief development is that the Old Salt, who, as you know,
left us after the Ranch, has written to me to say that he has definitely
decided to clear out as soon as somebody can be found to succeed
him; and this makes it very difficult for me to do the same, without
putting an unfair strain on the rest of the establishment, especially

Godfrey and Joey. There are so many cross-currents and cross-loyalties; I suppose I've never been up against quite such a tough problem in my life, and at present, in spite of what I've written to you before, I don't honestly know what I ought to do – 'ought', in the sense of doing what an honest man and a gentleman should do. Therefore, I suppose, it is best to wait.

You said the Ottawa speech was praised, and I've just got *The Times* of 4 August, which commends it. But – this is so typical – the passage in it which all the papers I have seen comment on approvingly, is the very passage on which *I* set most store, but which he cut out as being 'pompous', and never actually said! I knew, fortunately, he was going to garble it, and told the Press people to stick to the typed copies, which I gave out in advance.

It is the impossibility of making him realise this side of his position that defeats me. All the work his private secretaries have to do centres round that – the fact that he *is* the future king – and not round his individual personality; and as he makes no effort except in the direction of expressing that personality, in one form and another, and usually at the expense of the other thing, one is continually trying to carry water in a sieve. In fact, one is like a jockey trying to induce a race-horse to race, whose only idea is to stop in the middle of the course and perform circus tricks; or an actor-manager, whose Hamlet persists in interrupting the play by balancing the furniture on the end of his nose.

We got here yesterday morning; and I think it just as jolly a spot as I did before. I have just torn up a letter offering HRH, for about £7,000, an island of 750 acres, complete with a house of eleven rooms, garden, orchards, steam-launch, sheep, cows, pigs and poultry. From the photographs it looks delightful; but for my hatred of salt water, I believe I could live there quite happily.

They say that for four or five months in the year you can count with absolute certainty on the weather – sunny days and coldish nights – and though they get so little rain, they all have beautiful gardens; and of course the country itself is lovely, though perhaps too full of pines to suit you. Moreover, they are never worried by flies or mosquitoes, and the winter climate is much milder than in England, with practically no snow, though in the Rockies, a few hours away, you can get as much winter-sporting as you want. If only the inhabitants were less dreary, it would be as good a spot to live in as any in the world; but that is a big 'if', though I believe that outside Victoria itself there are a lot of nice people who have squatted here recently.

We had a delightful day out at Colwood, my favourite golf-links (rather like Swinley, only the trees are twice as big), playing a round before lunch and another after in absolutely perfect weather. The Prince and I beat Joey and Prince George, in a four-ball four-some, which we have never contrived to do before. As an antidote, the day ended with a heavyish dinner at Government House (the Lieutenant-Governor of BC lives here, a dear old Scotchman called Bruce[1]), and a ghastly ball organised by the ex-Servicemen's league, from which I have escaped.

Fix up anything you like for when I come home. If you don't feel like Scotland, and would rather go somewhere else, I wouldn't mind a bit. Let me know definitely before we sail (7 September) where you will be when we reach London.   Love, T.

On 18 August Joan wrote again, this time from Escrick Park. Thence she reported that Tommy's brother-in-law Melville Balfour (married to his sister Daisy) was 'if anything worse, and it's really almost uncomfortable staying there, his bad temper has become so chronic, and his manner of speaking to Daisy and the servants so awful – and it doesn't seem to matter who is there or what the occasion is. Poor Daisy looks ill and worried to death, and all ordinary conversation is almost impossible.'[2]

Then Joan reverted to the matter most on her mind. Shrewdly divining that Tommy's worries had been exacerbated by the stress of being at sea (which he always hated) combined with the pressure of frantic activity on landing and the excitement of his frank conversation with Baldwin, she again asked him to hold on:

18 August 1927   *Escrick Park*
                                            York

The more I think it over, the more I feel that it was impossible for me to send you a cable, 'I agree', as you asked me to, in my situation. I feel that if you had talked the whole thing over with me, as you did with S.B., had given me all the facts and what plans or rough ideas you had for the future, *before* you left, and had then asked me to cable approval on your definite decision – I could have done so with my

[1] The Hon. Randolph Bruce (1863–1942) had emigrated to Canada in 1887 (the year Tommy was born), had worked in railways and mining, and was Lieutenant-Governor of British Columbia 1926–31.
[2] Melville's condition was partly due to the fact that he had been gassed and shell-shocked in the First World War.

eyes open, and having had time to understand and think it all over. As it is, there is so much I don't know, and so much that I should like to talk over with you first, that I feel I cannot honestly say 'Go ahead' – and be ready to go ahead *with* you, without any doubts or misgivings as to whether it is all being done in the right way or at the right moment.

You must remember that we have been very definitely settled down in one way of life for practically seven years, and it's difficult to change it all in one moment without a certain amount of reflection. You know, darling, we do agree pretty well over most of the essentials of life, and I'm not likely to want to go against you in anything as a whole. Therefore I feel you must allow me to have some say in settling the details in this matter, and the how and when it is to be done. I do feel you have a certain amount of faith in my judgement, and that's why I do long to be able to talk to you, before you do anything. I do feel I might find it a little hard to forgive you if you do anything precipitate and I am not in complete agreement and knowledge of the facts . . .

I don't know enough about it to know if I'm asking something very hard of you – or spoiling you of the satisfaction of your decision. I hope you will get this letter with my last, as I feel you may have thought me a little hard and unsympathetic from that one – which I am not. I do love you enough not to want to make things harder for you than need be, and I want you to do the same for me.

All my love, darling, and take care of yourself, and don't curse me for not being able to say I agree definitely yet. J.

To Joan

23 August 1927   *Canadian Pacific Royal Train*
In the Rockies

My darling, We left Victoria in the small hours of this morning, after quite an amusing dance at Government house. We were all very sorry to go – it has been the most glorious weather all the time we were on the Island, and the people there are much the nicest of all the Canucks. Much good golf – I am playing quite well, all things considered – and on Sunday afternoon Joey and I had an amusing time trolling for salmon.

This is one of the great sports there, and though one can't call it fishing, it is quite good fun to do once in a way. We were taken charge

67

of by three Canadians called Henry and Arthur and George – I never got their other names – and set off in a small motor-launch up one of the arms of the sea which run into the Island, rather like Norwegian fjords, all along the coast. We were each given a very stiff seven-foot rod, with an enormous reel, holding several hundred yards of fine copper or steel wire, to the end of which was attached a spoon about six inches long.

You let out about 120 yards of line (which, being metal, sinks to a great depth), light a pipe and admire the scenery while your launch chugs slowly up and down the fjord. The water is full of salmon of several species, waiting to go up the rivers, and they run pretty big. During the afternoon we landed six or seven, the biggest a thirty-pounder which I hooked. He was a fine fish, and it took me seventeen minutes to get him into the boat. Joey got a good eighteen-pounder just as it was getting dark, and the others were all small.

Henry and Arthur and George, who were capital chaps but seemed to me to have very rudimentary ideas about fishing, made things more lively by getting wildly excited whenever a fish struck, beating the successful angler very hard on the back, pushing his rod up and down to what they considered the most suitable angle for playing the fish, and doing an increasing war-dance up and down the very narrow boat, shouting, 'My, that's a dandy! My, that's a big fish!' long before it was possible to get any idea of his size. On two separate occasions they all three fell upon the fish simultaneously with two gaffs and a large landing-net, with the inevitable result that he escaped in the mêlée. However, it was all very good fun.   Love, T.

To Godfrey Thomas

25 August 1927   *Canadian Pacific Royal Train*
                                      On line in Alberta

Dear Godfrey, I've been idle about writing, but it has been glorious weather, and as HRH insists that he and I can beat Joey and Prince George at golf, I have been in demand as a fourth ball. We've only done it once so far, but we are both improving, so there ought to be more victories in store.

The last fortnight has really been very pleasant, without any mishaps. The Prince got off two speeches to the Canadian Clubs in British Columbia better than I have ever heard before, and on each occasion pushed the unwilling Prince George up to break his orator-ical virginity, which he did quite gracefully. Everybody enjoyed

Vancouver Island – the Lieutenant-Governor, Bruce, is a real treasure, and quite won HRH's heart, so that he did everything the old man asked of him, almost to an embarrassing degree, for he was always popping in and out of cathedrals and hospitals without our knowing anything about it.

After an inauspicious beginning, what might be called the domestic side of the trip has lately been markedly better. I have felt at many times extremely depressed, not only about this particular expedition, but about the future generally. So often, as you probably know better than I do, one feels that any honest work one may have done is just sheer waste: as a stage-manager might feel if his Hamlet persisted in breaking off the play and balancing the furniture on the end of his nose, or doing even worse things. There was some very bad furniture-balancing on the way out, which threw me into a state of bolshevism from which I am only just recovering; and another thing which annoyed me furiously was the omission from the Ottawa speech, at literally the last minute and on the ground of 'pomposity', what I had emphasised as the most important sentences in the whole thing – sentences, by the way, supplied almost verbatim by the Colonial Office and not by myself, so I have no personal feelings about it. Instead, a very weak joke was substituted impromptu – not an unsuitable one for, say the Commercial Travellers' Festival Banquet, but utterly out of place at the Government of Canada's ceremonial board, in their own Parliament buildings. However, as luck would have it the Press, in almost every case, adhered faithfully to the 'advanced copy' I had given out; and I have smiled a grim smile on observing that the one passage selected for praise and comment by both the Canadian and home newspapers was the passage which was never spoken.

However, in this particular school it is not the Recitation Prize but the Good Conduct Prize which really matters at the present moment. I have high hopes, in view of recent talks, that we may yet get away with the latter, or at any rate with an Hon. Mention. But – 'the devil was sick, the devil a monk wou'd be,'[1] and the devil talking heart-to-heart in the monastic seclusion of a CPR train may become quite different in the glare of the footlights of Montreal.

I was very sorry to see the last of the Admiral. He ran the show quite first class from start to finish, and triumphed over a decidedly difficult situation. Joey has been in capital form throughout, though, like me, feeling at times a bit like the late Colonel Esmond in the

[1] From Peter Anthony Motteux's translation of Rabelais' *Gargantua and Pantagruel*.

famous chapter where he renounces the cause of the Stuarts for ever.[1] Angus has been a great standby. I had a long talk with him on the verandah of the Vancouver Club the other morning. He rejoins us on the boat and is going to try, during the voyage, to expound his views of the duties of the Heir Apparent in Canada, and life in general. They are extremely sound views, and as Angus is the least pompous of men, knows Canada backwards and is *très bien vu* with the Prince, he may do some good.

I like this country much better than I did in '24, and I warn you that some autumn before long I shall demand two months' leave and bring Joan out here for a week at the Ranch and a spell in Victoria.

Love to Diana. Yours ever, A.L.

To Joan

28 August 1927   *Canadian Pacific Railway*
Nipigon

My darling, I got a very wise letter from you last night, dated 13 August, from Holton, for which I am very grateful. You will, I hope, have guessed from my cable from Victoria and my last letter that there is now no risk of my doing anything sensational before we get home. I feel rather remorseful at having threatened it just now and hope it hasn't worried you a lot. But, at Ottawa and indeed during all the first part of the trip, I was feeling very hopeless, and probably saw things in too lurid a light.

Now, though I can't deny that I feel much the same as I did then about the whole problem of the ultimate future, I realise that there is' no immediate need for me to do anything in a hurry – particularly in view of what I told you about the Admiral. It did me good unburdening myself on S[tanley] B[aldwin]'s broad bosom; and, having told him – the only person who ought to be told – just what I believe to be the truth, I cannot do much more at the moment except try, so far as I get the chance, to steer things in the right course. As a matter of fact I have had several such chances lately, and have had two or three very straight talks, which I think made some impression. Anyhow, I have no serious complaints to make about the way the trip has gone during the last fortnight, and he has been very reasonable to work with.

---

[1] In W. M. Thackeray's *The History of Henry Esmond, Esquire.*

The cold fact remains that, as Joey and I both agree, it would be a real disaster if, by any ill chance, he were called on to accede to the throne now, and neither of us sees any prospect of his fitting himself any better, as time goes on, for what is, ultimately, his job in life, and ours – i.e., making a good, or at any rate a safe, king.

The difficulty in making up one's mind about this sort of problem is in striking the right line between one's appreciation of it when one is fed up and things are temporarily going worse than usual, and when one is fairly satisfied and things are going temporarily better than usual. My mind is running on mining metaphors just now, since we went over a very interesting mine a few days ago, and I see myself as a miner working away at a rich reef, which everybody believes is going to continue indefinitely to yield wonderful results, but which I happen to know is almost bound to peter out abruptly before very long. Well, anyhow, I have warned the Chief Director, and there is something to be said for the point of view that, having done so, it is my job to go on picking out as much precious metal as I can from my particular part of the reef, while it lasts.

So, on that assumption, I have recently done him what is probably the best short speech I shall ever do in my life. He is to deliver it at the Canadian Club in Montreal, and he is really tickled to death with it – though it is essentially serious and contains practically no jokes. I have no doubt he will make a good job of it. It comes off on 2 September, and if you see any allusions to it in the English papers, you might keep them for me.

I wonder if you will be in London when we get back. I hope so, though if you are up north, you mustn't come all the way back on purpose. If you haven't said this in any of your letters, send me a wire to Southampton, on board the *Empress of Scotland*.

An uneventful day in Winnipeg yesterday, ending with a ghastly dinner at the Government House (Province of Manitoba) at which we got nothing to drink but tepid water and a ghastly mixture of ginger-ale and grape-juice. Poor old G., who is not used to teetotal drinks, is convinced that he will develop typhoid as a result of it.

Joey is casting hungry eyes on the typewriter, so goodbye, my darling, and much love. Your letter was a real help to me. Thank the children for theirs. I ought to have written to them, but so far as I can recollect have sent them quite a few postcards.　　　　Bless you, T.

2 September 1927 Ritz-Carlton Hotel
Montreal

My darling, I bought you a blue fox today – rather a nice one, so far as I am any judge. I hope you will like it – anyhow I expect you can change it quite easily if you don't. The Prince had just bought three or four silver foxes at the same shop – beauties, but terribly expensive, so I got a reduction on mine. But I can't think of anything to get the children; there are no toys here that one couldn't get cheaper and better in London, and no 'native products' which would amuse them, except moccasins, which I've already sent them.

The speech at the Canadian Club today went off very well; he really took an immense amount of trouble over it. I brought him home from dinner soon after midnight last night, and apparently he sat up till past four working at it. Anyhow, the result was A1 – very well delivered, and no unsuitable interpolations. There was an audience of about 1,200, all businessmen (no women), and they received it with rapt attention and great applause.

I must say, what Baldwin calls the 'impressive loyalty' of Canada *is* most impressive, and moves me very much. They sing 'God Save the King' as if it really was a prayer, and with their whole hearts in it. Their devotion to the British throne is entirely genuine, and almost an article of faith. It makes one feel – particularly when at some western station you see a crowd of people who've ridden in forty or fifty miles just to get a glimpse of the two brothers – that there must be something worth working for in an institution which stirs a fine people so deeply. For they *are* a very fine people, underneath the crudity and lack of culture which is natural to any young nation that has been too busy wrestling with the forces of nature to think of polishing itself.

Our days here – which I had felt very anxious about – are passing away quite satisfactorily, with no snags ahead so far as can be seen. He is unquestionably much more controlled in every way at the moment – we are all quite bewildered by it; he has even consented to give a dinner party to the 'best people' of Montreal on Monday. It will probably be pretty heavy, but will do a world of good.

This will be positively my last letter, though I hope to get one or two more from you before we sail on Wednesday.

Bless you, my pretty; only nine days now before I see you again. T.

The party landed at Southampton on 14 September. Once again Tommy came home with his job intact – but only just. What bound him to the Prince was a mixture of loyalty and patriotism: loyalty to, and affection for, the man, and devotion to his country and to the ideal of monarchy, both stiffened by a powerful sense of duty. His disillusionment was far-advanced; yet he knew that (as Joan told him) his influence on the Prince was more valuable than that of any other member of the staff, and he perhaps still had faint hopes that he could bring off a miracle. No doubt he was also shaken by the realisation that he had thrown his own marriage into danger.

The Prince, for his part, had no inkling that he had almost lost a valuable lieutenant, and later in the month he wrote a line of thanks from Scotland:

Prince of Wales to A.L.

Monday, October 1927   *Balmoral Castle*

My dear Tommy, As a matter of fact I've been meaning to write you these last days to thank you ever so much for all your help and companionship (does that sound too much like Toc H?!)[1] on the Canadian trip – thank you is a bit weak but I guess you know what I mean and anyway I do thank you very sincerely. It was a bit of a strain and a rush for all of us but we remained a cheerful and peaceful party to the end – and *your* speeches were better than ever – you're amazing and that's that. And now I hope you've forgotten all about me and our work and that your '*va*-cation' is doing you good. It's been wild and cold up here, and we had a heavy snow all yesterday which did in all stalking today. But I've had three days on the hill the first two blank but three stags on Saturday and the fourth shot was to finish off a wounded beast – so the old hands aren't as shaky as I thought!

All quite fairly peaceful up here and the family being gentle to George and myself. We were out *dancing reels* (not Charleston) the first three nights which was a lot of gaiety for this locality, not 'gaiety' in the sense it comes into the story of the old Irish laundress! Still they were not bad parties and some attractive people to meet.
Hasta luego.   Yours, E.P.

---

[1] The Christian movement designed to bring people of all denominations together for social service.

EAST AFRICA
1928

By 1928 the Prince of Wales, in his own words, had begun to find England 'a little cramped', and he decided to indulge his 'recurrent wanderlust' by means of an expedition to East Africa, to which he was drawn also 'by reasons of Empire'. With him would go his brother, Prince Henry, Duke of Gloucester, who wanted to organise a safari of his own. The Governor of Kenya was then Sir Edward Grigg (known as 'Ned'), who had been the Prince's Military Secretary from 1919 to 1921, and had recently been inviting him to pay the colony a visit.[1]

According to Godfrey Thomas, the idea for a tour 'suddenly germinated in HRH's mind', so that plans for it had to be laid with some haste, and it fell to Tommy to make many of the arrangements. He himself eventually travelled as one of the party, acting as Principal Private Secretary; but, long before they left at the beginning of September, he was making positive suggestions to Grigg about the nature of the visit.

To Sir Edward Grigg

16 June 1928   *St. James's Palace*

Confidential

Dear Grigg, As regards Prince Harry, I can be fairly definite. He will be at your disposal for the first two or three days after our arrival in Nairobi, and after that you will see him no more. He proposes to go off on safari with Brooke [a young man whom he had taken on from

---

[1] Sir Edward Grigg (1879–1955) had been a classical scholar and journalist before joining the staff of the Prince of Wales in 1919. In 1923 he married the Hon. Joan Dickson-Poynder. He was Governor and Commander-in-Chief of the Kenya Colony 1925–31, and in 1945 was created the first Baron Altrincham.

the 20th Hussars] and the best white hunter they can get, and to be quite independent of the Prince of Wales and the rest of us. He will hitch on to our column when and where he best can, at the beginning of December – probably somewhere in Northern Rhodesia, but it all depends on the elephants. Anyhow, the point is that you, and we, can wash our hands of him. As he definitely wants to make serious shooting the cornerstone of the whole trip, so far as he is concerned, his plans seem to me eminently sensible; and I have no doubt you and others in High Places will be relieved that he has taken the whole business into his own hands.

About the Prince of Wales, I cannot be so explicit. My general philosophy, based on my experience of the last two transatlantic trips I have done with him, makes me sum it up in the comforting phrase, 'It will be all right on the night.' I can say with perfect truth that I have never seen the Prince do such good work, or play his part with greater advantage to himself and the British Empire, than on those occasions when he has had no set programme, and has himself fixed up a plan of campaign with the man on the spot – the Governor, or whoever it may be. I quite realise, however, the drawbacks of this manner of working, from your point of view, especially in a country where communications are liable to be interrupted, and plans have to be made in advance to some extent. But, if I may put it crudely, we have got to lump that, for he is quite determined not to pin himself to anything till he has had a good talk with you; and, as I say, in the long run the disadvantages of the system are compensated by the un-doubted improvement in the return on one's capital.

Chesterton says somewhere, 'Stone me if I attempt to prophesy,' and I say it too. But, so far as I have been able to gather the Prince's intentions, I envisage them more or less like this: a 'khaki' arrival at Mombasa, as simple as possible; go straight up to Nairobi, and there 'get down to it' with you; in the intervals, attend, say, a garden party, a large dinner-party or two, or any other such social and unofficial functions as you think fit for bringing him into touch with the white population of the place. After say five or six days of the ordinary life of Nairobi (with as much golf as the weather will permit), move on to one or two populous centres recommended by yourself – e.g. go and stay with the Francis Scotts for a day or two, if they could have him.[1]

---

[1] Lord Francis Scott (1879–1952), a son of the sixth Duke of Buccleuch and a formidable soldier, had married Lady Eileen Elliot in 1915. Arriving in Kenya in 1922, they had astonished the neighbourhood by building their house Deloraine on two storeys. Like Joan Lascelles, Lady Eileen was the daughter of a Viceroy of India (Lord Minto).

The Prince has told me explicitly, several times, that he has no wish to do any big-game shooting on a serious scale. We have impressed on him that, if he changes his mind suddenly about this, he can't expect people out there to produce elephants and rare antelopes at short notice. But I think he means it; he is definitely bored by shooting and fishing. But he is *crazy* about golf.

[There follows a long discussion of health hazards, and the question of whether or not they should take a doctor with them. In the end it was decided that they should not.] Another obviously important point is how much, or how little, HRH ought to show himself to organised gatherings of natives – one which I know you have already raised. I can't contribute much to this, because I obviously know nothing about it; but I talked to Amery about it last week, and I understand he is considering it seriously.[1] It is, of course, a clear case where Ministerial advice is necessary.

HRH is quite determined *not* to take any uniform more elaborate than khaki, and any advocacy of full-dress uniform will only put him out of heart with the whole trip and badly blunt the edge of his present intense keenness for it. It seems, no doubt, a small peg on which to hang the success or non-success of five months' travel; but remember, the bringing or not-bringing of elaborate uniform is for him the shibboleth of the whole business. He planned and initiated it himself from the very outset; he conceived it as a strictly 'informal' (to him, the most blessed word in the language) tour; and, in his eyes, the moment full-dress uniform is included in his luggage, that informal character is irrevocably gone.

The logicality of this attitude is probably doubtful; but my point is that the attitude is, for good or ill, a firm reality, and consequently can't be left out of account. So long as he lives he will never, I am convinced, do one tenth as much good when there is a formal atmosphere as he will when there is only a barely-perceptible whiff of formality. It may, possibly, be a weakness in one called to his particular job; from my own experience in India and elsewhere I know very well, and I have often told him so, that you can't keep the British Empire going without a lot of formality; and, personally, I like formality. But the fact remains that he is at his worst on a formal occasion, at his best on an occasion which is (even if only apparently) one of his own fashioning. And his best is such a good best that my own belief is that it outweighs the harm done by abrogating that

---

[1] The Rt. Hon. Leopold Amery (1873–1954) was then Secretary of State for the Colonies.

outward regality to which we have all been accustomed in his predecessors. (I am unashamedly conscious of the fact that the logical consequence of this line of thought would be the thesis that when the time comes, he must be crowned in a billycock hat. But I can't help that.)

My duty to Lady Grigg, in which Joan joins me. It will be very nice to see you both again.   Yours, A. Lascelles.

To Joan

7 September 1928   *SS Kaisar-I-Hind*
                                                         Marseilles

My darling, So far no misadventures. The Channel was quite choppy – enough to make walking about the boat difficult; but I took a Crippen tabloid [a patent preventer of sea-sickness] before embarking and never felt the least qualm – in fact, felt well and hungry. Ordinarily, I should have been as sick as a dog; they certainly are magically effective, and apparently leave no ill effects. We had an excellent dinner in the train, and a good night in a new sleeping-car, which is better sprung than usual. Here it is pretty hot, and we don't leave till five a.m. tomorrow, so shall probably have a stuffy night. The ship is pretty full, and to those used to large Cunarders – I think I'm the only one who's ever been on a P. & O. before – she seems very small and cramped. God bless you, my darling. I am glad we are fairly off, because every day now brings us nearer to getting home.   All love, T.

8 September 1928   *SS Kaisar-I-Hind*

My darling, Lovely weather all day, and a pleasant temperature, which is very welcome after the volcanic heat of Marseilles yesterday. As the ship was not due to sail till four this morning, we all dined at a place called the Hôtel de la Réserve, right out on the far side of the town, where we had a really delicious meal, on a cool terrace hung with lanterns. At the end G. was presented with a bill for 2,340 francs – about £19[1], which, for a shortish meal for six people, three bottles of champagne and about half a bottle of old brandy, was pretty hot. HRH, who has a praiseworthy dislike of being robbed

---

[1] Perhaps £220 in 1989 values.

77

more than necessary, contested it *à poings fermés*; and we then discovered that one item in the bill, which was as long as your arm, was the refreshment of no fewer than *four* French policemen, who had attached themselves to us surreptitiously, and who doubtless thought it a first-class opportunity of having a good blow-out at the expense of the *Prince des Galles*. As the latter hadn't left his ship till 8.30 p.m., which must be long past the dinner-hour of all French policemen, and had, moreover, neither asked for nor been informed of their presence, it was certainly a little hard to expect him to feast them on quite such a lavish scale. Anyhow, he failed to come up to expectations, and as a result, after a regular Locarno of international argument, the bill was reduced by about 750 francs.

All the same, it is a charming place to dine, and if we are ever stuck in Marseilles, we must recollect it. I daresay you know it already.

We are just through the straits of Bonifacio. I'd forgotten how lovely the north coast of Sardinia is, though it don't look as though the whole length of it contains enough nourishment for a single goat. By the way, I breakfasted off fresh sardines, and very good they were.

This ship is pretty full; but our deck-chairs have been isolated on a small deck just below the bridge, to which the vulgar are not admitted. This is very pleasant, though I have nothing against the passengers *en masse*, who seem a typically respectable crowd of returning officials, soldiers etc. with wives and children.

G. lent me Isadora Duncan's[1] *My Life* this morning, and I am now half-way through it. I started it reluctantly, thinking it would be great nonsense; and some of it is, but it is a most original book, and really is a very interesting revelation of an extraordinary creature. The account of the Duncan family descending on Athens and trying to live the lives of Greek citizens in the fifth century BC is one of the most entertaining bits of biography I have ever read. I think it would amuse you, and advise you to get it from the library. You might ask Helen if she knows who is the man called 'L', who was the father of her children who were killed in the motor accident. If she says, 'Craig', tell her to guess again, as it obviously was *not* Craig.

[1] The American dancer (1878–1927) who brought her passion for Greek dancing to Europe and had a strong influence on the development of the ballet there. Her memoirs, published in 1927, gave only the sketchiest account of the vicissitudes she suffered. Her first child, Deirdre, born in 1910, was fathered by the impresario Gordon Craig, and the second, Patrick, born in 1913, by the American millionaire Paris Singer. Both children were drowned in a freak accident when their car rolled into the Seine in 1923, and Isadora herself also died in a motor accident at Nice on 14 September 1927.

10 September 1928 We get into Alexandria about five tomorrow evening, so that we shall be able to dine ashore. Their Royal Highnesses have now realised what everybody has told them for months past – that they will find nothing whatever to do in Cairo at this time of year. So we are dividing our three nights in Egypt as to two at Alex and one at Cairo, instead of vice-versa, as originally planned. I am glad, for I have no doubt Cairo will be intolerably hot.

The voyage has been quite uneventful. We passed close under Stromboli, but it gave no sign of life. There was a slight swell for a few hours this afternoon, when we came opposite the Adriatic, but otherwise it has been perfect weather, and not too hot. Already we seem to have been travelling for months, and I cannot believe we were at Brancaster a week ago yesterday. TRH are obviously chafing under an exercise-complex – God knows what they will be like after a fortnight in the *Malda*.

Goodbye, my darling, you were very good all that last week, and I was grateful to you, for I minded going away unspeakably. Bless you always, and tell me all you are doing. T.

12 September 1928   *The Residency*
                                                              Alexandria

My darling, We landed yesterday afternoon in really lovely weather, with quite a cool breeze, and drove all through the town to this house. Masses of policemen everywhere, but I must say, the populace seemed most friendly and even enthusiastic. Hoare[1] is a nice tousled little man, whom I've known by sight in the Travellers' for years, with a vague manner, which covers, I think, an efficient interior. He is quite free from fuss, and looks at everything with a light-hearted detachment, which is just what one wants on these occasions. She is a nice, quiet little thing, and a childhood friend of Joey's, which helps; she was one of those Corfe Castle Bentincks.

It is a pleasant little house, very plain and white and unpretentious, with a small garden and bad surroundings, being overlooked by many other villas. But we are quite comfortable, and all our party except two servants are housed here.

Here are two rather dull p.c.s for the children – it is too hot to go

[1] Sir Reginald Hoare (d. 1954) served for nearly 40 years in the diplomatic service before joining the family bank in Fleet Street.

out and look for more, and we are due to start for [King] Fuad's[1]
lunch in an hour.   Bless you, my darling, T.

13 September 1928   *HMY Kassed Kheir*

My darling, King Fuad seems to have nothing but red ink on his
house-boat, but I daresay it will do as well as any other. I find it every
difficult to get up any enthusiasm about Egypt; partly, no doubt,
because of the season of the year, but also because these tours, and
the continuous society of the principal members of the party, always,
I find, engender a sort of coma of blasédom, which only disappears
when one steps ashore at the end of them, or in those brief periods, as
at the Ranch, when one can get right away by oneself for a few hours.
I am beginning to understand, in fact, how easily the wooden face of
royalty is acquired.

But, I believe the visit has been very successful; I have certainly
been surprised at the behaviour of the crowds, both here and at Alex;
they were quite large, and markedly friendly; quite a roll of continuous applause all down the streets as we drive along, and no
hostility at all that I have seen.[2]

Luncheon with Fuad passed off quite comfortably; he gave us a
delicious meal, and his palace was nice and cool. I found myself
between Zulfikar Pasha, the Grand Chamberlain, on whom I aired
my French, and Hassanein Bey,[3] his lieutenant, whom you probably
met – a charming and intelligent man who has come up here to look
after us.

We were away by 2.30, but did not escape without a return call
from the King, who followed us to the Residency after half an hour's
interval. He seemed in high spirits throughout, and showed himself
very genial and bonhomous. I only realised when I was dressing for

[1] Fuad I of Egypt (1868–1936) had been proclaimed King in 1922, when the British
protectorate came to an end. Known as 'the barking king', because the legacy of a
throat wound caused him to emit harsh, unintelligible noises at moments of stress,
he had already disconcerted his royal visitor on a previous occasion, when the
Prince of Wales, returning from his tour of India in 1922, had called on him in
Cairo, only to be baffled by his explosive utterances.

[2] After the end of the Protectorate in 1922 there had been a good deal of anti-British
agitation, and the Prince's visits to Egypt were intended to improve relations
between the two countries.

[3] Sir Ahmed Mohamed Hassanein Pasha (1889–1946), former fencing champion of
Egypt, made many notable journeys of exploration, and became Governor of the
Egyptian Royal Household in 1936. He was awarded the KCVO in 1927. See also
page 83.

lunch that I had omitted to bring with me my Order of the Nile, or whatever it was that he gave me in London, of which I probably ought to have worn the *bouton* in my button-hole. However, he made no comment on my omission.

Later in the afternoon we played golf on the Alex links – a sad change from Brancaster; after being five up on Prince Harry, I allowed him to beat me, largely because I again sprung the muscle in my back which I strained at Brancaster; however, I shan't want to play any more golf for three weeks, if then, so it will have ample time to mend itself.

We left Alex early this morning, and had a hot and tedious journey; it is very dreary country, nor did my first view of Cairo impress me much. The Residency, of course, is all shut up, but we are very comfortable in this immense and heavily-gilded house-boat, which needs no description, as you know well enough the kind of thing it is. After luncheon to the Museum; and I must say, some of the Tutankhamen trophies are worth a good deal of travel and discomfort. I forget if they were all on view when you were here; but to me much the most beautiful things in the whole collection are the alabaster vases, which are superb; and next, the four guardian angels who kept watch and ward round the body. Some of the jewellery, too, is very lovely, but I hadn't time to do more than run my eye over it. Thence to the Muski with Prince Harry, where I was profoundly bored, as I always am in any shop, occidental or oriental, while countless carpets were unrolled for his inspection. Apart from one or two of these, I saw nothing at all that I had any desire to buy, and a vast deal of extremely dear, nasty rubbish.

I have now come back to the boat with Hoare, till we dress to dine at the Gezira Club, while a Wenlockian sunset of the Chinese-white and grey variety unfolds itself along the opposite bank of the Nile. Tomorrow we 'do' the Pyramids before breakfast and entrain for Ismailia. I am looking forward to the fortnight on board the *Malda* with feelings of the utmost possible dejection. However, it will certainly be the worst period of the whole trip, and it will be something to have it over and done with.

Private. HRH, for some unfathomable reason, has insisted on making a new will, and, to my great annoyance, has made me one of his executors. I have no idea what the will contains, but it is not a job which I wish to take on in the least. Apart from the fact that it will involve me in a great deal of trouble (and probably acrimonious controversy with the rest of his family!) if he should be unfortunate enough to pre-decease me, it is yet another obstacle in my path to fresh fields and pastures new, which, at the moment, seems once more a very alluring one. G. is my partner in the undertaking, and I have insisted on a solicitor known to us all being nominated as a third.

Goodbye, my pretty. I'll write again from Port Sudan. I think you had better go to the expense of sending me a code wire, however brief, to Government House, Nairobi. I don't like the feeling of being out of touch with you so long.

I am very well, and not minding the heat at all – it is no worse than a Bombay February, if as bad. Bless you many times, my darling. T.

14 September 1928   *British India Steam*
                                                        Navigation Co. Ltd.
                                                        SS Malda

My darling, I climbed to the very top of the Great Pyramid and down again before breakfast this morning. It is hard work, but worth it; I liked them, and I liked the Sphinx, but all desert things should be seen in the half-light and not in the full glare of day – even with heavily-tinted goggles like mine – which are a *great* success.

This isn't a bad ship, if only she were going the right way. We are, I think, more comfortably housed than we were in the *Kaisar*: my cabin has two windows, one looking forward, which is a great luxury, but even so, I can see we are going to be pretty hot. However, I am very well so far. Bless you, my darling, and much love to the children. T.

16 September 1928   *SS Malda, Red Sea*

My Darling, We get into Port Sudan tomorrow morning, and it will be a relief to go ashore for a few hours, though it sounds a God-forsaken spot. It has been really very hot these last few days, with a following wind all the time, but the Captain thinks we shall find it a bit cooler after tomorrow. I am quite well in spite of it, but, oh dear, I am certainly getting too old for the society of the Windsors; they bore me stiff, I am afraid, and as you know, I am not good when bored. That particular aspect of the tour will, of course, improve when we get ashore, where one sees comparatively little of them conversationally, and we are not faced with any really long journeys by train; but at the moment I feel that even the society of Chadwyck-Healey[1] or Major Balmaine would be rare and refreshing fruit. It really will

[1] Chubby Chadwyck-Healey, with whom Tommy had shared digs at Oxford.

be out of the question for me to embark on another of these pilgrimages, apart from other considerations.

I forget if I mentioned Hassanein Bey in my Egyptian letters. He said he didn't meet you when you were there, but you have probably heard of him. He is King Fuad's Vice-Chamberlain, talks perfect English – he was at Balliol just after my time – and is *persona grata* with all the British community. I made great friends with him, and he has promised to come and see us when he is in London next spring. He is a great traveller, having done some remarkable desert-exploration, for which the Royal Geographical Society gave him their gold medal.

One trip which he never mentions is a minor expedition on which he foolishly allowed that shameless woman Rosita Forbes[1] to accompany him. It wasn't anything remarkable, but she, as you remember, made a tremendous Press stunt out of it, and then wrote a book in which she refers to Hassanein, who did the whole thing, as her *dragoman*. Of course Hassanein, who is the son of a distinguished sheikh, and a Moslem of high degree, got into terrible trouble with his relations. But he never said a word, for which Cairo gives him full credit, and, after two years, went off alone and achieved a really dangerous and difficult trip. He has published a book on it called *The Lost Oases*, which I know you would like, as it is delightfully written and full of very good desert-descriptions and curious lore.

He told me, when we were talking one evening about the more mystical side of Egyptology, a strange thing about Carnarvon.[2] After Carnarvon's death his nurse told Hassanein that for the last few days he had begged her never to move out of his sight – 'for,' he said, 'if once I am unable to keep my eyes on you, I shall go.' So she never left his room, till one night she went for a moment into the dressing-room, to boil something on a spirit-lamp. She had no sooner gone than every light in the hotel went out; she could find no matches, but she rushed back with the burning lamp; when she got to the bedside, he was dead. Hassanein also said that Howard Carter had told him

---

[1] English traveller and writer, 1890–1967. In 1920 she disguised herself as a Moslem to travel in the Libyan desert. Her books included *El Raisini, the Sultan of the Mountains* (1924) and *From Red Sea to Blue Nile* (1925).

[2] Fifth Earl of Carnarvon (1866–1923). A dedicated Egyptologist, he financed the excavations by the archaeologist Howard Carter (1873–1939), which led in 1922 to the discovery of the tomb of Tutankhamen. Most of the sinister stories about the boy pharoah, which Tommy here relates with such relish, have long since been discredited.

that he had found on Tutankhamen's cheek traces of a scar in exactly the same spot as that on which Carnarvon was bitten by the fatal mosquito; and that a mummy, noted for its malevolent powers, was on board the *Titanic* when she went down.

If you see Sarah, tell her Joey is really very well, though like me a good deal bored. Dinner-time has come while I was deciphering the wireless [messages], so I must stop. Good night, my darling. I feel I ought to write to the children, but am not in the mood at present. I'll try to find some postcards for them, tomorrow.   Bless you, T.

19 September 1928   *Red Sea*

My darling, We are due in Aden tomorrow afternoon, so another stage in this weary voyage will be over. It was terribly hot all down the Red Sea till yesterday afternoon, when we mercifully lost the following wind which had dogged us till then, with the result that the temperature instantly dropped a bit, and today, though it is still very sticky, is comparatively pleasant.

Frank Balfour[1] came on board at Port Sudan and took charge of us for the day. He was very agreeable, and I liked him better than before. In the evening we all went up to the Club, where Joey and I were put down to play a gruelling set of lawn-tennis with two ladies who were far better than we were. It is very difficult to see the ball at all in that hard, glaring light till one gets used to it. It is certainly a most God-forsaken spot. Frank told me he is moving on shortly to be Governor of Mongalla, between the south end of the Sudan and Uganda. He seemed pleased at the idea, but I gather that everybody in Port Sudan will be sorry to lose him. Phyllis is at Ooty till November.

There is a nice Irish doctor on board, one Burkett, who appears to be the great medical expert in Kenya. I had a long talk with him on medical matters generally, and he told me, among other useful information, that nobody need ever get fever in Africa if he will only take five grains of hydrobromide quinine night and morning, with a glass of water and on an empty stomach; and that if it is taken in that way, it has no ill effect on one's general health. So I am telegraphing to Grigg's secretary to have a bottle ready for each member of the party when we reach Mombasa. The Governor of Uganda, who is

---

[1] Lt. Col. Francis Balfour (1884–1965) was Governor of Red Sea Province, Sudan, 1927–28, and Governor of Mongalla Province 1929–30. He married Phyllis, daughter of the second Viscount Goschen.

also on board, is taking steps to provide a doctor when we are up there, and I don't think there will be any difficulty about taking one when we start south. Burkett says we should certainly be well-advised to have one handy in case of emergency, but that that particular trip is really quite healthy at that time of year, and there is no reason why it should not be delightful.

Have you ever read Olive Schreiner's *The Story of an African Farm*, which I have borrowed off Joey?[1] If not, you had better buy it in Fisher Unwin's cheap edition – 'Cabinet Library' – for it is a remarkable, Brontë-esque book, and some of it really beautiful – e.g., the chapter called 'Waldo's Stanger', which is an extraordinary bit of work for a woman of about twenty, as she then was. It made a great sensation when it came out in the Eighties, and I don't wonder. Like the Brontës, she often writes very crudely, and even ridiculously. Her attempts at a love-story, which fortunately don't begin till the latter part of the book, are lamentable, and her psychology is right off the rails, but, as a whole, I think it is a great book.

I have written a letter to the children, addressed to Lavinia (John will get the next one), which I shall send separately. I suppose it will still be another fortnight before I hear anything from you, though I hope there may be a telegram at Nairobi. I shall think of you all leaving Brancaster on Saturday.

I am, inevitably, thinking a good deal about the future again, but from quite a different and more dispassionate angle than last year. This time, there has really been nothing to cause one active worry so far – indeed, I am so hardened by now that I expect nothing *will* worry me. That is the serious part of it, and I am inclined to think that the truth is that, apart from any consideration of whether the objective results are satisfactory or not, I have been private-secretarying quite long enough, no matter who the Principal may be. Very few men, I expect, can go on doing it indefinitely, unless they are pronouncedly of the E. Marsh[2] type; there are too many continual restraints of one's own will, and too much repression of one's own standard of values to make it really healthy.

I am meditating a letter to Walter Riddell,[3] who, of all the men I

[1] Olive Schreiner (1855–1920), the South African author and early champion of women's rights, published *The Story of an African Farm* in 1883.
[2] Sir Edward Marsh (1872–1953), scholar and civil servant, worked for Winston Churchill during much of his early political career. His reminiscences, *A Number of People*, were published in 1939.
[3] Sir Walter Riddell (1879–1934) was Principal of Hertford College, Oxford, 1922–29.

know is the most likely, I think, to be able to suggest some alternative which might suit us both better – and even give you a garden. I shall send you a copy of it when I write it – it will be purely what the diplomats call a *ballon d'essai*, so don't imagine that I am going to take any rash step before I get back; but time is getting on, and if we are ever going to pursue a new path, I feel it will have to be in the next few years or never, and there is no harm in exploring the ground. Since I left England, one or two possible, and pleasant, jobs which I might get have occurred to me, and they are all in that sort of semi-academic world in which Walter R. moves and is a considerable power. Moreover, Brancaster showed me how jolly an interregnum of five or six months at Sutton would be, before the old man [his father] departs and before John goes to school. I feel that the next few years, which will never recur, are those that may count most in my whole relationship with him hereafter; and that relationship can never be really satisfactory in ordinary London life.

However, all this is purely nebulous at present, so, as I say, don't be in any anxiety about sudden developments. One thing which has started my thoughts this way is the realisation that I can never again go off on one of these trips and leave you and the children for so long. And, unless I clear right out, I don't see how I can escape them. Bless you always, my darling. T.

25 September 1928   *SS Malda*

My darling, I have had a bad week, feeling very ill and melancholy; nothing serious – only the natural reaction of my liver to the continuous Turkish bath of the Red Sea; too much sweating always saps my small stock of vitality. But I am much better now; after rounding Guarda Fui, we ran into the tail-end of the monsoon, which brought the temperature down at once, though it brought also an unpleasant swell for the last two days. Now, however, that has abated, and we have got quite pleasant Mediterranean weather, with a barely perceptible sea. Nothing, however, can ever make life on the ocean wave anything but a nightmare to me; fair weather or foul, I loathe ships and everything about and around them. I don't know what I wouldn't pay now for the boon of walking round one small grass field, or for ten minutes in the pine wood on Sutton Hill.

Whenever I am away from you, which I am determined shall never happen again, I always start re-casting the future. That proves, I think, that there is something wrong with the present. Once I am home, the ordinary London day, pleasant enough, with the sure knowledge that you and the children will be there when I get back to Hyde Park Square, and the prospect of two or three jolly weekends, or maybe a Brancaster or a Loch na Bo in the near future – it all acts as a kind of drug, making one feel, 'Oh, well, this is pleasant enough'. And the foreground of Hyde Park Square and of our own life makes the background of York House and its inherent unsatisfactoriness and futility seem something of little account.

That's why I find it so difficult to tell you, in the middle of it all, what I am feeling; it's not because I don't want to tell you, for I've never concealed anything *definite* from you for ten minutes; but somehow, leading that curious kind of double life, the York House side of it seems so remote and unreal the moment I step off my bus in the Bayswater Road, that I find it impossible to formulate, even to myself, just what my feelings are. It is only when I get a detached view, as on these tours, that I get at the truth.

Last year, I admit, when I wrote to you from Canada, I allowed the question to become coloured by personal currents (mixed metaphor, I know); I had lost my temper with the Prince, and I mistook that for the mine, whereas it was only a more or less casual match. Moreover, I'd no business to spring it on you suddenly, with Caroline still pending, and you were perfectly right to stop me; not only from your point of view, which was absolutely legitimate, but (even though this may not have occurred to you at the time) because I was approaching the thing by entirely wrong methods – making a *personal* question of it, and planning a melodramatic exit, which I now know would have done no good to anybody.

After your letter brought me to reason, I made up my mind to lock the whole thing up for a bit, and try to start afresh; all this last year, I have just gone on from day to day, just not thinking about it, and assuming that I should still be treading the same path this day ten years.

Well, there comes this trip, bringing me back again into the position of an active and (*pro tem*) chief private secretary, in constant and direct touch with the man who pays me; with it comes the inevitable stock-taking. There's been nothing, so far, to annoy me. I feel just as friendly towards him as I ever have felt, or shall feel; and I'm not letting the fact that the sea gives me the heebie-jeebies influence me; but the conclusion I keep on coming back to, and cannot get away from, is that ten years of this 'personal staff' work (I'd had one and a half years with G. Lloyd, remember – a different business, I grant, but nonetheless working solely for *one man*) is as much of my life as I want to give to it, and that, as regards this particular private secretaryship, the longer I stay at it, the less good I shall be, either as a private secretary, or to myself, or you.

A good private secretary ought to be whole-heartedly devoted both to his man and to his aims. I'm very far from being either, I fear, and the result is I'm always having to be deceitful, which is very bad for one. Even if I were red-heatedly convinced that Monarchy is a flawless and indispensable institution (which I'm not), his interpretation of the duties and aims of royalty is utterly discrepant from mine.

It is like being the right-hand man of a busy millionaire, when one is not at all certain that capitalism is a good thing in itself, and is anyhow quite sure that this particular capitalist is practising capitalism on thoroughly unsound lines.

Apart from principles, too, if he's not intended by nature to be a prince, I don't think I'm intended to be anybody's personal employee. As I grow older, I'm finding the strain of submitting incessantly to small caprices more and more trying to my temper. Why *should* I undo an hour's work just because another man suddenly decides he wants to play golf at three instead of five? Why *should* I continually hang about on one foot or the other because another man can't take the trouble to go and change his clothes in time? Small things, I know, and things that other men have to put up with; I've put up with them quite patiently for eight years, and now I find they are slowly but surely sapping my temper. And I would sooner die in the workhouse than that you and the children should ever think of me as a bad-tempered man.

Lastly, all the savour has gone out of the work, even when there is enough of it to keep me occupied, which isn't often. Time was, when I got a real thrill out of the speeches; I can't raise a spark of interest in them now. And, on this trip, which sounds so fine on paper, the bald truth is that I shan't really have a hand's turn to do from start to finish, beyond keeping a simple diary, cyphering a few telegrams about trains and dates, and giving my clerk an occasional handful of letters, which can all be answered by a printed form.

My own view is, then, that within, say, the next year or so, I must move on. It will be easy; I shall merely tell him that I am through with private secretary-ing, as a profession, and want to do something else, though I don't quite know what. I think he will be sorry, but I believe he will be quite sympathetic, and accept my reason, which is fundamentally the true one.

I certainly shan't ask him to find me another job; and if I can get reasonable assurances elsewhere that I am likely to be offered other jobs, I should dearly like an interregnum in the country with you and the children before they grow up.

Detailed plans for the future can only be discussed properly when we are together. For the moment, the keystones to that future are that we have, between us, £3,000 per annum (less income tax) without counting Sutton; that, after nearly nine years, I can say more unhesitatingly than ever before that I personally (that is, so far as my own personal happiness is concerned) want nothing out of life except to live with you and the children in surroundings where we should all be content – preferably, of course, in the country. I don't see that this is an unrealisable ideal, or at any rate that it is not one which could be modified to fit in with the kind of work I might be able to do. Whether such work could be made to bring in as much as my present salary, I doubt. The thing we have got to thrash out is, how many hundreds a year are we justified in paying for what would be, certainly for me, and I believe for all of us, a happier life? And, again as far as I'm concerned, a healthier one; this present job is pushing me down the slope of middle age much quicker than it ought to.

Each succeeding year I want more and more to have all the spring and all the autumn to ourselves. Don't you, my pretty? Other people have to do without it; yes, I know they do, but how many other people can you think of who want so very little else besides each other, as we do? Not many; and it seems such a pity to waste anything so rare, if one has been miraculously given it.

Goodbye, my darling. There is such a heap of things I want to know: what Mrs Pawle answered, how your golf prospered, whether you went to Holcombe, how the motor was after its visit to Johnson's garage, and how you got through the migration back to London: how your winter plans progress, and whether you still love me as I do you. T.

PS I forgot one point, though you have already made it to me, last summer: it seems pretty certain that trips such as this will constantly recur, probably every autumn, USA, India again, and Australia. I quite definitely will *not* embark on another, and, so long as I am paid by him, how can I refuse?

PPS If you go down to Sutton in October, plant a *lot* of bulbs under the apple trees and in the long grass by the side of the church walk.

8 October 1928   *Government House*
Nairobi

My darling, I probably shan't have time to make this a letter, as I must go down-town and buy a pair of mosquito-boots before lunch, and the mail closes immediately after. As a matter of fact we haven't seen a single mosquito since we left England, but we are sure to meet some in Uganda when we go there next week. At the races the other day I had a long talk with Jex-Blake, the doctor who married Muriel Herbert, and he confirms that nobody who takes quinine regularly in feverish places need ever be afraid of getting seriously ill, though he might have a mild go of fever. He is a charming man; we talked Einstein and astronomy through three very indifferent races, and he told me that modern philosophers are inclined to believe that the universe is finite – which is a comforting thought, as the notion of endless space, or endless time, has always seemed to me particularly terrifying.

The incoming mail has been 'over-carried' to Bombay, which means, I suppose, that they forgot to change it into the right boat at Aden, and that it has gone all the way to India. So I don't know when I shall hear from you again. They never seem to get an inward mail here more than once a fortnight, though it goes out every four or five days. I don't understand it.

Gloucester went off on safari yesterday, and if he doesn't turn it up, we shan't see him again till the first week in December, which is a relief. He's not a bad chap at all, and he has the right sort of ideas in his head as to what he ought, or ought not, to do in public – like the Duke of York[1] – so he is not much trouble.

The Prince of Wales, too, has gone off with Joey and the Delameres[2] for a few days on their farm, so there is a blessed calm over the whole house – very welcome to me, as I have a fair amount to do, fixing up the future and smoothing out the past. I am much afraid he may want me to go up there tomorrow, but if not I shall enjoy a quiet week here, till we start for Entebbe, the capital of Uganda, on the thirteenth.

---

[1] Later King George VI, to whom Tommy became Assistant Private Secretary in 1936, and Private Secretary in 1943.

[2] The third Baron Delamere (1870–1931) was a pioneer and pillar of Kenya society. His first wife, formerly Lady Florence Cole, died in 1914, and in 1928 he married Gladys Markham, a forceful lady thirty years his junior, who after his death became Mayor of Nairobi.

This place has a delicious climate now – like Delhi in January, only not so hot at midday or so cold at night; one is . . .

I've been irretrievably interrupted. So sorry, my pretty. God bless you. Mail just going. T.

To the Hon. F. C. Lascelles

26 October 1928
Government House
Entebbe, Uganda

My Dear Father, We came on to Uganda from Nairobi on 13 October, and after a few days here started off up-country with the Governor, Sir William Gowers,[1] who came out in our boat and is not at all a bad chap, though very susceptible to female charm, which is a dangerous trait in a governor, especially one whose own wife lives permanently in Paris, as is the case here.

It is a much nicer country than I anticipated; not unpleasantly hot, with frequent heavy showers of rain, which rarely last more than half an hour and usually occur at night. As a result the whole country is as green as Ireland, a very welcome change after the dried-up plains of Kenya. Nor do I think it is less healthy than any other tropical country. There is always the chance of getting fever, of course – malaria and blackwater – but the risk is very much reduced if one takes ordinary precautions, such as taking quinine regularly, wearing mosquito-boots in the evening and sleeping under a net. (As a matter of fact, I've scarcely seen a dozen mosquitoes since I landed in Africa, though it don't follow that they have not seen me.) Sleepy sickness is a very small risk, unless one happens to be permanently stationed in one or other of the few infected areas. Almost the first man I met here was a man I'd not seen since Oxford, and he, after nearly twenty years of Uganda, looks a great deal better-nourished than most of my contemporaries.

We came in a sort of penny-steamer across Lake Victoria, an all-night journey, and started inland a few days later. This trip was rather marred by the sudden illness of poor G. Trotter, who had suddenly developed a weak heart and will have to go home as soon as he is fit to travel. He was very bad indeed for a day or two, but is now safe in hospital here, and going on as well as can be expected.

---

[1] Sir William Gowers (1875–1954) was Governor and Commander-in-Chief of the Uganda Protectorate 1925–32.

We began by going up Lake Albert and then up the Victoria Nile to the Murchison Falls, which very few people have ever seen. They are most imposing, though one cannot get very close: the whole of the River Nile goes through a cleft eighteen feet wide. The pools below are swarming with crocodile, and HRH shot a large one, though I did not see the incident. We also saw a number of hippo on the way up, and a few elephant coming down to drink.

The next day we went down to Lake Albert again, *en route* for a camp about five miles from the shore, where it was expected to find plenty of elephant. Some good bulls were seen on the bank some way above our landing-place, and HRH was put ashore to give chase, with Salmon and Pete Wilson, two noted white hunters in these parts. Pete is a most interesting chap – an Australian by birth, and tough as nails. He has killed upwards of 800 elephants, the majority poaching in the Belgian Congo, though latterly he has been in the service of the Uganda Government as a game-warden. He has walked right across Africa, from East to West, and back again, several times, and once spent a year living with the Pygmies, all by himself. He told me that nobody understood their lingo, not even the neighbouring tribes, and that they were so treacherous that he knew very well that if he shot badly and failed to provide them with meat, they would very soon make meat of him. He also told me some very curious things about the way the Belgian officials run their Congo territory. We were, of course, within a few miles of their eastern boundary.

HRH secured one of these tuskers, after a very long walk, which tired him so much that he didn't leave camp the next day. I gather that the actual shooting of it was a comparatively tame affair. He had another try the third day, but saw nothing. Meanwhile Piers Legh relieved me on board the boat, where I was helping the doctor look after G., and I went up to the camp for the final day there.

That evening at dinner plans for the final day were being discussed; it was agreed that HRH must try to get another elephant, and after some discussion I consented to make one of the party, on the distinct understanding that he should take the first shot. I had no rifle of my own, and really have no desire to shoot an elephant, though I was anxious to see how it is done. Later, it was decided that the Governor should also be of the party, which in my opinion made it much too large.

However, we set off at 6 o'clock next morning, the arrangement being that the Prince, under Pete's guidance, should take the first elephant that presented itself. All being well, I, who had armed myself with a double-barrelled .470 belonging to Shiffner, the Governor's ADC, was then to run on with Salmon and take my chance of getting another elephant out of the herd, if there was a herd.

After walking about one-and-a-half hours, not bad going, through high grass, we came on recent tracks and droppings of elephant, and not very long after, we walked round a clump of bushes to find ourselves looking straight at the ribs of an old bull, not more than eighty yards away. He had only one tusk, but that was obviously a very good one, and as he stood there he offered the best chance of a heart-shot imaginable; and all these elephant-hunters tell one that a single heart-shot is worth a dozen in his head or anywhere else. Moreover, an elephant who has got it in the region of the heart is hardly ever known to charge or give any trouble.

Any of us could have shot him three times over, but the Prince chose that moment to start an argument as to who was to take the shot, and tried to induce me to. I have seldom been angrier with anybody, because we had definitely made the agreement I mentioned above, and nothing is more infuriating and futile in any form of shooting than this kind of messing-about at the critical moment, whatever people's motives may be. By the time I had convinced him, somewhat forcibly, that I meant what I said, the elephant had seen us and moved on, not in the best of tempers. I then retired firmly to the rear of the procession, lest there should be any more nonsense of this kind, and we resumed the pursuit. The order of march was then: the elephant, which was lost to view; Pete; HRH; Salmon, a few paces behind; a group of native gun-bearers; the Governor; and myself, each with our own gun-bearers.

We had now got into rather a nasty bit of country – clumps of solid bush, which made it impossible to see more than a few yards ahead, with only a narrow path between them. It was obvious, even to me, that we had lost the initiative, and that the elephant, if he felt so disposed, could get us on the hop; and this is exactly what he did.

We had pushed on, feeling our way blindly, as it were, and the head of our little column had just got round a circular clump, when I heard a peculiarly unpleasant scream, which I guessed from descriptions was the trumpeting of an extremely angry elephant extremely close at hand. I could see nothing immediately ahead, and the next thing I became aware of was being violently charged, not by the elephant, but by the Governor of Uganda, who was a few feet in front of me just round the bush.

Apparently the elephant, who had been thoroughly annoyed by

the previous encounter, had lain up for us, as they sometimes do (though rarely), and as soon as he caught sight of Pete and Co., had charged them incontinently. Pete and Salmon, with great gallantry and presence of mind, seeing that things were looking really ugly, instantly stopped in front of the Prince and fired simultaneously. Both shots were a trifle low and got the elephant in the extreme upper end of his trunk. Salmon, luckily, had a double-barrelled rifle, and got off his second barrel instantly, and this third shot turned him. Afterwards we measured the distances: he was exactly nine feet from Salmon and Pete, and eight yards from the Governor and me. The natives, having delivered their guns to their owners, dived for dear life into the bushes – and small blame to them.

I, meanwhile, having been propelled round the clump by His Excellency's onset (it is only fair to the latter to say that he did entirely the right thing – he couldn't have let his rifle off without killing somebody, probably the Prince of Wales), was waiting in considerable anxiety to see round which side of the bush the elephant (who had all the time been hidden from me) would choose to appear, and reminding myself of expert advice that, when confronted by angry tuskers, it was no manner of use trying to get up a tree, and the only hope of escape was to plunge into the thickest place that might be handy and hope that he would hurt somebody else.

However, as he didn't materialise, and as the heavy firing which had developed on the other side seemed to be getting a little further off, I remembered my arrangement with Salmon and ran forward. After a few yards I found myself in open country, over which Salmon and a posse of his armed natives were skirmishing in open order, running like stags and firing as they ran at the retreating stern of the elephant some eighty yards ahead of them. So I ran too, as if the devil was after me, hoping to register my own bullet on his backside before it was all over; but, unluckily, just as I was fairly in the firing-line and not unduly blown, he slowly collapsed and turned over on his side.

By the time Salmon and I got up to him, he was about finished, though the three or four natives discharged their rifles into his forehead to make sure. The three frontal shots had done no more than turn him, but as he turned, it seems, Pete, having got his magazine rifle loaded again, had just had time to give him a broadside more or less in the right place. This shot and a series of bullets in the stern sufficed to stop him. He was a very big elephant, and his single tusk weighed just under 100 lbs, which is well above average.

The whole incident only took about five minutes. It might easily have ended in favour of the elephant. If Salmon had happened to have a magazine instead of a double-barrelled rifle, there is no doubt he would have come on, and in that case someone must have been badly hurt, if not killed. It was the third shot that made him think better of it and swerve away. As it was, both the experts, who, when it was all safely over, were considerably rattled over what might have been, agreed that in all their experience they had never had to shoot an elephant at closer quarters – though I have no doubt that if they had been alone, and not responsible for HRH, they would have jumped aside the moment the elephant began to charge, and plugged him in the side as he went by.

I shall very likely never go elephant-hunting again, and it was an extraordinary piece of luck coming in for an exhibition of that kind, though I do regret not having been able to see him at the actual moment he charged. However, the scream of rage he gave was well worth hearing, and was not a sound one is ever likely to forget.

We then had breakfast, and the native trackers were sent out to find out what had become of three or four other elephants which had been feeding close by before the battle began; but there had been so much firing that they were apparently properly scared, for after about half an hour the trackers came back to say that they had moved very fast and were still going on several miles ahead. So we decided to go back to camp, on the chance that trackers who had been sent out on the other side might have brought back news of another herd; but this also came to nothing, and the day's sport ended with some rather mild guinea-fowl shooting just before sunset, and a native N'goma, or dance, after it. The next day, we struck camp and came back here.[1]

Will you send this letter to Admiral Sir Lionel Halsey at St. James's Palace, as I shan't have time or energy to write another account of the episode? He might then return it to Joan, but I don't think he had better show it to anybody else.

I hope you are keeping well and will not have a hard winter. Giving Lonsdale[2] the Garter is an incredible piece of tomfoolery, and

---

[1] In his own memoirs *A King's Story* the Prince described this incident as 'a terrifying experience' which made him regard elephants with new respect. In October 1929 he had a section of the single tusk made into an ashtray, which he gave Tommy as a souvenir, remarking in a letter that this was 'the only possible form of mounting ivory that I can devise – anything else is to my mind frightful.'

[2] The fifth Earl of Lonsdale (1857–1944), soldier, master of foxhounds, and owner of more than 150,000 acres of land.

I think poor Baldwin must be mad to shove that ass Willy Peel[1] back into the India Office, or Londonderry[2] into any office at all, except perhaps a lost luggage office.   Your loving Tommy.

To Joan

30 October 1928   *Kitale, Kenya*

My darling, We left Uganda last night, after playing golf at a place called Jinja, famous as being the only links in the world that has a local rule allowing one to lift without penalty from a hippopotamus footmark. The links stand literally at the beginning of the Nile, where it runs out of Lake Victoria over the Ripon Falls, which are nothing more than glorified rapids.

Uganda is a beautiful country – in an early Wenlock way perhaps the most beautiful I have seen. There has been a full moon this week, an African moon, light enough to read by, and as it is always dark by 6.30, whatever the time of year, one saw plenty of it. Most evenings Joey and I have driven back from Kampala to Entebbe, after seeing Gerald [Trotter] in his hospital, about that time; the road runs all along the side of the lake, and I shall never forget the fairy-like beauty of it all, with the horizon, in spite of a cloudless sky and the brilliant moon, continually glowing with far-off lightning – a curious effect, which I have never seen before outside of Covent Garden theatre. But it is a *béauté de diable* – very sinister, and unfriendly: you never forget that malignant death is lurking just round the corner. I can't imagine, for instance, walking about it alone with any pleasure; one would always have the feeling that the country hated him, as something alien, and was only waiting its chance to blot him out. The people, too, get terribly weary of the inevitable sameness of the weather; year in, year out, one day never varies perceptibly from another. None the less, if they eliminate the fever-scourge (as, in the process of time, they doubtless will) I can't imagine a pleasanter winter resort for anybody who wants to sit quietly in the sun and stare at a blue sea, without any risk of a bitter wind, as there is on the Riviera.

---

[1] 1867–1937, Secretary of State for India 1922–24 and 1928–29. He was created first Earl Peel in 1929.

[2] The seventh Marquess of Londonderry (1878–1949) was appointed First Commissioner of Works in 1928.

Here, we are back in the highlands of Kenya; beautiful distances, with ranges of blue hills beyond rolling plains, but, as always here, drab foregrounds and middle distances. Rather symbolic of the whole country, that – the far prospect is fair enough, but the present reality dusty and dreary. Tomorrow we move down the line to Eldoret, a similar nucleus of white settlers, spend the weekend with the Francis Scotts a little further on still, and so back to Nairobi for one day and then off to the Mount Kenya district for another two days.

I get so very tired of this constant travelling, and of the necessity, from my point of view, of always having to be thinking five days ahead, like a harassed chess-player. Joey has taken over all the financial side of the business now, from G., and will probably do it rather better. He is in capital form just now. He came to breakfast today looking more than unusually like something off a fishmonger's slab, and complained of troublous dreams, particularly one where he found himself in bed with Joan Grigg. 'But,' he added, 'it was all purely platonic. She only came there to tell me how much she hated Kenya.'

Well – if it comes to that, 'Going abroad is bad enough, but when it comes to the Colonies . . .' to quote Conrad's [Russell] farewell letter to me. I continually find little pictures of England flashing in front of my eyes at odd moments – the road winding up the hill from Sutton cow-leaze; Melbury in the evening; or the view from the ninth green at Brancaster. I don't know what I wouldn't pay for a quiet week at Sutton with you now. However, we'll have one, early in February; and it can be very delicious down there then, with the Chase and the Vale just beginning to stir in their sleep.

The film 'Simba' you talk of was shown privately at Government House, Nairobi, one night, in the presence of various shikar experts who knew all about the making of it. I gathered that it is by no means as truly 'face to face with nature' as it professes to be, and that a number of the pictures are actually fakes, while many others give an entirely false impression through the skilful use of extremely strong telephoto lenses. There is a lot of very boring padding, too, and even I could recognise that a considerable amount of it was taken in country very different from where it professes to be.

31 October   *Eldoret*

We had an awful evening at Kitale, a so-called ex-service dinner of about 150 of the local settlers, all very good chaps, but two-thirds of them were tight before the soup was off the table, and the noise for the rest of the evening was deafening. We then went on to a ghastly ball at the club, an entertainment which will be repeated here tonight, and tomorrow night, and the next night, at Rongai. This evening, however, it will be prefaced, thank God, by dinner in a private house. One result of G.'s collapse is that I must now take turn and turn about with Joey for the night work.

Thanks for the cutting about Keats's Shakespeare, which interested me. As far as I remember, Keats himself said that what really opened the flood-gates of his poetry was reading 'The Faerie Queen',[1] but no doubt Shakespeare had a great influence on him too. I don't suppose anybody who has written English poetry in the last 250 years hasn't owed something to Shakespeare, directly or indirectly. 'The Eve of St. Agnes', still the best romantic poem in the language, is steeped in Shakespeare; so is most of Matthew Arnold and Tennyson. But of course, the Xanadu theory can be pushed too far: after all, only a limited number of combinations of intelligible words are mathematically possible, and a certain amount of what seems to be repetition is bound to happen, just as it does in music.

I am glad you got a day's hunting at St. Fagan's, and the old gent you met was quite right: I've always told you you had a very good seat on a horse. Also that you met Nellie Grant.[2] Everybody out here has the greatest admiration for her: she must have had a remarkably hard life, and has been so plucky and efficient all through. I've not heard anybody say the suspicion of a hard word about her, though all her friends are very exercised about Elspeth's future. Personally, I would almost as soon see Lavinia on the streets as trying to earn her daily bread as a journalist in New York, but perhaps I am prejudiced against American Press life.

I knew my Aden letter would not come as much of a surprise to

---

[1] In *John Keats* (1968) Robert Gittings wrote: 'The spark undoubtedly fell when [Charles Cowden] Clarke, one evening in the old arbour at school, read Keats the "Epithalamion" of Spenser. Keats was so enchanted by this new poet that he took away with him that night the first volume of "The Faerie Queene", which, said Clarke, "he ramped through . . . like a young horse turned into a Spring meadow."'

[2] Mother of the author Elspeth Huxley, Nellie Grant had emigrated to East Africa with her husband Jos in 1912. After establishing a coffee plantation at Thika, she bought a new piece of land at Njoro, in the Rift Valley, and when Jos drifted off into other projects, struggled manfully to set up and run a farm there. Elspeth, then 21, was about to leave for London and begin her career as assistant Press Officer to the Empire Marketing Board.

you; but don't think it is in any way a hysterical outburst this time. In sickness or in health, at sea or on land, in London or on tour, I am really quite convinced now that I can't go on, and I am sure that when we've really talked it out, you won't ask me to. I've got nothing new to say on the subject, so won't start it all over again. But when you talk in your letter about some arrangement whereby Godfrey [Thomas] and I should take turns over these tours – that, I'm afraid, can *never* be made workable. A Viceroy could never keep a secretary who begged to be taken on tour only when it suited him; and you yourself wouldn't keep a nurse who stipulated that she should never be asked to go to the country. The Prince's theory now is that Godfrey should be kept practically entirely for the routine work at home, and that I should specialise in the overseas trips. There is, on the face of it, nothing whatever unreasonable in that – if the two of us are prepared to work on those terms; if we are not, then we have no right to stay on, any more than a sailor who, for private reasons, don't want to be sent to a foreign station, has any right to stay on in the Navy.

Even if we *were* to take turns – an arrangement HRH would never agree to – even that wouldn't do for me; I really could never go on even one of these expeditions again. I can't tell you how indescribably I mind the separation part of it; and, leaving that out, it is hard to make anybody understand the awful physical strain on one's whole system. Don't think I am ill – I am organically as sound as a bell; but I do seriously think that a few more spells of this sort of thing would, in a lesser degree, of course, affect me permanently in the same kind of way as it has Gerald.

Even in the worst parts of the war – and I was a good bit younger then – I don't remember ever feeling such acute mental and physical exhaustion. Even if it don't permanently affect one's general health, I know it has already affected my small stock of sociability. I always come home feeling that I never want to see a lighted candle for months and months, and that the sound of dance-music will make me scream; and that makes me a poor companion for you. Nor can we kid ourselves with the idea that there are not likely to be many more of these jaunts. The Prince is so bitten with this country that he seriously discussed coming back here *for another three months after South Africa*!! Only the advent of the point-to-point season turned the scale. Only two things keep him at home now – riding races, and F.W.[1]

---

[1] Mrs Freda Dudley Ward had become the Prince's mistress in 1918; she was one of the strongest influences in his life, and their relationship lasted until 1934.

Both those sheet-anchors may part any moment; hunting, as distinct from point-to-points, has already faded out of the picture, and he himself admits that F.W. won't last for ever. He is already busy fixing up plans for a long stay out here next year, and talks also of other visits to Australia and Canada in the near future – besides, of course, the ever-present menace of USA.

Well, there it is. So please do believe me when I say that I shall have to settle the thing pretty soon after I get back, one way or the other. Once he definitely asks me to come off with him again somewhere next year – probably here – I shall have to take it on, *or* definitely ask to be set free. Not, as I said before, on any controversial grounds, but simply because I myself am not strong enough, or, for private reasons, not free, to go on being a private secretary on the lines his plan of life demands. That is to say, it would all be quite friendly.

Give me credit, too, for not being unemployable (though, by God, I shall be, after a few more years of this). I'm always being given to understand that I've made a fair success of this job, though I know very well in my own heart that I passed high water-mark some time ago. I've done no good work for a year. I've got a fair number of acquaintances, and honestly, without over-estimating my own capabilities, I really don't think we need be afraid of my being unemployed very long, though I hope I might be for a bit.

Goodbye, my darling. It would be such a comfort to talk to you just for ten minutes. Bless you a million times. T.

Before Tommy could despatch this letter, he received a cable from Joan, evidently supporting him in his decision to resign, and he added the following postscript:

2 November 1928   *Deloraine*
Rongai
Kenya Colony

I was on the point of sticking this up in the train when I got your code telegram, which makes much of the letter unnecessary. Still, it is just as well you should know what a menace these annual tours are likely to become.

I was very glad to get the cable – thank you for it, my darling. If you are really prepared for the resulting dislocation, I should like to have it out with HRH on the boat going home and give him till Easter to find somebody to replace me. That would involve trying to let Hyde Park Square for the whole summer, and our spending it between Sutton and Brancaster; to me that is an ideal prospect, but if for domestic reasons you would rather wait a bit, send me a cable and I will say nothing till after I get home. But the boat is a first-class place for getting the job over, as, once we are in London, God knows when I shall be able to get an hour alone with him.

It will be painful, for I believe he will mind parting with me; but I shall take the line that I have now been ten years on the staff and, in my own interests, must go back to regimental life, so to speak – an argument which he quite understands and will sympathise with. He will probably ask if I would come back again some day in the future, and though I've no intention of ever doing so, at present, I can't very well refuse point-blank. However, all that can take care of itself, and I am quite certain I can settle the whole thing amicably. The person who will have hysterics is poor old Godfrey – not because he is especially attached to me, but because he will have to run round in circles more furiously than ever, trying to find a successor. Though he may already have his eye on somebody – I gave him the broadest possible hint not to look on me as a permanent limpet last autumn.

We got here – the Francis Scotts' – this morning; much the most attractive country I've seen yet, and he has built himself a very delightful house, though ruinously expensive – they say it cost him £15,000. He is in terribly low water just now, too, both his wheat and maize crops having failed disastrously through quite unexpected drought, involving him in a loss of some £7,000. I like him so much, and he has been delightful to me ever since we first found him in Nairobi. But, like everybody else, he has gone and got 'just a few people in to dance to the gramophone after dinner' – which means another 4 a.m. bed, I suppose. She hasn't appeared yet. I fancy she spends a good deal of time in bed these days.[1]

I had a pleasant ride with a man called Joyce – a settler in another part of the country; a very nice man, and, in the course of the ride, I found that his father was Clanricarde's agent, quarrelled with him, brought an action for libel against Clanricarde, and was completely broke in the resulting litigation, which the wicked old man, with his millions behind him, took to every conceivable court of law.

Tell the children I've got some elephant's whiskers for John and a bracelet made out of the tail-hairs for Lavinia. I'll send them next mail.

[1] Elspeth Huxley also reported that Lady Eileen spent a great deal of time in bed, and that, when she had finished her bath, she required her maid to come and pull out the plug for her.

P.S. Supposing we *do* spend such a summer as I suggest, I will guarantee to give the children regular lessons in arithmetic, history etc. I should love it. We could get a sort of general syllabus out of Miss Bernan – and we'll do such a lot of botany!

To Godfrey Thomas

10 November 1928   *Government House*
Kenya

Dear Godfrey, We start the great trek on Wednesday. All last week reports about the state of the roads were most gloomy, and people shook heads and said we should have to give it all up. Latterly, however, the short rains seem to have let up, and for the last few days things have been steadily improving. Anyhow, we have now got Denys Finch [Hatton][1] to take charge of us. I *fiche* myself completely of all anxiety, for I know nobody in the world who inspires me with more complete and child-like confidence than he does. He was always a remarkable chap, but he has come on tremendously since the days when I used to know him in England. He has organised the whole expedition for me, down to the last sheet of bromo; my only anxiety is that HRH is continually being told of some indispensable gadget for safari by his club-friends, and rushes off and buys it, only to find that Denys has already ordered several last week.

The procession will be an imposing one: four touring cars and four lorries – it sounds an immense convoy, but everybody says it is if anything slightly less than most parties of the same number usually take for this trip, especially at this time of year, if they are ever rash enough to go at all. And we are now entirely self-contained, so that if we stick in the mud, or there are lions in the path, we can settle down for the night quite comfortably where we are, without bothering to plough on till we reach the next prepared camp.

Our total European strength is now: HRH, Joey, Denys, self, COPHO (which is Burt's name in the Government code book) and a sergeant in charge of the four King's African Rifles lorries which

[1] Denys Finch-Hatton (1887–1931), the celebrated pilot and white hunter, was the second son of the thirteenth Earl of Winchelsea. In 1928 he was nearing the end of his long affair with the Danish settler and author Karen Blixen (1885–1962), also known as Tanne, or Tania, and by her combination of pen- and maiden-name, Isak Dinesen.

have been loaned us. The other servants I am sending round to Beira by sea, where the Vice-Consul has got to get them up to Livingstone by rail, and luckily the boats and trains run kindly, so that we can keep them here till we go, and still get them to Livingstone before our own arrival.

[On the proposed visit to South Africa, which never came off.] I dread that period, for everybody agrees in saying Johannesburg is a foul spot, and now old G. has left us, I feel bound to take turn and turn about with Joey at the night-life, and for me it is no life, but sheer, lingering death; tight women do bore me so terribly at any time, and the nighter the tighter, so to speak.

We have been fairly good here – fairly. But I shall feel no pangs at all when I see the last of Nairobi, though there are bits of this country which I should have been very loth to leave twenty years ago. As it is, with the calculating eye of middle age, I find myself always conscious of the serpent only half-hidden in the most Eden-like patches: the hectic flow of nervous conversation; the no less hectic flow of sun-downers, moon-risers and star-palers; the pale-faced children; the farmyard morals of their elders. I don't blame them, God knows – it's the Equator, and I should be every bit as bad myself if I stayed here: the continual struggle against debt with all but a very few; the constant dread or reckless disregard of malaria – see what I hope will be the most telling passage in the farewell speech HRH is to make tomorrow (of which, by the way, only God and Lord Delamere know how sick I am); the all-pervading 'eat and drink for tomorrow we die' philosophy. And yet, in spite of it all, I have seldom come across a more lovable and forgiveable set of people than these East Africans. It's a very funny place.

Africa, on the other hand, can be intoxicatingly beautiful – far more so than, say, India; but she never for one moment lets you forget that you are an alien. Everywhere you get the feeling that the country is fundamentally hostile, and that death from sun, bug or wild beast is waiting to spring on you round the next corner. It is that, I think, far more than this 'altitude', to which they attribute every ill, which plays the devil with their nerves.

It is too near dinner-time to start talking politics; and, as Ned Grigg is going home on 1 December, you will hear all you want from him. They [the Griggs] have both been exceptionally kind to me. An old friend of mine, who I found had spent the last fifteen years in Uganda, said to me the other day, 'The angel Gabriel couldn't govern Kenya.' I never thought of Gabriel as a proconsul, but the aphorism is a profoundly true one. And yet, I dined the other evening

103

with Ewart Grogan,[1] who from being the Cecil Rhodes-to-be of East Africa has become a sad and sour bore, and he spent the whole evening trying to convince me, till I literally fell asleep, that there are no problems in this country which a child could not solve on its slate. But then he is an Irishman, and a disgruntled one at that.

Tell the Admiral I had two devilish good days trout-fishing under the shadow of Mount Kenya this week – the only breath of sport, save for our historic day's elephant-hunting, that I have had yet; except in so far as onlookers see most of the game. Love to Diana. Enclosed is for Michael [Thomas's son].   Yours, Tommy.

PS A boy, or son, in the vernacular is a 'Toto'. The natives, it appears, refer to the Heir Apparent as 'Georgie's Toto'. Nobody has yet had the courage to break the news to him, but the discovery is a constant source of joy to both the Acting Comptroller and the Assistant Private Secretary.

To the Hon. Frederick Lascelles

17 November 1928   *In camp, Babati*
                                                        Tanganyika

My dear Father, I had two afternoons trout-fishing before we left Kenya. We were staying in the Mount Kenya district, ostensibly for the local race-meeting, but when I discovered that there was a nice little stream running below our host's farm, I gave the races a miss and stayed behind to fish. It was a rapid, rocky stream, never very wide, and much overgrown, which made casting very difficult, especially as, on local advice, I put on a small salmon fly – a yellow-winged thing I found in my book something like a Black Goldfinch. It worked well, for I had out seven little rainbow before it got dark, which it does punctually, and very rapidly, at 6.15 in this part of the world. None of them differed from another by more than an ounce or two, and all were about half a pound, but very strong and lively. I lost one bigger fish, which took me under a submerged tree and broke me. He must have been 1 lb, which is about as big as they go in this river.

---

[1] The settler celebrated for his feat of walking from the Cape to Cairo, but a bitter opponent of the Kenya Government, and often at loggerheads with other white leaders.

Next day Piers Legh and I were taken off to a larger river, the Naro Moru, where there are said to be trout of 5 lbs and more. This was a bigger affair altogether, with great deep pools and an extremely strong stream, which made wading quite dangerous in places. It would be a really first-class river if its banks were not covered, with such impenetrable jungle that it is quite often impossible even to see the water, let alone get down to it, for several hundred yards at a time. The only practicable way of fishing is to walk along till you find a gap, made by animals going down to drink, and then get into the water and wade as far down, and then up, stream as is feasible.

We got there late, and as it was a dark afternoon, with heavy clouds and some rain, we did not get much fishing. People have no idea of time out here, and none of their watches seem to go at all. However, I got a nice fish of about 1¼ lbs fairly soon, casting up stream, and then, in a very awkward place, completely tunnelled by trees, so that one could only switch the fly downstream and pay out line at the end of each cast, I hooked a good fish, who promptly ran out about thirty yards and then threw himself right out on to the opposite bank. I could do nothing, as both trees and rocks made it impossible to move, so could only shout loudly for Legh and my host, to whom I had lent my landing-net. They were some way off, but eventually arrived at the double, imagining that I was treed by a buffalo or a leopard, which is a not uncommon occurrence on this water; and after a good deal of crashing-about one of them managed to struggle into the water below me, and we got the fish safely out. He was a picture of what a rainbow trout should be, and must have weighed very near 3 lbs, but unfortunately nobody had a weighing-machine on the spot. It was then beginning to get dark, but I got another fish, the double of the first, before we knocked off.

We started off on our long overland trip to Broken Hill from Nairobi last Wednesday. The road on the first stage, to a place called Kajiado, was reported to be so bad after the recent heavy rain that we gave up the idea of trying to motor, and went round by train, this being the only bit which can be done by railway. We were well advised, for we heard that another party, who tried to get through by road, became helplessly stuck and spent the night in the ditch. At Kajiado, however, we got out of the rain-belt and found lovely weather and a good road, so far as mud was concerned – though of course it is nowhere anything more than a track, and often terribly rocky, especially when it crosses dry river-beds etc.

On the second day, when we reached a spot about ten miles short of the Tanganyika border, Finch-Hatton was told by some natives on the roadside that there was a herd of elephants quite close by. As we were in a Game Reserve, there was no question of shooting one, but we thought we would go and have a look at them. Grigg, the Governor of Kenya, had lent us a cinema-camera, and it seemed a good chance of getting some pictures.

I took charge of the camera, while the others brought rifles, in case of trouble. After walking for an hour or so, and having seen nothing but impala, baboons and a wart-hog, we decided to make for the road again and pick up the motors. We had hardly turned when we came on a bull-elephant, feeding quietly about 100 yards away. The wind was right, so we got up to him, and from the shelter of some bushes both Finch-Hatton and I got a lot of pictures at various ranges, down to about twenty-five yards, without disturbing him.

A second elephant was standing about 100 yards off. As we had got no full-face photos, nor any of him in motion, we cast back a few hundred yards and got up to him also from a different angle. The wind was still good, though inclined to be uncertain, and the cover not so handy. However, we walked up to within about sixty yards, and I started filming him. He must have heard the whirr of our camera, or very likely saw enough of us to make him suspicious, for after a second or two he swung round, spread his ears, cocked his trunk and bore straight down to where I was standing, at a slow walk.

He looked so magnificent through the view-finder that perhaps I let him come rather nearer than was prudent, as he was clearly not in the best of tempers. Finch-Hatton, who was at my elbow, sent the Prince and Legh quietly away, and then whispered to me that it was time to clear. It certainly was, for when I put the camera down from my eye (it is one of those things you hold against your nose and look through a miniature telescope at the side of the machine), he was not further away than the length of a cricket-pitch, and still coming on.

We slipped behind the nearest bush and made off as quietly as possible, but not quite quick enough. Unluckily, the wind went wrong at that very moment, and he got it. He gave one scream, and started after us at a good trot – trunk up, mouth open, ears right forward – a real charge, meaning business, and a very fine sight, though too adjacent to be altogether pleasant.

On such occasions, as you probably know, it is no use trying to get up a tree, as, unless it is a very solid one, he will have the tree down or shake you out of it. The best plan is to dive into some thick place, into which he is not likely to follow you, as he is apt to hurt his tusks in thick stuff. So we scattered and ran like stags for about 200 yards, without gaining much on him.

The Prince was close alongside me, and as there was no very good cover for some little way, I was getting quite anxious, when Finch-Hatton very wisely decided to stand and shoot, Reserve or no Reserve. He gave him one in the ear, standing about three-quarters broadside to him at about forty yards, which sufficed to stop him. I don't think he will be much the worse for the shot, as he would have dropped if it had touched his brain, but he swung round at once and left us in peace. We heard afterwards that there is a rogue-elephant round there, which has been chasing motors down the road, and this was probably our friend. Anyhow, if only our film comes out, it ought to be a really fine one, worth perhaps quite a bit of money. Finch-Hatton, who has done quite a lot of this kind of work, covering people taking photos for museums etc., says he has seldom seen a better chance for pictures at close quarters. But it is not a game I propose to make a habit of.

23 November 1928   We have had several long days after rhino, buffalo and lion, all very interesting and full of incident, but HRH got no shot till two days ago, when he secured quite a good lion. We had roped into our party a certain Baron Blixen,[1] a very fine shot and hunter, who has been at the game for a long time. Incidentally, he married as his second wife Emily Alexander's daughter,

[1] Baron Bror Blixen-Finecke (1886–1946) had sailed from Denmark for East Africa in 1913 already engaged to his second cousin Karen Dinesen. The couple married on the day she landed in Mombasa – 14 January 1914 – and went to live on a coffee-farm near Nairobi. Blixen soon won a wide reputation as a hunter and philanderer dogged by shaky finances. As Elspeth Huxley remarked, 'on safari, he chased lions and sometimes ladies, but in between his creditors chased him.'

Finch-Hatton had first met Karen in 1918, and after a while he made a habit of returning to her home outside Nairobi between his safaris. Her divorce was made absolute in 1925, but although Finch-Hatton continued to live with her, they never married. In 1928 Baron Blixen married Cockie Birkbeck, the divorced wife of another settler.

The Prince of Wales's visit in the autumn of that year raised latent social tensions to a high pitch. Both Blixen and Finch-Hatton were engaged to organise safaris for the Prince, and the new Baroness Blixen went to some of the parties *ex officio*; but Finch-Hatton made sure that his lover was not left out: she dined with the royal party at Government House, Nairobi, and on board their train; then she entertained the Prince to dinner and to a specially laid-on *ngoma*, or native dance, at home.

'The Prince of Wales *is* really absolutely charming,' she wrote to her mother on 14 October 1928. 'I am so much in love with him that it hurts.' 'The dinner on the train,' she reported, was 'frightful, but still very congenial'; her own, on the other

Footnote continued overleaf.

Jacqueline Birkbeck, she having also parted from her first husband.

Blixen plastered the whole countryside with dead zebras and kongonis, and spent the small hours of the morning watching the result. When we got down to the chosen district from our camp, about 7 a.m., he reported that he had harboured no fewer than four lions in the neighbourhood of various kills. We had a long hot walk of about three hours, but eventually got to the valley where he had seen these lions. As there had been some hitch about getting enough native boys to act as beaters, Blixen, Legh, the local game-warden and I had to take it on.

I had only a shot-gun, though they say that at close quarters that is the most deadly weapon of any, so I stuck pretty close to Blixen, who is a dead shot. HRH and Finch-Hatton were posted at the end of the valley, and we then advanced up it, barking like dogs and making other noises calculated to rouse a sleeping lion and push him forward. Right at the end of the beat there was a loud *woof* in a patch of thorn at my elbow, and out came a lion and lioness. Whether we had not barked loud enough, I do not know, but unluckily they broke back and disappeared in the direction from which we had come too fast for anyone to get a shot at either of them.

We then went on to the next place, a long strip of grass with a narrow spinney about half way down it. This time only the bold Blixen was required as a beater; he was pretty sure that one or more lions were lying up in this patch of bush, so, the wind being convenient, he advanced on it from the up-wind end while we crouched in the grass at the other. The manoeuvre was quite successful, for a lion came out broadside to the Prince at about 100 yards and made off down the valley. He missed him with his first barrel, but knocked him down with the second – a good shot, as the animal was then 140 yards off and moving fast through fairly long grass. He lay for a bit, but as we approached went on a bit and then turned on us, evidently prepared to charge. As a matter of fact, he could not have done much, as his hind leg was broken, but we did not

---

Footnote continued.

hand, was voted by the Prince the best he had had in Kenya. Seven sat down, with Karen next to her royal guest at one end, and Tommy beside Finch-Hatton at the other. The eighth place had tactfully been left open, in case the Prince wanted to bring a lady with him.

Disaster struck both Finch-Hatton and Karen only three years later. In 1931 he was killed in an air-crash at Voi, and she was driven home from Africa by bankruptcy; yet in later years she made herself world-famous with *Out of Africa* (1937) and other books.

know that, and he looked nasty enough. The Prince gave him two more, both right in the chest, and the second killed him stone-dead. He measured 104 inches, an oldish beast, in good condition. He was skinned by Finch-Hatton's boys in about twenty minutes, while we ate our luncheon. There were two more lions in the same patch, which broke on Blixen's side, but too far for him to do any good.

We have a few more days in camp ahead of us, and then resume the journey southwards, going by train from Dodoma to Kigoma, where we get a steamer to take us down to the southern end of Lake Tanganyika; thence by motor to Broken Hill, perhaps shooting a bit on the way, and so down to the Cape by train. Our boat sails on 11 January, and should be at Southampton by the 28th.

Perhaps you would send this letter on to Joan.

Your loving Tommy.

Only the first part of this journey took place as planned. The party went on to Dodoma, but there they began to receive doom-laden messages from England, bringing the news that the King had fallen gravely ill – and there the Prince let fall on Tommy what he described as 'the last straw on my camel's back':

It was finally broken by his incredibly callous behaviour when we got the news of his father's grave illness. I remember sitting, one hot night, when our train was halted in Dodoma station, decyphering, with the help of dear Denys Finch-Hatton, the last and most urgent of several cables from Baldwin, begging him to come home at once. The Prince came in as we finished it, and I read it to him. 'I don't believe a word of it,' he said. 'It's just some election dodge of old Baldwin's. It doesn't mean a thing.'

Then, for the first and only time in our association, I lost my temper with him. 'Sir,' I said, 'the King of England is dying; and if that means nothing to you, it means a great deal to us.' He looked at me, went out without a word, and spent the remainder of the evening in the successful seduction of a Mrs Barnes, wife of the local Commissioner. He told me so himself next morning.

Joan Lascelles to A.L.

26 November 1928   *3 Hyde Park Square*

My darling, On Friday night all the papers were full of alarming bulletins about the King, which made it look as if he might pop off at any minute, and though it's the last thing to be desired, I almost felt pleased at the idea that it might shorten your trip. The ideal thing would be for him to be ill enough to bring you back, and recover as soon as you were nearly home again!

Meanwhile terrific gales have been raging all the weekend, so no mail has turned up yet. I'm sending you off some books I've got you for your Xmas present. The one I loved, and think you will probably like best, is *Memoirs of a Fox-Hunting Man* by Siegfried Sassoon.[1] It has got tremendous charm and simplicity, and gives a real feeling of the country, and will probably make you feel very homesick, but as you won't be away much longer after you get it, that won't matter so much. Dixon the groom is one of the most charming characters I have ever met, though he hardly speaks two words all through the book. I think that its real charm lies in the fact that he makes you feel all his characters and country without any elaborate descriptions.

I also send you *Orlando* by Virginia Woolf with some misgiving, as you may be exasperated by it. It must be taken as a purely fantastic story, with some of the most beautiful and vivid descriptions I've ever read. It is entirely modelled on Vita Nicolson, makes no bones about it, and gives photographs of her as illustrations.[2]

I gathered from Godfrey on the telephone tonight that you are waiting at Dodoma for news of HM. They say he's a bit better today. One can't quite visualise the future for England if he don't recover. However, it's no good writing about that.

Good night, my darling. You feel a long way off, and I expect you feel it still more in the heart of the African back of beyond. It seems almost too absurd to be true that you should be there, and rather pointless! It's getting late and I must go to sleep. J.

Joan's wish was fulfilled to the letter. The King did not die, but he was ill enough to bring his eldest son rushing home. The royal tour ended prematurely as the Prince and his entourage hastened by train to Dar-es-Salaam, and there boarded the light cruiser *Enterprise*, which steamed all-out up the Indian Ocean and the Red Sea, through the Suez Canal and along the Mediterranean to Brindisi, covering 4,700 miles in eight days.

As they came speeding home, Joan wrote three further letters

[1] This minor classic became one of Tommy's favourite books.
[2] The novel, in the form of a biography stretched over four centuries, was inspired by the author's friendship with Vita Sackville-West (1892–1962), who had married Harold Nicolson in 1913.

which graphically expressed the apprehensions felt by millions of King George's subjects:

I don't think most people have realised till the last few days how serious the illness was all last week, as the bulletins have been very guarded and non-alarmist, and several people have asked why the Prince was coming home . . . Undoubtedly one of the few romantic things of modern days is wireless – and one has realised it in the last few days. The bulletins have been given out at one and nine o'clock, and it is rather thrilling to think of people all over England sitting and listening, first to the chimes of Big Ben, and then waiting breathlessly for the announcer's voice. I spent last weekend with Bid, and one felt the force of it in the depths of the country, where one would otherwise have been without news. They have got a large set there, and I still take a childish delight in twiddling the handles . . .

[At a New English Society concert] they played 'God Save the King' at the end, which they have never done before, and everyone sang it in the most moving way. It all somehow feels like moments in the war. It is really rather wonderful to think of the King, living quietly and unobtrusively all these years, doing his job, and then to realise at moments like these what he means to the whole nation, and it is all utterly spontaneous. I took Ma to read the bulletin this morning, and there was a continuous stream of cars and people moving along in front of the Palace to get the news. One can't help feeling that no republic could ever mean the same thing, and that a king provides a heart for the nation in a way nothing else can. One had forgotten in these democratic days that so much can still depend on one man.

I hope you won't think this a morbid outburst, but it's very true of the general feeling, and I thought you would be interested to hear what people are feeling. It makes one feel that it is a cause not to desert lightly, but perhaps that's mob-psychology!

I met sweet old Lady Airlie yesterday outside a shop, and she came out with an entirely unsolicited dewdrop about you. She said she was so thankful that you were with the Prince at this moment, and that she had been talking to Baldwin a night or two ago, and had started to say something of the sort to him, and that she found, as she said, that 'she was carrying coals to Newcastle', as he agreed with her so warmly and said that you were the only person who had any imagination or were of any use in the entourage, so that I don't think, whatever you decide about the future, you really need feel that the last eight years have been wasted in any sense – and if anyone can influence him in the right direction at the moment, I am sure you can.

Joan's letters travelled by hand of Godfrey Thomas, who set off on 7 December to meet the royal party at Brindisi. There Mussolini put his own train at their disposal, and this rushed them to the Channel coast. At Folkestone they were met by the Prime Minister, Stanley Baldwin. When the Prince reached Buckingham Palace on the evening of 11 December, his father recognised him, but next day lapsed into unconsciousness, and was saved only by an emergency operation to drain an abscess in his chest.

By the time the travellers landed in England, they were exhausted.

To the Hon. F. C. Lascelles

12 December 1928   *St. James's Palace*

My dear Father, We got home late last night, and I am very glad to be stationary once more. Travel in a modern cruiser at 27 knots is not jam; the noise and vibration are something beyond belief, and the heat below insufferable. We spent a day with the Lloyds in Cairo, and found them both very well. George seems quite contented with the present state of Egypt.[1]

The King sounds better today, but I am afraid he is by no means out of the wood yet. Things being as they are, I shall not try to go away before Christmas. I am sorry not to get down this Sunday, but, things being so unsettled here, it is not advisable to go far out of London.   Your loving Tommy.

The next day – 13 December – Nellie Grant came to tea, and for the evening Joan had laid on a grand family reunion, the Chelms-fords, Maclagans and Balfours all coming to dine and hear the traveller's tales.

Thus Tommy's plan to 'have it out with HRH' during the voyage home was blown away, and the crisis forced him to suppress his own worries for the time being. But it was the Prince's callous reaction at Dodoma, on hearing the news of his father's illness, that finally turned Tommy against him.

For Tommy, that Christmas was a traumatic one. He reached

[1] Lloyd was by then High Commissioner for Egypt and the Sudan.

Sutton run down by the strain of the journey and his impending resignation, and he had hardly arrived when his father, then eighty, was stricken by severe pains in the chest and shortness of breath. Daisy Balfour and Fergus Nixon (Tommy's sister and brother-in-law) also arrived. Nurses were brought in, and it was soon clear that the Honourable Frederick had not long to live. 'The old man is trenchant as ever in his utterances,' wrote Tommy to Blanche (in Cairo) on 23 December, 'and takes a delight in discussing his own funeral – "Understand that I want no flowers or any nonsense of that sort. And now that tree is down in the church walk, they will have to carry me round by the top gate." At night he sometimes wanders a little, but very little, and as a rule his mind is as clear and vigorous as ever.'

As his father's life ebbed away, Tommy himself went down with a ferocious attack of influenza; and the Prince, hearing that the family were in such straits, wrote with characteristic generosity:

December 1928   *St. James's Palace*

My dear Tommy, I'm so sorry I didn't see you before you went away for Xmas but it was a rush and (what with Buckhouse and 'shopping' calling) I was hardly in at all. But I do want to thank you for all your wonderful help on the East African trip and hope you aren't too run down though I know you are a bit and that you are laid up in bed now. It was a nightmare that last fortnight with the cypher cables and the vibration. It took me two days to become normal and I've got two days hunting into me this week which has helped a lot though I was stiff and out of practice.

The King wasn't so well yesterday but the news seems better this evening and I hope to get away for the weekend's hunting – and now I hear your poor old father has been very ill and that his heart won't last out very long. I am so sorry for your anxiety though I guess it wasn't exactly unexpected. What a worry one's family become when they get old.

I am sending you an *'old-fashioned'* match-box to replace the one you lost on safari. You'll be surprised the trouble I had to find a suitable one this type of match-box being so *'old-fashioned'*!! It won't have the same sentimental value as the old one but I hope will be as useful and much used.

Hoping you will soon be fit again and with my best wishes for 1929 to yourself and Joan.   Yours, E.P.

The old man held out till the last day of the year – and after his death Tommy wrote again to Blanche:

My dear B., I expect Helen has already written to you. He had no pain at all, I think, the last week, though I went to bed with 'flu on Christmas Day and so never saw him again; but that mattered little, as I gathered that he was very wandery all those last days, and hardly knew if one was in the room or not. The important thing was to have been here the week before, and I am very glad that I was.

Till the end, nobody could say for certain what the issue would be – a partial recovery, not impossible with one of his strength; long weeks of invalidism; or, what actually happened, the sudden stopping of a heart worn out by *anno domini* and bronchial trouble. On the afternoon before he died, everybody in the house – Hollick [the doctor], the nurses, Daisy and Fergus – came into my room and reported him markedly better and clearer in the head; we again canvassed the possibilities of his being, some day, able to potter about the garden again. Two hours later he had another short, and probably quite painless, bronchial attack, and his poor old heart stopped for ever.

His situation after the first attack of angina, was, in fact, very much the same as that of the King; it was a question of whether his strength, aided by nursing, strychnine, oxygen etc., would or would not enable him to gain enough ground to counteract the weakness of the heart, for perhaps another six months or a year. Personally, I felt and indeed hoped it would all end fairly soon, as he would never have been happy as an invalid; but one could be sure of nothing, and to have attempted forecasts or even estimates of his condition would have been futile.

Two days before Christmas, for instance, he sent for me and told me he was positive he would be dead before morning, and I was to fetch the parson – which of course I did. Next day, he woke up looking and feeling more sprightly than he had been since he first fell ill, and was very annoyed that he had been proved wrong in his forecast. 'I can't understand why I'm not dead. Now, I don't think I shall die' – and from that moment, I believe, he decided *not* to die. Anyhow, I don't think he ever alluded to it again. But, as I say, his mind began to get very hazy shortly after that, and he lived mostly in the past. Characteristically, he never left the plane of ordinary day-to-day conversation with any of us. His last words, about quarter of an hour before he died, were 'Well, I think I will turn in now. You can put out the lights.' But I don't think anything was in his mind more than going normally to sleep.

I have had a great many letters, from relations and neighbours; he was certainly a great landmark in this part of the world.

[The author here gave some details of the will, in which his father had left him the house.]

If I can escape from the royal kraal, as I am now trying to do according to plan, we shall come to live here for the summer and autumn. My idea is to sink about £1,000 in the more obvious and necessary improvements which this house needs to make it habitable. I shall then, I believe, have little difficulty in letting it for quite a good rent. This country is alive with retired generals etc. looking for just this type of house and garden; but I shall get nothing for it in its present state. I shall not sell it except in the last resort, though I may have to do this some day.

As you say, it is astonishing what a permanent, and mellow, background the old man had come to be in the landscape of one's life, and here especially there is an hourly sense of loss in the absence of the familiar door-bangings and stumpings. Love to G. T.

PS There is no question of anything in this house being moved or destroyed before you come home in the spring.

RESIGNATION
1929

Tommy's determination to resign badly unsettled his colleagues. Both Godfrey Thomas and Admiral Halsey revealed that they too had been considering the same action, and for much of January 1929 agitated letters sped back and forth as they tried to decide what to do. But Tommy was first in the field, and on 30 December 1928 Thomas wrote from The Residentiary, his in-laws' home at Chichester:

> My dear Tommy, I read your letter coming down here in the train yesterday. It may surprise you to know that, by a strange coincidence, I was on my way to break to Diana [his wife] my decision to seek a new job, or at any rate vacate my present one, some time during the coming year, as gracefully as possible and with minimum inconvenience to HRH and all concerned.
>
> While you were away in Africa I had time to see things in their proper perspective, and the strain of the last six weeks, with the ever-present possibility of our translation to a higher sphere [that is, of Edward becoming King], has brought matters to a head in my case! My reasons are obviously the same as yours – I too have for some time past ceased to do my job to my own satisfaction, and know that it is time to go. But as the real reasons which underlie the situation in both our cases are those that cannot very well be given to anyone outside the walls of your house, I haven't yet clearly thought out how I'm going to set about it . . .   Yours ever, Godfrey.

Next day – the last of the year – Tommy's hand was strengthened by the death of his father. This gave him the pretext he needed – an ideal excuse for seeking a change of life. Yet Admiral Halsey was appalled by the news that he meant to leave so soon and, when he

Sutton Waldron, the Lascelles family home near Blandford, in Dorset, left to Tommy in his father's will.

Joan Lascelles reading to John and Lavinia.

Above
Canada, 1924: the Prince with Tommy and Sir Walter Peacock,
Secretary to the Duchy of Cornwall, in Vancouver.

Left
John and Lavinia on holiday with their mother at Cacouna on the
St Lawrence river.

Aboard the *Berengaria,* en route for New York, September 1924: the
Prince of Wales with Gerald Trotter, Tommy and David Boyle.

The Prince with Tommy in America, 1924.

The indefatigable tourist: the Prince touring the Chicago stockyards
with Louis F. Swift, 1924.

Above
Fruity and Lady Alexandra (Baba) Metcalfe leaving for India,
September 1925.

Left
High society, June 1924: the Prince arrives with Admiral Halsey for
the christening of the Hon. Piers Legh's daughter.

Uneasy alliance: the Prince with Stanley Baldwin, the Prime
Minister, flanked by Fruity Metcalfe and Mrs Baldwin.

East Africa, 1928. The Prince outside Government House, Nairobi,
with Sir Edward Grigg, Governor of Kenya.

On safari: the Prince with a trophy, East Africa, 1928.

Tommy as best man at the wedding of Bunt Goschen and Vivienne
de Watteville, 1930. The bridesmaid is Jean Meynell, Bunt's niece.

Left. Lord Bessborough, Governor General of Canada, lays the foundation stone of the new armoury of the Victoria Rifles of Canada in Montreal, June 1933.

Right. In his element: Tommy on the Bonaventure river in Canada.

Left. The King is dead: the body of George V lies in state in the chapel at Sandringham, January 1936.

Below. The former King Edward VIII leaves Windsor Castle after making his Abdication broadcast, December 1936.

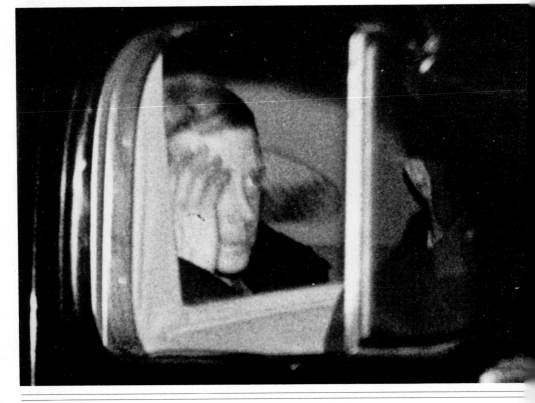

wrote on 6 January 1929 from his home at Biggleswade, the Old Salt displayed almost pathetic loyalty:

I am not over-buttering the bread when I say you will be the very greatest loss to the whole structure of HRH's success in his capacity as a speaker, and he will lose a splendid adviser on many subjects . . . Believe me, I am feeling exactly the same as you feel about the whole business, with the one exception that you are nearly sixteen years younger than I am, and therefore you have, apart from your own loyal aspect, to think a bit about your own career, whereas mine is over and done with.

What I feel is that if, between us, we can make HRH realise that he is doing himself and the Monarchy no good by his present outlook on society life, by boldly saying what is our unalterable opinion of his daily life, we shall be doing a very great and valuable service to our country. I am prepared to face any music if I can possibly do ultimate good to HRH, and therefore, indirectly, to the whole structure of the Monarchy and Empire.   Yours ever, Lionel Halsey.

A week later the Admiral wrote again, urging a delay at least until the end of the month, so that a concerted campaign could be mounted; and on 15 January, with telling clarity, Thomas set out his own thoughts, which closely matched Tommy's own:

My dear Tommy, Needless to say, I am in entire agreement with every single word you have written as to the general situation, and I readily admit that, as regards your own personal position, your arguments are unanswerable. There are special circumstances in your case, and your father's death, coming at this moment, gives you an unrivalled excuse for making your 'change of life' *now*. What is more, it enables you to clear out gracefully as far as the outer world is concerned, and with tactful handling, any mud that your resignation stirs up need not spread beyond York House. You are clearly the first to leave – I was about to write 'leave the sinking ship', which would be a brutal and perhaps unfair thing to say – but at any rate the ship that you and I know we are unable to navigate, and which, if we continue to try to control in our present frame of mind, will very soon run on the rocks.

For the rest, it is obviously impossible for us all to leave in a body. Such a step would, as you say, produce a first-class public crisis, and would serve no useful purpose. I've known HRH for some fifteen years and have served him for ten, and in spite of his failings am devoted to him. Quite apart from our feelings of private friendship, I'd do anything to help him because of what he stands for, and what he will succeed to.

I know that I cannot help him if I stay, so like you have decided to go, but I owe it to him to make the order of my going as easy for him as possible. The only solution appears to me that you should leave in the near future, but that before your actual departure, we should – with the help, I suppose, of the PM – fix on somebody, acceptable of course to HRH and the Powers that Be, who is prepared to be the Lord Stamfordham to the future sovereign. Where he can be found, Lord knows, but the problem can't be insoluble. Suppose last summer we had both been killed in the smash motoring down to golf: something would have to have been done then.

I must obviously stay on for a bit longer. Quite apart from the fact that I haven't got your opportune excuse, I couldn't go now in the present state of uncertainty, as, whatever happens, HRH will have to try and adapt himself to a lot of new things this summer, and it wouldn't be fair to him to bring the whole house tumbling about his head.

I hate the idea of a break-up, but the more I think about it, the deeper grows my conclusion that it is the only thing to do. Like you, the fact that I was serving the future King of England has kept me going through many a difficult period when my patience was strained to breaking-point – and, like you, those two words, and the traditions attached to them, theatrical as it might seem to the Prince, mean so much to me that I simply can't sit here and see the whole show going downhill, after having regretfully come to the conclusion that no influence I can exert will have any effect, and that I am merely regarded as 'old-fashioned'.

HRH, knowing so little of English history, alas, will always go on believing that provided he carries out his public duties to the satisfaction of the Press and the Man in the Street, his private life is entirely his own concern. I'm terribly sorry for him, but unless someone can succeed in disabusing him of this *idée fixe*, I can see nothing but disaster ahead.   Yours, Godfrey.

Tommy's draft letter of resignation was dated 31 January 1929:

Sir, If we had ever reached Cape Town, I had meant to tell you on the voyage home that it was time for me to leave your staff. As things turned out, I could not bother you with it just then.

Counting my time in India, I have now been ten years doing

personal staff work, and it is high time I did something else before I get too old. Very few men can go on being private secretaries all their lives, and I am not of them. I have done my best, while I have been with you, but for some time past I have known that I have worked the private secretary reef out, so to speak.

Quite apart from that, I am not the right man for you. You have got your own views about life in general, and about how your work should be done; it is not my business to say whether they are right or wrong; but I should be utterly in the wrong myself if I didn't let you know that I don't agree with them. I cannot go on working for any man, and taking his money, unless I see things more or less in the same way that he does. It is not fair to either yourself, Sir, or to me, that I should go on trying to do your work.

I hope you will agree to my leaving as soon as somebody else of whom you approve can be found to take my place. As a result of my father's death, various circumstances make it necessary for me to let my house in London and go and live in Dorset for a while. I won't bother you with all that now; but this of course will be the only reason I shall give anybody else for my leaving York House.

I am more sorry than I can to have to write this letter, Sir. But I want you to believe that I have thought about it for many months before doing so. Yours, AL.

PS I have told the Admiral and Godfrey that I am writing to you.

Tommy showed the draft to both Thomas and Halsey, and the Admiral suggested that he should omit any mention of his real reason for leaving, as, 'without that, it is a letter he can show to anyone, and it won't do any harm from a public point of view.' The true reason could be given in another letter, or at an interview. It is no longer clear whether or not Tommy accepted this advice; but in any case he sent the note before the end of January. The Prince's first response was to ask Gerald Trotter to find out what it was all about. Tommy, however, insisted on confronting the Prince himself:

I refused to discuss it with G., and that evening or the next the Prince himself sent for me. The resultant interview was the most exhausting experience I have ever had. I did not consider myself as any longer in his service, and, when he asked me why I wanted to leave him, I paced his room for the best part of an hour, telling him, as I might have told a younger brother, exactly what I thought of him and his whole scheme of life, and foretelling, with an accuracy that

119

might have surprised me at the time, that he would lose the throne of England.

He heard me with scarcely an interruption, and when we parted, said, 'Well, goodnight Tommy, and thank you for the talk. I suppose the fact of the matter is that I'm quite the wrong sort of person to be Prince of Wales' – which was so pathetically true that it almost melted me. The next morning he sent me a message to say that he accepted my resignation, and would like to give me a motor car, as proof that we parted friends; which I in turn accepted in the spirit in which it was offered! So I, an inverted Falstaff, retired into the wilderness at the age of forty-two (less my wages of £1,000 a year) and left Prince Hal to work out his own damnation. I have never had any doubt in my own mind that, by so doing, I served him better than I could have by staying acquiescently on his staff.

At once Tommy sat down and wrote to Stanley Baldwin:

4 February 1929   *St. James's Palace*

Private

My dear Prime Minister,
This is merely to let you know that I have had the interview of which Admiral Halsey spoke to you the other day; that I said everything which was in my mind, without any beating about the bush; and that it was very kindly received. We parted on friendly terms; though whether what I said will have any permanent effect, I cannot of course say.   Yours sincerely, A. Lascelles.

So ended his first period of royal service, to his own great relief, but to the dismay of his former colleagues. From Craigweil House at Bognor, where the King was convalescing, Sir Clive Wigram wrote on 24 February 1929:

My dear Tommy, I have [been] meaning to send you [a] line to say how very sorry I am to hear about your departure. I regard it as almost a national tragedy. Your steadying influence on that young man was the best. Have you read the *Sphere* of the 16th, on the back of the page with a picture of the Prince arriving by train to hunt? It is very well written, and shows what the staff of these Princes are up against. Unfortunately the writer hits the nail on the head every time, and his criticisms are very fair and just. They will let down the Monarchy if they are not careful.

Well, you will be a great loss, and missed by many who have had the pleasure of working with you, but by none more than by

Yours ever, Clive Wigram.

In the event, both Godfrey Thomas and Admiral Halsey, disgruntled though they were, decided to soldier on. Tommy, with no job and no plans, withdrew to Dorset, and for the next two years did what he had long said he wanted to do: lived in the country with his family. At first he had to clear up his father's affairs and reorganise the house. After that, he did exactly what he always planned to do, given a sabbatical: he worked at improving the house and garden, and enjoyed being with the family. He read many books aloud to the children, took them for walks, taught them tennis and cricket on the grass court. He implanted in Lavinia the seeds of a lifelong love of gardening, and taught her to ride on John's strong-minded grey Welsh pony called Joey, thereby starting another passion. He also instructed her in the basics of a musical repertoire by whistling theme tunes, which she had to guess. He greatly treasured this period – the first in his adult life when he had not been under pressure of work or war.

It seems strange that no writing survives from these years. Several times – as on the 1927 tour of Canada – he had suggested that he would love to settle down and see if he could make a career as an author; but nothing emerged from this apparently golden opportunity. The truth (which perhaps he now discovered) was that, although his natural expression in letters and journals was delightful, he ironed all the life out of his writing if he tried to improve it for publication, and by excessive polishing killed it stone dead.

So little ill-will was there between him and his former employer that he continued to help the Prince with speeches, and in the summer of 1929 received a typically warm message of thanks:

Prince of Wales to A.L.

29 June 1929

Middleton
Sunningdale
Berks

My dear Tommy, I was rather rushed last week or I would have written before to thank you very much for taking the trouble to send me some admirable dope for that very tricky speech at the East

African dinner. It was grand stuff and went down far better than the nasty food provided by the Hotel Cecil. But honestly Tommy I think I did get away with it thanks to your help and I'm most grateful.

I enclose a letter from that fellow Anderson (that death-white hunter with a game leg) who we met in Nairobi and lives near here and is a golf rival. He was at the dinner and is a tough bloke and wouldn't write a thing he didn't mean.

How are you Tommy? Leading the quiet life in the country I guess and I sincerely hope feeling much fitter than you were in consequence. The summer is passing far quicker than I thought it would and this place has been a godsend and I've been able to slip down for golf a good deal – but I've had a lot of tiresome things to do and boring people to see as well and I'll be glad when August comes. I don't know if you and your wife would like to come here any weekend next month (July) but I'd love to have you both come so please tell me if you could make it. I have this house till end of July and the golf is good as you know. Either of the last two weekends of July would be best but any would do if you can come. Yours, E.P.

To Helen, on her Fiftieth Birthday

2 October 1929 *Sutton Waldron*

My dear Whelk, Quinquagesimally molluscous, it has befallen to me to write letters for many curious occasions, but never, so far as I recollect, for one such as this; and, having got thus far, I realise, with a certain sinking, that I shall now have to write one each year, till 4 April 1933 is safely past; while, four years and one week after that date, I shall have to sit down and write the answers to similar letters to me.[1] It is a distinct relief to feel that no silver weddings are due till 1936, but after that they will come thicker and faster than one cares to think; and I had forgotten, God help us, the comings-of-age of nephews and nieces, which all begin but a few months after D[aisy]'s fiftieth birthday. The future, in fact, is repulsively big with festal anniversaries; but the Ancient Whelk, with the cunning long peculiar to its hoary antiquity, continues to get there first, and to skim with predatory paw (in so far as whelks have paws) the untainted cream off the pot of congratulation.

[1] First, for his three other sisters' fiftieth birthdays, then for his own, on 11 April 1937.

If Joan and I can make it any richer by adding our blessings, you have them in full measure. I know nobody who has better reason to be proud of his or her fifty years. All love from us both and the children. T.

To Letty Benson

30 December 1929   *Sutton Waldron*

My dear Letty, Handkerchief-day seems to come round very quick as the years go on, but the receipt of it is none the less welcome, for noses run just as fast as the years.

The 1929 vintage is an exceptionally fine one, rich, colourful and heavy-bodied. I think there are now in my drawer no less than a dozen from your vineyard, and there ought to be two more, one lost in the wash and one out fishing; at this season of the year our thoughts turn naturally to Absent Handkerchiefs, do they not?

Stories reach me of your having acquired a plot of land in Gloucestershire, not so very far from here. Is there any truth in it, and if so, how far has the plot thickened? Are you living on it, and where is it? The sale of our house in Hyde Park Square, and consequent release of our furniture etc. there, has advanced us one stage more in the long adventure of 'getting straight'; but the garden is still a semi-wilderness, and the schoolroom will leak till the end of time, or until I can afford to build a room over it. However, a few drops on the head enliven lessons, and are good for the little ones' chevelures.

G. G. Goschen [Bunt] was here a little while back, quite untouched by Time's effacing fingers. He said to me in his artless way, 'How is it that all the people who were at Oxford with us have become ugly old men, and you and I have remained young and beautiful?' I don't know so much about me, but certainly he, and the Baroness Wenlock, are the two people who snap their fingers at age more effectively than all the rest of the world. Aunt C.'s feat of finding, buying and establishing a brand-new home, in an unknown corner of England, with all the enthusiasm of a bride of twenty, is really a wonderful one. I anticipate a flood of Late Wenlocks between 1930 and 1940, which, in extent of canvas and thickness of paint, will outweigh all the others put together. God bless her; and you too, for that matter, and a happy New Year to you.   Yours, Tommy.

No one now remembers how Tommy met Vivienne de Watteville, a glamorous and exciting girl who in 1929, at the age of twenty-eight, had already proved herself as writer, photographer and big-game-hunter, and who lived on the island of Port Cros, off the South of France. In the autumn of 1929 she came to stay at Sutton Waldron, and, without telling either party, Tommy began to think that she would make an ideal wife for his dear friend Bunt Goschen – but, before he could introduce them, fate brought them together anyway, at a concert. Years later Vivienne used to say that if Tommy had not written the letter below, she and Bunt might never have married.

To Vivienne de Watteville

15 February 1930   *Sutton Waldron*

My dear Vivienne, If you saw it in a book, you would say it was foolish, and that the world was not so small as all that. Yet the fact remains that the blond and blue-eyed stranger whom you met at the Albert Hall the other day was very nearly my oldest friend.

I am glad you had the sense to introduce yourselves to one another – it saves trouble, because the next time you came and stayed here, we should certainly have asked Bunt Goschen to come and meet you; now we shall be spared the tiresome preliminaries of introduction.

Joan and I went over to lunch with Lady Goschen, his sister-in-law, yesterday. Bunt was there, and while telling us about Kreisler [the violinist who had played at the Albert Hall] said he had met there a young lady who lived all alone in the heart of darkest Africa, and from whose hands lions and elephants fed like birds. 'That,' we said, 'was Vivienne de Watteville' – and so, apparently, it was.

It was a very fortunate chance for both of you; for you are very obviously creatures of the same genus, and probably species too. Don't lose sight of him; he is one of the real sunshine-makers of this world. I have had more childish amusement (which is the best sort of amusement) out of the many hours I have spent with Bunt during the last twenty years than I shall ever get from anybody else's company. He is, moreover, a very genuine musician.

When are you coming back here? There are many changes. Two days ago I pulled up the path at which we worked so hard last August. I am sorry, but a path there will never fit into the general scheme.

Joan sends love, and says she meant to write to you at Christmas, and wishes she had. Yours, Tommy.

This letter had the effect for which its author had been fishing: the couple got engaged early in the summer, and were married in the autumn, with Tommy Bunt's best man.

To Vivienne de Watteville

13 May 1930 *Sutton Waldron*

My dear Vivienne, You are quite right to marry Bunt. I believe you will be very happy together. Your news was a great joy to Joan and me, all the more because we had been hoping to hear it.

I suppose I know Bunt better than anybody else does – even better than his brother. So if ever you want any guidance in the proper treatment and control of him, you must come to me. He is often a bit of a nuisance about the house, especially in his comings and goings, though he has got much better about this; and anyhow, he can't borrow your clothes, as he used to borrow mine.[1] You had better not leave him alone with the elephants, for he would certainly make even greater demands on their friendliness than you did.

I wonder so much what your plans are, beyond Bayreuth. I hope none: it is so much better to have no plans till they are forced on one. In the interim, both or either of you can always come here for as long as you fancy, any time this summer. I hope you will; it is not an island, but it is not a bad place for those who do not want to be pestered by the world at large, and we now have a very good piano and a rejuvenated gramophone.

It would be fun if we could all meet somewhere in Bavaria or Austria after you have done your Bayreuth and we our Salzburg – Munich or Vienna or some such place; or even Tenschau, if we get there. But you must come to England soon, and then we can discuss all these things.

I have asked Bunt to come down here this week or next. It is quite evident that you have made him immensely happy – as, indeed, he ought to be. And I feel sure you are equally so. Hold on to it, and go on being happy for many years. Yours ever, Tommy.

---

[1] The two men had once shared digs in London.

To Letty Benson

25 December 1930   *Harewood House*
                                                          Leeds

My dear Letty, You train your handkerchiefs well. I took them both
to church this morning – it seemed cruel to separate them so soon –
and, so instinct with the Christmas spirit are they, that with the first
notes of *Adeste Fideles* they leapt in their several pockets like young
rabbits; or like that precocious child of Elizabeth's in the Bible.

Their bravery, too, is a lesson to all of us. They show no sign of
having been born in this squalid and murky year of 1930. Nothing
faint-hearted and bearish about them; they are coloured like the
wings of celestial Bulls, and no Nose which seeks comfort in them
could fail to be uplifted. Their message is, Gather ye rosebuds while
ye may; in other words, let us live happily on our capital for ever
after.

There are not many signs of the old order changing here, however;
in fact what changes there are, are all to the good. It is a delight to see
this beautiful house improved so unobtrusively and skilfully; bath-
rooms liberally scattered where they ought to have been put years
ago; pictures rescued from dark corners and hung where they were
originally meant to hang; and rooms which were always kept locked
now made habitable. He has done it all very well.

What promised to be a shattering journey here – seven hours with
three children – turned out quite bearable; indeed, they arrived in
such good shape that as we drove through the wintry streets of Leeds
John [aged eight] exclaimed, 'What a beautiful town! I shall spend
my honeymoon here.'

I have not even a clean Christmas card to send you back; so I must
pass on the characteristic one I had from old George Gerard. They
are spending their Christmas in Switzerland, and it may be a
momentous one, for when I last saw Bunt, he told me that they had
decided that the work of creating young Fritz Goschen (whose
birthday must fall in the summer holidays) would be seriously
undertaken at the festive season. Being Bunt, he will probably bring
it off exactly as he wishes; anybody else who attempted to dictate to
Fate in this way would certainly be punished with twin daughters at
Easter.[1]

Give my love to Belvoir; and thankyou, dear Letty, for your
unfailing memory.   Yours, Tommy.

[1] The Goschens' son, David, was born on 19 October 1931.

CANADA
1931–1935

It is no longer clear how Tommy got the job of Private Secretary to the Earl of Bessborough, who was appointed Governor-General of Canada in 1931. It may have been that he exploited a family connection – for through Joan he was a cousin of Bessborough's, whose mother, like Joan's, was a Guest. Equally, it may have been that Bessborough, looking round for a secretary, heard good reports of his work at St. James's Palace.

Canada was then in a phase of political stability, and Bessborough, who had served for three years on the London County Council and for eight years as Member of Parliament for Dover, proved an industrious, if not inspirational, Governor-General. Yet if Tommy's post at first seemed something of a come-down after his position in the Prince's household, he soon discovered that in one way it was curiously similar – for although the Governor-General was not a member of the Royal Family, his job was to represent the Crown, and, as Tommy found to his delight, the Canadians were then still stirringly loyal to the King, so that he himself was once again working to preserve and put over the ideal of monarchy.

From his letters home, it is clear that Tommy's arrival in Canada gave him severe culture shock: levels of education, political awareness and conversation were far below those to which he was accustomed. Yet, once he had adapted to new conditions, he made many friends. For the Prime Minister, R. B. Bennett, he conceived a considerable regard, even if he later came to modify his approval; and his relations with Bessborough seem to have been entirely cordial, if not fired by much admiration or personal affection. He did not share the Governor-General's passions for the theatre and cricket, but as a subject to fall back on he at least had hunting –

for in earlier days he had been a passionate rider to hounds, and Bessborough, in his youth, had carried the horn for the pack founded by his father in Kilkenny.

Travelling ahead of the rest of the family, Tommy reached Ottawa in March 1931. For the first few months he rented a house belonging to Willis O'Connor, one of the Canadian ADCs, in the smart residential district of Rockliffe; but in the autumn of 1931 he and his family moved into Rideau Cottage, a comfortable, medium-sized house, clad in timber and surrounded by a wide verandah, in the extensive, park-like grounds of Government House (Rideau Hall), a mile or so from the centre of the capital. The cottage was only 400 yards from Government House, but pleasantly isolated by trees, and the family enjoyed all the amenities of the main establishment, not least an indoor tennis court, a covered curling rink and a private skating rink on which, in winter, furious games of ice-hockey were played and dances were held to the strains of an ancient gramophone.

For Tommy, the highlight of each summer became his fishing expeditions – first to the Jupiter River, and then to the Bonaventure, to which he was invited every year by a business friend. There he enjoyed the best salmon-fishing he had ever known – and in general his time in Canada gave his passion for fishing full rein. On the lawn outside Rideau Cottage he would spend hours teaching the children to cast, with a small piece of paper tied to the end of the line, and often acted as the salmon, rushing about with the end of the line in his mouth; and his own outstanding skill with the rod was memorably caught by the second Earl of Bessborough (son of the Governor General) in his memoir *Return to the Forest*: 'He seemed to have the knack of throwing a fly so attractively, that is to say, so accurately and unostentatiously, that the fish could not resist it.'

To John Gore

26 April 1931　　　　　　　　　　　　　　　*Government House*
　　　　　　　　　　　　　　　　　　　　　　　Ottawa

My dear John, I have really been pretty busy ever since we arrived, acquainting myself with office routine, and with individuals; but I think that, if times remain fairly quiet, I shall soon be able to do all that is necessary with a comfortable margin of leisure. When the

128

House is sitting, as now, I go with His Excellency three mornings a week to his office in the Parliament buildings, where we are at home to such Senators and Members as care to interview us. This takes up a good deal of time, but serves a useful purpose, in getting both parties mutually acquainted, and is a custom much valued by Canadian legislators. They are good chaps, in general, and have plenty to say for themselves on all kinds of unexpected topics. Whether it is the result of the climate of this Continent, or a characteristic of a young and vigorous civilisation, I find that the average man who comes to see one plunges into conversationally deep water far quicker than his counterpart at home. At York House, one would be paddling about in the shallows of small talk for minutes, before the objects of the interview, or any real interest in the life of the visitor, became apparent; here, the cards are on the table in the twinkling of an eye.

Politics are much more eighteenth century, too: there is plenty of good Whig and Tory rancour about, and no bones made about it. But what strikes me as most remarkable is the astonishing patriotism of nearly everybody; no nonsense about Monarchy, and the Monarch's representation, being a creed outworn. It is a red-hot article of faith. Formerly, having first set foot on this Continent in those United States, I was disposed to think that much of this was just vulgar royal-snobbery; but it isn't – it is a genuine survival of that curious phenomenon of Loyalty, which has made, and blotted, so many pages in human history. And, what is specially significant, is that it isn't merely the sentimental flap-doodle of the man in the street: the higher up you get in the intellectual scale, the stronger you find it. I am not sure that it wouldn't be an immensely statesmanlike move for Buckingham Palace to be picked up and replanted in Canada for a generation or two. I feel pretty sure that if the British race has any future left to it, that future lies in this Dominion, politically, economically and eugenically. Australia is down and out for many years – they're a bad breed anyhow; India is a Lost Dominion; New Zealand is too far away to matter, and South Africa, besides being torn by racial problems, doesn't really matter a row of beans, except to metallurgists.

The Norman Kings found eventually that they must remove from Rouen to Winchester and London; perhaps some day the present Dynasty will be forced by circumstances to exchange Windsor, England, for Windsor, Ontario. When that happens, I shall go quietly back to Sutton, Dorset – and what an infinitely pleasanter land to live in I shall find it.

Domestically, I have been fortunate, through the untiring efforts of kind friends, in securing, with a minimum of trouble on my part, a really charming little furnished house, where I can settle Joan and the family immediately on arrival; and a most superior cook, late the property of Mr. Minister Herridge, who has recently become, almost by the stroke of the same pen, the brother-in-law of Premier Bennett and his Government's representative in Washington. I cannot possibly afford to hire either the house or the lady for more than the summer months, but it is a great relief to have got a comfortable home together, and I haven't time to hunt round after alternatives. What will happen after this temporary asylum is closed to us, I have no idea; but the Ravens always come, if one plays Elijah with sufficient conviction.

For the moment, I am comfortably and economically boarded at Government House, where My Lady keeps a devilish good table.[1] I work pretty hard at office and social duties, and play an occasional game of golf or tennis, outdoor and covered. So far, we are all quite happy, and the three boys we brought out from the Navy, 11th Hussars and Coldstreams [the ADCs] are really a most delightful trio – all of them, in their different ways, amusing companions and easy to control.[2] They have the merit, too – outwardly at all events – of being much attached to me. I am a far bigger swell than I thought I was. I am a Deputy-Minister, and treated with immense consideration by Ministers without a deputy. I am not yet quite clear what this means.   Yours, A.L.

The rest of the family sailed to join Tommy on the SS *Duchess of Richmond* in May 1931. They found the cabins comfortable and the food good; but the voyage was very rough, and the children were sick and got colds. Their nursery-maid Doris Titcombe, a Dorset girl, was wonderful: a natural sailor, she kept everyone else going. 'I don't think we shall ever regain control of Caroline,' wrote Joan in a letter home. 'After her first seasickness she quite recovered and attended every meal with Doris and was the centre of attention of all the old gentlemen on the ship, and returned laden with oranges and barley-sugar to the cabins where the rest of us lay in a state of coma.'

[1] Lady Bessborough was French, the daughter of a Parisian banker.
[2] David Fuller, Robin Steuart-French and Sir John Child, Bt.

130

John Lascelles (aged nine) to Helen

6 June 1931   *Government House*
                                                       Ottawa

Dear Aunt Helen, We have not had a very nice journey, it was all right till we got beyond Ireland and then it began to get rough. When we were half-way across we got into the tail-end of a storm and the Captain was rather anxious. On the last day Dad came on at Quebec, the same evening, when it was too cold to go on deck.

We arrived at Government House in time for lunch and spent a few days there. We have a very nice house. It has a verandah that looks over a small lake. On the other side of the lake there is a thick wood with a lovely sandpit in it where we have great fun. There is a lovely big playroom down in the basement and it is very cool there in hot weather. There are some lovely walks round here and once we saw a skunk up in a tree. Another time we saw a jack-rabbit as big as Toby.[1]

The other day Dad went with Lord Bessborough to Quebec and had dinner on the *Empress of Britain* and made some speeches, and at the end of them the Captain, who is a Scotchman, got up and said that Jacques Larrier was really a Scotchman called Jock Larter, and Dad said everybody laughed like anything and the Prime Minister of Quebec laughed the most.

There are crowds of squirrels and chipmunks here. Some of the squirrels are black. There are some lovely birds too.

With love from John.

To John Gore

25 June 1931   *Government House*
                                                       Ottawa

My dear Johnny, Ottawa is a very beautiful place. It is now past its best, which is early spring; but I have never seen such lovely and varied lights as one gets here, from flaming sunrise to flaming sunset,

---

[1] A brave but recklessly aggressive wire-haired fox-terrier, Toby had travelled out to Canada with the family, and went back with them to Sutton Waldron (after six months' quarantine) when they returned home. In 1936, when Tommy let the house and moved to London, the dog was 'given away'. Lavinia suspected that he had been put down, but never knew for sure, and was heartbroken at losing him.

and its admirable cluster of public buildings, perched on the hill above the great shining river, make a fine middle distance at all times of day. I am sorry we shall not be here in September, when they tell me it is lovelier still. The weather is not disagreeable either: three perfect summer days, with fresh winds, are regularly followed by a forty-eight hours' gradual stoking-up, at the end of which there is an apocalyptic thunderstorm, with torrential rain, when the cycle begins again. The only trouble is that dressing becomes difficult; a thin tropical suit, indispensable on Monday, is a menace to comfort or health on Wednesday. You would find yourself banding your belly with more than usual care if you were to spend a summer here.

We shall have to come back for a day or two sometime in July, to entertain Their Majesties of Siam, whose impending visit is giving me a good deal of trouble. I am told that they are sweet, delight impishly in finding work for European servants, when they get the chance, and make a practice of demanding boiled eggs at all hours of the day and night, no matter how well you feed them at table. The present King's grandfather had 687 sons, his father a mere four score; he is the son of a brother and sister, and his Queen is doubly his first cousin. It is not surprising that he has no children; but, since the royal family now numbers over 20,000 souls, this don't signify. He used to be inordinately fond of golf, until one day the Queen beat him, five up and four to play, since when he has given the game up. He now enjoys going out to *look* at golf links, poking the bunkers with a stick, and explaining how he would play each hole. *O-wa-ta-na* Siam, as we used to sing at my private school. I suppose my collection of useless baubles will be enriched by a White Elephant, Fourth Class.

We shall move into Rideau Cottage in the autumn, which means a very considerable saving to me, the Comptroller, who thought to go on occupying it indefinitely, being about to perish miserably. He is a very tiresome little man, and has succeeded in getting on everybody's nerves. I have had my dog Toby clipped, as he was feeling the hot days, and he now looks like something in a bottle in a medical museum.[1] For myself, I have been feeling much more robust since I allowed the doctor to inject ten doses of iron and arsenic into my arm. I believe it is a good egg.

Did I tell you of the resentment roused by Randolph Churchill[1] in this country? The Torontonians nearly lynched him after a particu-

[1] 1911–1968. Son of Winston Churchill, he was then an aspiring but unsuccessful politician, trying in vain for a seat in Parliament, and already in trouble with his father over his extravagance.

larly offensive speech, and said some very hard things about him in their Press. He came to stay here for a few nights, slightly punctured and piano, and, when he wasn't holding forth, I liked him. But the moment any remotely political topic came up, he became like a dipso in the presence of drink, and quite insufferable. He is a dirty boy, too, and slovenly.   Yours, A.L.

To Conrad Russell

16 October 1931   *Government House*
                                                               Ottawa

My dear Con, They [the politicians preparing for a General Election] have made England very ridiculous with all their silly manoeuvrings. Everybody thinks it absolutely childish nonsense, and very dangerous nonsense, too. And Lloyd George's wireless manifesto, as published in today's newspapers, beats the band. Why is the man allowed to use the BBC for propaganda of that kind? Really, it reads like the ravings of a lunatic. A prominent doctor told me the other day that, reading between the lines of the bulletins about Lloyd George, he had come to the conclusion that he was finished; if so, he is being an unconscionable time dying. There is not much chance of the evil *he* has done being interred with his bones; we shall feel the weight of it for many a long year yet. To think that poor Guido Fawkes should have been put to death so elaborately, and that Lloyd George, who has done the State infinitely more mischief than all Guido's gunpowder could have done, is allowed to die in his bed, and will as like as not be buried in Westminster Abbey.[1]

Private advices from the States continue to show that they are in a state of hysterical panic there, in financial circles at any rate [after the Wall Street crash of 1929 and the ensuing Depression]; they have lost all confidence in their bankers, and, as they have long known both their legislature and their judicature to be thoroughly corrupt,

---

[1] The career of David Lloyd George (1863–1945) was by no means finished; but after a serious operation in 1931 he withdrew into the role of an elder statesman. In the end he declined to be buried in Westminster Abbey, choosing instead that his grave should be at Llanystumdwy, the village in Caernarvonshire where he had been brought up.

His broadcast of 15 October 1931 does not now read like the ravings of a lunatic. A sober address on the dangers of international tariff barriers, it ended, 'Protection is the impending peril. I should use my vote to avert that calamity.'

they haven't much to lean on, poor things. Latterly we have had several 'prominent London businessmen' passing through here. Most of them go home via New York, and they all say in their Collinses [thank-you letters] that the 'tone' in Wall Street is far worse than it is in London. 'Our civilisation is at stake,' is the burden of innumerable public speeches on this Continent now; such speeches end, as you may guess, with the original statement that if only we all pull together, everything will be lovely. I always wonder exactly what we ought to pull: our legs, perhaps, or even our rhubarb.

If our civilisation is at stake, I, for one, have no inclination to pay a large price to redeem it. For quite a while I have thought it high time we thought about getting a new one.   Yours, T.

To Letty Benson

15 March 1932   *Government House*
                                   Ottawa

My dear Letty, Four zero days running, we've had here, but it's the wind which nips the ears, not the temperature. Even so, I find it a warmer place than London. Linlithgow[1] was here last week – is he a friend of yours? And Winston,[2] with Miss Diana, a nice girl, but my, what a rattle. Talk, talk, talk, till you look for a green baize cloth to throw over the cage. I have just finished *Brave New World*.[3] I suppose *all* babies will be made that way soon. A pity, for, as the Two Black Crows say, the old way was such fun.   Yours, Tommy.

23 March 1932   *Government House*
                                   Ottawa

My dear Letty, We are having a long snowy March, and all wondering, not too hopefully, if spring is far behind or not even over the horizon. This place wouldn't be so bad if it weren't for the electric shocks. All through the winter, whatever you touch shocks you: you

---

[1] The second Marquess of Linlithgow (1887–1952) who became Viceroy of India in 1936.
[2] Winston Churchill (1874–1965) was then Conservative Member of Parliament for the Epping Division of Essex, but held no political office.
[3] Aldous Huxley's novel had just been published.

hand your wife a hairpin, you brush a hyacinth with your nose, you (inadvertently) make contact with the footman's fingers as he hands you the cutlets – out pops a great blue spark, and you jump like a c. on h.b. It really wears the nerves to fiddle-strings; and latterly – I suppose the magnetic pole has been extra peppy – one can't even walk along the carpeted passages without going like a horse with string-halt, for every second step the nails in one's shoes get off with the nails in the floor, and you get a shock right up the leg. The only compensation for this intolerable nuisance is watching visitors who haven't been told about it. They are curiously shy of mentioning it, I notice; perhaps they think it is due to some lapse of their own hormones, and the less said about it in public, the better. But if ever you come here in winter, you look out.   Yours, Tommy.

To Maurice Headlam[1]

2 August 1932   *Hotel Tadoussac, PQ*
                                                              Canada

My dear Maurice, Every good fisherman lies awake at night and builds his airy castles, of a day on a noble river full of fresh-run, friendly fish. My castle came suddenly solid this week, and stayed so, not for one day only, but for two and a half.

I have a friend in Montreal, a worthy man and wealthy, who, with five others of the same type, has for a number of years held a lease of some ten miles of the Bonaventure River – flowing, as you may know, from the north to the south of the Gaspé peninsula, to discharge its gin-clear water into the Baie de Chaleur. At a point some seven miles from its mouth they have built them in a pleasant clearing a cluster of green and white log bungalows; and here, with an admirably organised fleet of canoes and guides (the Canadian for ghillies) they meet each midsummer for a month of what, I would say, is very nearly the best salmon-fishing in the world. Each week one guest, or occasionally two, is invited to join them; and this week I was the man.

I reached their camp at 4 p.m. one afternoon. In twenty minutes, with my light 14-foot rod (really a two-handed trout-rod), whose reel

---

[1] 1873–1956. A leading civil servant, he had been Assistant Secretary to the Treasury 1920–26, and in 1932 was Comptroller-General and Secretary of the National Debt Office. In 1934 he published *A Holiday Fisherman*, which established itself as a firm favourite in the field.

holds nearly 150 yards of line, and the very considerable stock of salmon flies which I always carry ('The time you want your fishing-tackle,' my father used to say, 'is when you go fishing. So why leave it at home?' My father rarely said anything about fishing that was not worth writing in a book), I was on my way to the beat that had been kept clear for me.

The vehicle was a fairly substantial canoe, manned by two French Canadians improbably named Campbell and Sinclair (the ancestors of about a third of Quebec Province were Murray's Highlanders, disbanded in 1759), born and bred on the river, and knowing every stone as we know our front door-steps. Like Youth and Pleasure, they stood respectively at the prow and at the helm, armed with long, iron-shod poles and light paddles. With the former they propel you upstream, over incredible rapids; with the latter, they guide you down, when the time comes to turn. Charming men, but with a disconcerting habit of looking down a pool and telling one – generally with ninety per cent accuracy – exactly how many fish are in it; I do not like to have the future revealed to me by such clairvoyance, which seems to me slightly indecent: a river's secrets are its own. The Bonaventure, too, is the last river in the world where I would forget my manners, for it is noble from its source to its estuary, and a prince among rivers – broad, strong and very clear, with the great features of the Spey, the breadth of the Tay, and the crystal clearness of the waters of Norway; lined with grand rocks, red and grey, above which the virgin forest piles itself, and offering, usually, a narrow beach of shingle where the fisherman may disembark to land his fish.

Twenty minutes' hard poling, through a perfect midsummer afternoon, brought me to my first pool, and, with a small Silver Grey, I threw the first salmon-fly that I had cast, save in imagination, since September 1929. A grilse of 5 lbs – the first killed on the river this year – took it very soon, and then I put on a slightly larger Jock Scott – size No. 1 – and the almost immediate result was a fish of 22 lbs, which, with my light rod, took more than the regulation pound-a-minute to kill.

(The method of fishing a pool, by the way, is to drop anchor out of the canoe and, beginning with a short line, to fish your pool till you reach your limit of casting. Then you up-anchor, drop about two canoes' lengths, and begin again with a short line. When you hook a fish, the anchor is hauled up at once and the men hold the canoe with their paddles, ready to follow the fish if he takes out an unhealthy amount of line – if necessary down the rapids to the next pool. When he has got reasonably tame, you are landed, and finish the fight on foot, usually over roughish ground. The gaff is not allowed, and I find that bringing a salmon to a landing-net is a much more delicate operation than bringing him to a gaff.)

The sun had now got below the high horizon of pines on the western bank, so I changed to a 1/0 Wilkinson (my favourite fly), and in succession caught a twelve-pounder and a nine – the latter every bit as lively as the twenty-two. During my whole time on the river I never saw a fish that was not bright as silver, nor killed one without sea-lice;[1] and the antics of the smaller fish – 10, 11 and 12 lbs – were such as I have never seen before save in rainbow trout in the early spring. They would run sixty or seventy yards time and again, and at the end invariably execute a double-somersault in the air, which, as A. P. Herbert's Topsy might say, was simply too cardiac for words.

So darkness fell: three fish weighing 43 lbs, and a grilse. We dropped down the river in the cool emerald twilight, I thinking that already my twenty-four hour journey was justified, and that a very fair basement had been built for my dream castle. I little knew how splendid a *rez-de-chaussée*, how solid a first storey, the next two days were to add to it.

They told me at dinner that night that the only standard English fly which was useless on the Bonaventure was a Durham Ranger. Therefore, the next morning being dark and cloudy, and I being my father's son, I began with a No. 2 Durham. Within an hour and a half it had killed me three fish – 21 lbs, 12 lbs, 13 lbs. Then another rose to it, but would not come again, so I changed to a Jock Scott, and he took it at once – 14 lbs, an incredibly active fish that might have been a 200-lb porpoise, the way he acted. Then luncheon; and, the day having brightened, I stuck to the Jock, who rewarded me with a twenty-pounder, a good fish lost, a twelve-pounder and a twenty-four pounder in quick succession.

I then had seven fish; and by the rules of the Club no man may kill more than eight in a day. It was barely 4.30 p.m., and my guides were confident that I should get my limit-fish within the hour. But the gods had decided to give me full measure that day: three times I hooked good fish, and three times did they let go, two of them after they would certainly have been dead had we been using a gaff instead of a net.

My guide grew gloomy. 'They're just Joneses,' he kept saying –

---

[1] Indicating that the fish had not been in the river long.

which I concluded was a topsy-turvy reference to the prophet Jonah. It was past seven, and growing perceptibly less light. Only some forty yards of water remained of my last pool. But, thirty-one years ago, I had killed my first salmon on a Dusty Miller, which has always been my good angel ever since (though, as I say, my heart belongs to the more carnal-looking Wilkinson). Ashamed that I had not thought of doing so before, I put on a Dusty Miller. A fish took him at the third cast, and, hooked right through the tongue, gave me little anxiety. He was 12 lbs. Eight fish, weighing 128 lbs. The evening and the morning were the first day.

The second was no less glorious, though less statistically imposing: seven fish weighing 75 lbs. I struck a run of 'July' fish, which, it seems, average about 12 lbs in this river. But I have no complaint of them, for every one, on my light rod, gave me more exercise and excitement than many a Scotch twenty-pounder.

This day was very fine and bright. I eschewed standard patterns and killed all my fish on a black-and-teal affair invented by an old Norwegian crony of my father's called Chadwick, and on a sombre fly that I've had for years and whose name I think is a Dark Fairy. I lost three fish, one of which gave me a warning that will last my lifetime. Ever since I started to fish, I've always fastened my line to my cast by a simple round-hand knot, round both arms of the gut-loop, and have never had a suspicion of trouble. This day, I must have greased the end of my line excessively: the knot slipped, and left my cast and a nice new 'Chadwick' in the mouth of a good fish. *N.B.*, therefore, that he who greases his line heavily must use a more elaborate knot, as I did forthwith.

The story does not end so happily as it began. The next, and last, day was very wet, with an awkward wind. I killed a fish early in the morning and lost another, thereafter moving only one fish till dark. But still – nineteen fish and a grilse in three and a half days – I make no complaint, and never expect to do better.

Note this, too: half my fish were killed on a treble-gut cast which, to my certain knowledge, was bought not later than 1902, and to which, in 1923 or 1924, I had attached a length of Japanese gut brought back from Japan by Lionel Halsey in 1921; the other half, on one of Mr Forrest's 'fine salmon' casts, which I've used at intervals over a period of four years. So much for the legend that gut can't be trusted after one season. My rod was bought in 1900, and several of the gut-eyed flies which I used must be older. My casting-line was new this year, but the backing – nearly all of which was often out – is as old as the rod.

Jane Austen wrote her novels without mentioning the Napoleonic War, and I write you this letter without mentioning the Ottawa Conference.[1] I don't propose to lower its tone now. If you have an opportunity, give it to John Gore, whose wife, being a better fisherman than he is, might enjoy reading it; and in return let me know if you have achieved anything on the Test or the Itchen this year.   Yours, A. Lascelles.

To Letty Benson

23 August 1932   *Jasper Park Lodge*
                                    Canadian National Railways

Dear Letty, The Baroness [Constance Wenlock] is dead; and I believe that, in all this foolish world, which never realises its own rare jewels, you and I and a very few others are the only ones who understand what that means. She was just a deaf old woman, for ever painting unframeable pictures; but if, in our own galleries of memory, we could substitute for her portrait that of any other human being, living or dead, would we do it? Not I; in all history, there is no individual for whose company I would exchange that of Constance Wenlock, and you, I believe, would say the same. What rare and wonderful people we have known in our forty-odd years; and how unceasingly grateful one ought to be for the one gift (which, thank God, He has given me) of being able to go on tasting all the mellowness of their memories and none of the bitterness.

Goodnight, dear Letty. If I had been on your side of the Atlantic, I should have been forced to ring you up on the telephone tonight. That being impossible, you will understand why I write.

                                    Yours, Tommy.

PS I don't even know where you live. You see – space severs one far more quickly from the living than time does from the dead.

---

[1] The economic conference held in July 1932 by members of the British Commonwealth, which established preferential arrangements for trade between Great Britain and the Dominions. Although Tommy did not describe the meeting to Maurice Headlam, he did send home a full account of it in letters and telegrams to Buckingham Palace; and on 26 August Lord Wigram, the King's Private Secretary, wrote to him from Balmoral: 'It was indeed good of you to give us this first-hand information, and the King and Queen are most grateful. We could picture, thanks to you, exactly what was happening.'

To John Gore

20 September 1932　　　　　　　　　　*Governor-General's Train*
　　　　　　　　　　　　　　　　　　　Approaching Medicine Hat

Well, Johnny, it is quite a while since I wrote to you, but no wonder. Since 15 August I have been touring this intolerably large Dominion, with little leisure to devote to private affairs. Apart from that, it needed a period to cool my anger with you. When we sang about Darwin, and Huxley and Ball, in Balliol quad one night, Julian Huxley burst out on us, white with anger, and said, 'I don't mind what you say about *me*, but I won't have you abuse my people.'

That is just where Julian Huxley and I differ. I don't care how much you abuse my People in your filthy news-sheet, but I won't have you saying things about *me*. I have said so a hundred times.[1]

Your cousin Vere is not at all a bad chap, and, in nearly all respects, an exceptionally good Governor-General. But he is no boy's horse, and he wants careful riding. Nothing in the world is more calculated to upset him, and to bring out the little weaknesses of his character, than, at the very moment when he saw himself with his finger on the Empire's pulse, closeted in his book-lined study with one Imperial statesman after another, to read, in a quasi-respectable London magazine the statement that his Secretary is the 'power behind the Throne.' I went cold all over when I read it. Fortunately, he tackled Joan about it, and not me; fortunately, though he said in his conversation with her, 'I believe one of the Gores writes for this paper – there are continual paragraphs about the Ponsonbys', she did not reveal any close intimacy with that particular Gore. But for some days thereafter I noticed a quite perceptible decrease of malleability in him, in matters which he is usually content to leave in my hands.

Seriously, and once for all, I ask you to believe that, apart from any contingent embarrassments, I definitely dislike seeing any comment about myself in the public Press. It is bad enough being constantly photographed, but that is one of the inevitable penalties of this particular type of profession. The other is not merely a penalty, but may quite well be a nuisance.

[On this, the Governor General's first trip to the West] socially, conversationally, gastronomically, they [the Westerners] have reduced me, after six intensive weeks, to a state of screaming hysteria.

---

[1] John Gore was then contributing the Old Stager column to the *Sphere*.

But there is no doubt that, if you are an Imperialist (which I don't think I am), you must admit them to be very sterling people in the west. Nonetheless, Ottawa, my cottage, and even the Rideau Club, now mercifully only eight days distant, seem to me as roseate a Paradise as Sutton Waldron usually does when I am in Ottawa. We were going to be away till 13 October – fifty-two solid days of touring. I warned Bessborough – knowing a bit about Western tours – that we should all come back stark, staring mad; but he said that the coming winter would be all the shorter if we stayed away longer. Mercifully, just as he – and much more she – were beginning to realise the truth of my prophecy, the unexpectedly early summoning of Parliament gave us a perfectly adequate excuse for cutting out nearly a fortnight; and now we have all reacted into the healthy end-of-term hilarity of small boys, who say each morning, 'Only eight days more.'

I must say, he is a most satisfactory Orator to work for – a beautiful delivery, and a very ready and happy wit for extempore introductions to more solid matter. I did not expect him, typical product of Pall Mall as he is, to go down well in the west, where, as you know, they are terribly suspicious of anything they can label 'dude'; but he has had a remarkable success almost everywhere. They are impressed by his dignity on the platform, and his 'geniality' off it, while they all consider him the most 'thoughtful and inspiring' speaker they have had as a Governor-General for many years. She, of course, invariably provokes enthusiasm of the 'My, but isn't she a lovely lady!' order, and works like a black; but she is a shocking bad traveller, poor thing, and, like him, nauseated by the standard of cuisine that we have to endure practically everywhere. So am I, for that matter – I frequently eat nothing but bread for luncheon, and man cannot live by bread alone. All the same, I am very well, and I believe I put on weight. Have I told you about my taking thyroid for the past six months? It has undoubtedly made an immense difference to my powers of endurance and general cheerfulness.

I cannot recollect your son's name; nor Jasper's, nor any bloody body's name, if it comes to that. We are getting old, Scaramel, we are getting old – though I am bound to say none of the frightful women I sit next to at luncheon can ever guess either my age or my weight correctly. (That is the sort of level to which my conversational standards have dropped.) And once upon a time, A and B and even C used to be quite glad when they heard I was to take them into dinner.

I knew I should never see Constance Wenlock again, God rest her witty, lovable soul. There was nobody that I ever met who had quite her quality. You are quite right – I was very fond of her – fonder than I have ever been of any blood relation in my life, save possibly little Mrs Nixon [his sister Maud].

Time to dress. I am so bored of having a choppy bath, with white horses breaking round the bush. But we always, thank God (and my own admirable staff work), tie up at night; Lady B. cannot sleep in a moving train. Nor can I.   Yours, A.L.

To John Gore

2 December 1932   *Hotel Pennsylvania*
                                                              New York
                                                    2,200 rooms, 2,200 baths

My dear John, It is typical of the age and the country that, with 2,200 rooms and 2,200 baths, this caravanserai only offers six writing tables at which a waiting guest may while away the time by correspondence. I have had to wait twenty-five minutes for what, in a rush-hour at the bogs of my private school, we used to call a 'vake'. The word, by the way, had a curious development, not without etymological interest. Originally and properly meaning 'a vacant bog' (as you will have guessed), it came to denote the bog itself. Thus, one would say, 'I always use the third vake from the end,' or, 'T.P. is awfully batey because Johnny Gore has carved his name on one of the vake seats.'[1]

I was particularly interested by what you say about Ronald Cruikshank.[2] There is no doubt that great numbers of the Frightened Rich are turning to God and trying to lay up treasure in Heaven, since Earth has proved such an uncertain repository. A group of revivalists, mis-calling themselves the 'Oxford' Group, has recently toured Canada and achieved remarkable success among the once-moneyed classes. I do not like their methods or their personnel (which has only a thirty per cent connection with Oxford, if that), and, personally, I would as soon reveal the state of my soul (which to my last breath I shall continue to call my own) to any save a few intimate friends as I would reveal the state of my bowels. None the

---

[1] Tom Pellatt, usually known as 'T.P.', was the eccentric but gifted headmaster of Durnford House, the preparatory school in Dorset to which Tommy had gone.

[2] Journalist and editor, 1898–1956. He was American correspondent of the *News Chronicle* 1928–36.

less, I recognise that the vast majority of my fellow-men will only do things in herds, and I think that any kind of spiritual revival, however vulgar and herdish in its beginnings, is to the good.

Yours, T.

To Helen

31 December 1932   *Government House*
Ottawa

My dear Whelk, Many thanks for your letter and cheque, which, after a good deal of arithmetic, I have distributed equitably in Canadian currency [to the children]. I hope you will get letters from the recipients in due course; it was good of you to think of them.

So far we have had, for the second year in succession, an unusually mild winter – only one short spell of 'zero' weather, and very little snow, so that we skate agreeably most afternoons, often in bright sunshine.

Joan, at the moment, is pretty well; but she has bouts of what the doctors seem to agree is a form of nervous indigestion which is apparently not uncommon in this land of low temperatures and hot houses. She is never well, and I fear never will be, when the thermometer gets into single figures, for cold has always affected her much as heat affects me. But the medicos (who are very good here, I think) are all agreed that there is nothing wrong with her organically or constitutionally, and the only trouble with her heart is that she has a 'systole', which, as you probably know, is nothing but a slight habit some hearts have of missing a beat now and then.

Of course, like all of us she is home-sick, and misses Sutton and the garden a great deal; but if she broaches to you the idea that we must come home before long, I should be grateful if you would discourage it. Whether I shall stay for the Bessboroughs' full term or not, I can't yet say, though if they can stick it, poor things – as they must – I should feel badly at deserting them, as they have done everything they can to make us comfortable. Apart from that, as I am saving money, and still the right side of fifty, I feel it would be folly to come home prematurely, unless some other worthwhile job were offered me. Moreover, having astonished the world by throwing up one job in what must have seemed sheer wanton-ness, I do not want to get the reputation of making a habit of it. And, unless things get much better (as I'm now inclined to think they *may* be beginning to – though it will obviously be a long and weary process), it would be difficult to live at Sutton with any degree of comfort.

The children are undeniably happy here, and John extremely so at his school. The standard of education may not be high in classics and maths, but they teach them good manners and a very fair level of general knowledge, I should say. I was pleased when he gave me 'A thing of beauty is a joy for ever' as a gibbet the other night, and knew where it came from, and, unlike the Eton boy in the story, has no temptation to say, 'What *are* Keats?'

So far, thank God, he has no trace of a Canadian accent, and his natural intelligence is so good that the fact of his not absorbing as much Latin grammar and arithmetic as English standards expect don't worry me much. None the less, I think I shall very likely ask Pellatt to take him for the final year before he goes up for his Eton entrance exam.

Your exhibition of children's books seems to have been most successful. I wish I had seen it. I suppose you found nothing of unexpected interest in the library at Harewood? It is unlikely that there would be much there, but you never know. I remember that when poor Vernon had the library valued, at his barrack of a house in Derbyshire, he discovered a collection of holograph letters from Voltaire, about which there was no record. He promptly sold them for, I think, several thousands of pounds.

When I was on Long Island the other day, I came suddenly on the old gates of Devonshire House which, though I had forgotten it, were bought by J. A. Burden for his house there – the house that was lent to the Prince of Wales in 1924. They look very well, I am bound to say, and the house is not unworthy of them; but the sight gave me an unpleasant shock none the less.

Bennett (for whom, incidentally, I have a great regard) has come back full of Harry [Harewood]'s praises; apparently he sat next to him after dinner at Buckingham Palace, and was much impressed by his knowledge of Canada.

A happy new year to you all, and love from us both. T.

PS I understand that His Majesty is being pleased to confer a CMG on me. You need not write a special letter of congratulation on this. As I forget who said in similar circumstances, 'I would so much rather have the Monkey, without the Goat.' I do not relish the prospect of having to tie the infernal thing round my neck every time I dine at Government House.

144

Since I began this letter the thermometer has dropped forty degrees in a single night, and is now ten below zero!

To John Gore

11 February 1933   *Rideau Cottage*
                                                                    Ottawa

There is almost a note of reproach, Johnny, in your suggestion that I am the only one of your acquaintance to preserve some appearance of cheerfulness these days. I am sorry not to be in the movement, but I can claim no credit for being thus in a class by myself. If you put me there, it is only, I am afraid, because you do not see me often, because one of my few social principles is that Letters – especially letters to or from those in exile – should be dedicated to the lighter, rather than the darker, side of life, which is at best sombre business for those who have left their youth behind them.

Letters to my friends have always been an almost sacred task to me. Like Henry, in 'Gentlemen Prefer Blondes',[1] I have ruined many a party, for myself and others, merely by arriving at it; but in writing letters I have generally done my best to apply what your major prophet, R.L.S., says about the task of happiness, and what Carlyle says about consuming smoke. A man has no business to put his bile on paper when writing to a friend; he might as well curse him at the breakfast-table. A letter, like a garden, should be a lovesome thing, God wot; the flowers, when a friend is taken round it, should be displayed, the weeds hidden. Good news should be put in letters; bad news, in communications to doctors or solicitors.

On this principle, which I now violate, I tell you – quite truthfully – that thyroid treatment has done me a power of good; I conceal the fact that it is all too likely that, when you next see me, I shall have a complete ratelier of false teeth. I tell you that Joan is coming home; but not – nor will you please tell anyone else – that I am worried to death at the effect the Canadian winter appears to have on her health; I tell you – at the risk of appearing complacent – that I have succeeded in saving £1,500 in the last eighteen months, but not that I lost £3,000 in a single day, two years ago, when the irrevocable bankruptcy of United Havana Railways was suddenly revealed.

---

[1] The first, and immensely successful, novel by the American author Anita Loos, published in 1925.

Similarly, though I often cheer Joan and myself by discussing the beauty that our garden-improvements at Sutton will have attained after a five-year maturity, I should think it the act of a bad husband to reveal to her that only a miracle can make it possible for us ever to live there again for any length of time – which, as it happens, is the only thing that I desire to do with any degree of intensity. [There follows much gloomy speculation about how the world is going downhill, financially and politically.]

Well, and after all, what does it amount to? The world is in a shocking state. Its past, which we happen to find so pleasant, is being buried in indecent haste; its doubtful future is coming to birth with exceptional travail. This is, no doubt, depressing for us who have had some affection for the dead King, and are not at all sure how the new one will treat us. But should it be any more depressing than the immutable facts of every man's life in every age? If we read the Psalms of David or the Book of Job, with the daily assiduity we give to a daily newspaper, we should find our reading matter no less full of potential sadness.

Death, possibly lingering and painful; the gradual loss of the faculties; the grasshopper becoming more and more a burden; the probability – calculated on a strictly actuarial basis – that in a few years' time our children may quite likely be a nuisance, if not a disgrace, to ourselves, or we nothing but a burden to them; the steady falling-off of old friends; the gradual closing to us of one place after another that has become a storehouse of happy memories; the growing conviction that love and laughter end finally and irrevocably with the Grave – are not all these hard facts, which are always just round the corner, far more potent agents of depression than economic catastrophes, or the passing of social, political and imperial systems?

Yet we have little tolerance of the man who allows them to monopolise his thoughts or influence his actions. Newspaper troubles, the troubles of the herd, can never be as poignant as the troubles of men and women. The tragedy of Romeo and Juliet is far more tragic than the tragedy of the fall of Rome. Kipling puts ashes on his poor old head because the British Empire is dying; but Kipling would forget about the British Empire if he could get back his dead son; and George Lloyd would forget about it too, if he could forget about George Lloyd. You dread the prospect of ten years' socialistic rule in England; but if the Angel Gabriel appeared to you and told you (no, not that you were with child by the Holy Ghost: no conception of yours could be immaculate, Johnny) that it rested with you to choose whether this should come to pass, or whether your son, or even mine, should be run over by a bus, I know very well what you would decide. And, being but a man, you would be perfectly right.

Yours ever, T.

To John Gore

12 April 1933

Rideau Cottage
Ottawa

My dear John, Yes, I mind the idea of never seeing Chelmsford again [he had died on 1 April]. He was, from the moment I told him I wished to marry his eldest daughter, an ideal and always helpful father-in-law. Under his frozen, early Roman exterior, he was a most human and affectionate man. My theory, well grounded, is that he would have liked to be very much closer to his elder daughters, to whom he was devoted, but for her [his wife's] inordinate jealousy. From what I have heard from Joan of her childhood, I believe this repressed both him and them like a black cloud. Poor woman, I don't know what she will do now.

I have heard no details of his death yet, save that he died suddenly. Daisy writes that she went to his funeral, but omits to say anything of his death – it is extraordinary how really intelligent people who have never lived long abroad can't grasp the elementary principles of writing letters to exiles.

Chelmsford was a really fine character, I think; in his imposing list of offices he did not, perhaps, achieve real success in any, and the world looked on him as a mediocre man; but he was a good deal 'greater' than many who have achieved greatness in our time. A slave to duty, and incapable of swerving one hair's breadth from his own principles, which were pretty rigid ones, he had only a moderate sense of humour, and no sense of flippancy whatever; but, in spite of that, I was very fond of him, and of his society – when alone with him.

Guendolen,[1] as you say, was one of the very rare. I have known none like her. In later years I fear I saw little of her – Algernon somehow put a thorn fence round her, which it was terribly difficult to penetrate. Put away at Sutton, there are over a hundred of her

---

[1] Lady Guendolen Osborne (1885–1933) had been one of Tommy's dearest friends and most faithful correspondents. A daughter of the tenth Duke of Leeds, she married Algernon Cecil in 1923, but had no children.

letters, mostly written in wartime, which, for wit and grace and wisdom, are second to no published collection of letters, ancient or modern, that I have ever read. She was, with Conrad [Russell], incomparably the best letter-writer of our day; better than Con, perhaps, for her letters have a literary style and variety which his, magnificent though they are, do not attain. I am glad to think I kept every line she wrote me, over a period of about fifteen years. I shall always be very proud of having had her friendship.

I have been very lucky in my friends. It is only rarely that I wish that old acquaintance might be forgot – as I did last week when I suddenly got a very cordial letter from Rupert Leslie, in Jamaica – I think I have only seen him once since Trinity days – written as if we had parted last month, and asking me to look after his sister (unmarried) and lady friend who are visiting Ottawa in May. He asked to be cordially remembered to Bessborough, a former brother officer in the Suffolk Yeomanry. 'I just remember him,' said Bessborough. 'They used to call him Bum-face in the regiment.' This, I fear, is the only time in two years that the Governor General has made me laugh spontaneously and unaffectedly.

John has come back from school really well; his doctor here, after a thorough overhaul yesterday, was delighted with him, and the boy really looks quite different. He is up to my chin now, and, though thin, is perceptibly thicker, and happy at his school to a degree that makes me sigh with envy, remembering my own miseries at his age.

This news will, I hope, do Joan more good than the doctors can, for I think worrying over John [who had been ill] last year – more than was necessary – was the main cause of her breakdown; if not the only one, for, apart from the inevitable boredoms of this place, I know of no other conceivable source of mental anxiety for her. Ours has been a remarkably happy life for thirteen years, and world crises interested rather than depressed her.

My love to Jenny, T.

PS A few weeks ago Bessborough said to me, 'Old Stager, in the *Sphere* – he's one of the de Greys, you know. Says etc. etc.' I said, 'Oh, yeah?', or words to that effect. The other day, J. B. Bickersteth,[1] lunching at Government House, said, 'I think that was mentioned (whatever it was) by Johnny Gore – he's the Old Stager in the *Sphere*, you know.' 'Of course he is,' says the Governor General, and,

---

[1] 1888–1979. A contemporary of Tommy's at Oxford, he made his career in Canada and from 1921 to 1947 was Warden of Hart House, University of Toronto.

turning to me, asked, 'Did *you* know who the Old Stager is?' I looked down my nose and said I thought I had heard it somewhere.

To Letty Benson

27 May 1933   *Rideau Cottage*
                                                                            Ottawa

My dear Letty, As a sleeping-partner (forgive me if I am indelicate) in a leading financial House, you will know that a dividend passed at the beginning of the year becomes all the more difficult to produce at midsummer, if it is Cumulative and Participating.

That is just my trouble now. Last Christmas, God forgive me (for you never will, Madam), I passed my dividend on Handkerchief Preferred; and how I am to meet it now, I do not know. Why I never wrote to you at the time is one of those things a man can't explain even to his Maker; it was inexcusable, and I make no excuses. It was the act of a Bunt. I never thought that I should fall so low. It will serve me right if next Christmas you send me a paper Doyley (or Doiley?).

It was a lovely handkerchief, too; just a *leetle* loud, perhaps, for a Secretary – a trifle passionate for a father of three – a shade frisky for one whose exact contemporary (Hon. G. Charteris)[1] is going to be a grandfather in about twenty minutes – but none the less an ornament to any nose. (I wish I had no nose; for the things I miss most in a strange land are English smells. There are no smells in this hard, dry land; and when you put your head out of your bedroom window every night – as I hope you do – before hopping into bed, you should sniff gratefully, and think of those who sniff in vain. Smells, and music, and a little honest, flippant dirt: those are the three things for which I really get homesick; and an old cock-thrush in an apple-tree at sundown.)

We are just back from the most shattering week of the year – Toronto races; which we try to pretend are Ascot, with our grey top hats and a drive up the course in a barouche with postillions, but which give me little pleasure, as I can't abide seeing horses galloping round a dirt-track instead of over Christian grass. And when we got back, after seven hours in the train, we had to go and prorogue

[1] The Hon. Guy Charteris (1886–1967), second son of Lord Ercho, had been one of Tommy's closest friends at Oxford, and had married Frances Tennant in 1912.

Parliament in tight trousers and tighter boots, at eight o'clock in the evening, when a gentleman should be thinking of his dinner.

And you, I see, presented Laura Charteris [Guy's daughter] to Their Majesties the other night. It seems incredible to me, who have never seen Laura save under a thick coating of mud, and with a hole or two in each stocking.

I have had a lonely three months, and an anxious six, for Joan was not at all well throughout the winter. But she really does seem better now, and I have just had a cable to say she is definitely sailing on 9 June, to join me at Quebec; and a few weeks after that I get my annual spoonful of jam in the shape of a week on the loveliest salmon river (the Bonaventure) that I have yet found anywhere.

Well, goodnight, dear Letty. Won't you come out here some day? I can't think what for, but won't you? Oughtn't you to show a brace or two of your boys the way round the Empire? And Marjorie [Anglesey, her sister] has oilfields in Alberta, too. Love to Guy.

Yours, Tommy.

To Maurice Headlam

22 July 1933   *Rideau Cottage*

My dear Maurice, Here, since you asked for it, is the story of a better week's fishing than the last. I shall tell it in detail, for, as Lord Tennyson might have said had his liver served him better, pleasure's crown of pleasure is remembering better things.

None the less the story, if it ends happily, is not all jam. [Here the author described at some length how his favourite 14-ft split-cane rod was damaged in transit to the family's summer cottage at Cacouna, 150 miles from Ottawa, where the people spoke a scarcely-intelligible brand of French, and how, in despair of getting the joint repaired, he took it to a local craftsman.]

So, attended by my daughter aged ten, we went in search of him. And, at the back [of a shop], up a rickety staircase, we found an old, old man who, from the debris that surrounded him, was all too obviously the village cobbler. My heart sank. 'Do you think he understands this sort of work?' I asked. 'He is very clever with his hands,' said Peter, and left us; but when he was half-way down the stairs he relented so far as to shout a further string of instructions to the old gentleman, of which I caught only the concluding sentence: '*Et prends garde, veux tu – c'est une perche très coûteuse.*'

Meanwhile the old man had snatched from my hands the *perche très coûteuse* and, turning it this way and that with senile gaiety, seemed to be saying, in a hideous parody of the Harley Street bedside manner, that the case presented no difficulty whatever. What he really said I cannot tell you, for throughout the whole interview I understood not a syllable of the running commentary he kept up.

He took up a rusty hammer and a long conical instrument ending in a point. Before I could say 'Jack Robinson', he had rammed the latter down the ferrule, into the very bowels of the split cane. This was more than I could bear, and I caught his arm. He was offended, and I feared he would throw up the case. But with a shrug of his shoulders he selected a less deadly weapon, and then began, with a touch of surprising delicacy, to tap the dent with his hammer. For several minutes he tapped without any visible result, while I stood by in silent agony; I felt as Dr. Jenner must have felt when he selected his infant son as the first subject for vaccination.

But the cobbler had the patience of the true artist: the third time he allowed me to look along the rod, the dent was perceptibly shallower. After a further interval, it was almost possible to get the middle joint in; and finally, after a shower of Cyclopean blows that made me groan till my daughter asked anxiously if I was ill, the dent vanished altogether. I felt certain that the last onslaught must have cracked the metal, but there was no flaw to be seen: the middle joint fitted perfectly, and the sun shone and the birds sang once more.

I pressed twenty-five cents into his hands. He was overjoyed. I said, '*Monsieur, vous êtes artiste,*' which may not be idiomatic French, but he understood it, and we parted good friends. There is a memorable passage in Queen Victoria's diary where she records that, on John Brown completing twenty-five years of faithful service, she gave him a leather blotting-book, with (I think) silver corners: 'The poor fellow said it was too much. God knows it was not enough.' Those were my feelings as I stepped out into the street; and you, perhaps, will believe, what others might think hyperbole – that no single interview in my whole life has caused me such an agony of mental apprehension as that one.

That was on Wednesday. The train that would take me eastwards to the Bonaventure was due to leave our wayside station at 4 a.m. on Saturday morning, and would land me on the river-bank – assuming punctuality – by 4.30 that afternoon. On Wednesday the sky was cloudless: the kind of weather which, if it preceded a fishing-expedition to Scotland, would induce one to console himself by saying, 'Oh well, anyhow it will be very nice lying in the heather by the side of the river.' But, as I knew from my last year's experience, it was exactly the weather in which, on these well-fed Canadian rivers, one looks to catch fish; here, it is not the sun but the rain that the occasional summer angler fears. And on Thursday the rains came – and continued torrentially all Friday. 'Done,' I thought, knowing that once the rivers do come down in spate, they don't clear in a hurry. 'Two more days gone.' For I heard that morning that the Saturday in my week would be a *dies non*[1], as the water had been let to an American party from that date, and our party would have to leave the camp at noon on Friday, to catch the only train.

I sought consolation by telling myself that after all the Bonaventure rose in the southern watershed of the Gaspé mountains, and we were on the north; that its valley was nearly 300 miles to the eastwards – as do men, passing Grantham in a golden sunset, say hopefully but without conviction, 'Ah well, it may have rained today at Perth.'

It looked bad; and it looked worse when, at 3.30 a.m. on Saturday, I rolled off the parlour sofa into the local taxi and found the rain still falling steadily. It was daylight when my train left; and every glance from the window showed some little stream rushing north to the St. Lawrence in a brawl of porter-coloured foam: hour after hour the same disheartening evidence of heavy spate.

Then at last came the moment when we crossed the range of hills and reached the land of southward-flowing waters, of those Homeric rivers whose names, like those of the Blessed Damozel's handmaidens, are sweet symphonies: the Matapedia, the Ristigouche, the Grand Cascapedia, the Miramichi. But it was not their names which exercised me that morning: it was their colour. The Matapedia comes first; the train swoops unexpectedly into its valley and runs by its side for miles. But one glance was enough; the Matapedia was full, but it was clear as gin. The rain had not crossed the mountains.

After that, the fact that the train left the junction for the final stage an hour late, and got steadily later all the way to Bonaventure station, was a matter of comparatively small moment. My casts were in soak, I was ready to step straight into a boat; at the worst, I calculated, I ought to be on whatever water had been left for me by 5.30 at latest, and that left me a full two hours' fishing.

As it turned out, it was almost exactly at that hour that my first cast was made, at the head of the best pool in the lower water, which a considerate host had earmarked for me. Two casts later I had risen

---

[1] An Etonian expression meaning a day off.

a fish, to a No. 1 Durham Ranger, which he refused to approach again; and perhaps two casts after that I had hooked another fish, which I duly killed – 12 lbs, sea-lice. It had been a nervous moment, making the first few casts with my split-cane convalescent; but it was as good as ever, and, though there is a slight but perceptible kink at the middle joint, it behaved perfectly throughout. With the sun setting, I changed to a 1/0 Wilkinson, on which I killed two fish and lost a third; and so to dinner. As we paddled home, I reflected that on the first evening last year I had killed three fish and a grilse; but then last year the train had not been late.

At dinner I heard the gossip of the river. They – six or seven rods – had been fishing a fortnight, and a wonderful fortnight it had been. I forget how many fish they had got, but I know that limit-days (eight fish) had been frequent, and that one chap had got forty-odd fish in six days' fishing.

The next day, the Sabbath, was a very lovely, but a very long, day, for fishing is not allowed on Sundays. This, I think, is partly because the members of the Club come of sound Presbyterian stock; and also from the more practical reason that the guides, who are all small farmers in the locality, have a pretty busy week – on the river all day, and 'boxing' fish in their spare time.

This boxing and despatching of fish is quite a business, as you can imagine when there are sometimes fifty or sixty salmon to be disposed of in a day. It has been admirably organised by Herbert Molson, my host, who is the presiding genius of the Club. He has built a first-class ice-house, in which the temperature is kept at about 33 degrees, night and day. (Ice, of course, is always easily obtainable in this country; they cut as much as they want out of the rivers in March, and store it in subterranean ice-houses.) Here every fish is laid, on a shelf marked with the guide's name, as soon as it comes in from the river, and it will keep perfectly fresh for a week or ten days. In the evening those who wish to send fish away write the addresses on printed cards, which are put in the window of the living room and collected by the sender's guide early next morning; a guest is invited to do the same, and at no expense to himself – noble hospitality. I sent away about a dozen fish to people in Ottawa whom I wished to propitiate, and all of them, after two and a half days in the train, arrived in perfect condition.

Early next morning – about 7 a.m. – the guides arrive, collect their respective cards (on which are written the weights of the fish to be despatched), and fall to making boxes out of the store of lumber kept for the purpose. All the guides are expert carpenters – one of them

153

makes all the boats used on the river, which are as good as anything produced by Messrs Salter at Oxford. The fish are packed, with ice and sawdust, in these boxes, which are duly collected by an old gentleman with a dray, driven to the station four miles away, and put on the midday train. As the supply of individual sendees runs out, surplus fish are sent to the big hospitals in Montreal, and a number are given away to the guides and to local farmers.

The noise of the guides at their box-making is a useful alarm-clock to wake one in the morning. But on Sundays the guides do not work, and on this Sunday it was the sound of gargantuan laughter that brought me from my bed. The Chief Justice of New Brunswick, who is exactly like Falstaff, and his friend Mr Harrison, who is the living spit of Sir Toby Belch, had met on the verandah of the central bungalow to enjoy the morning sun, and, not a jug of burnt sack, but two enormous jorums of rum and milk. There they sat in their pyjamas, two very jolly old cocks, patting their pendulous bellies and exchanging reminiscences of a humorous character. They pressed me to join them, which I did; but, though they are turned seventy and I not yet fifty, my stomach is not robust enough for rum and milk at that hour of the morning. (Falstaff and Toby, I may say, did not confine this convivial ritual to Sundays, but never failed to observe it on any day of the week.)

I was told that the next day, Monday, I was to go 'up-river' with Molson. This involves a boat-trip of some seven miles to the top water, which I had never fished before. Two rods go, each in his own boat, with a guide at the prow and another at the stern; a baggage-boat follows at its leisure with bedding, etc., and a cook. There are two beats, which the two rods fish alternately, sleeping the night at a small camp between, and returning to the main camp the following day. A prodigious number of fish had been taken out of the upper water this year, and it was confidently predicted that each of us would get his limit one day at least.

Camp-business, and the necessity for the guides packing up the accumulation of fish in the ice-house, delayed our start to what seemed to me a criminally late hour; it was ten o'clock before we got under way, and we had a journey of two and a half hours between us and our water. So, with two rods and reels in the boat, and a great quantity of flies, I settled myself in my seat as patiently as I could.

The journey itself was a glad experience.

It is a cloudless summer day, and the great cool, clear river – at any time of day it is delicious to drink, and until my last day there its temperature never rose above fifty – looks supremely beautiful. Fish are showing, birds singing, and there is unending pleasure in watching the guides: balanced at each end of the long, light boat, and handling their poles with unfailing skill, they drive her over fences of water and rock in a way that makes you feel you are on a horse. But in such weather it is hot work, and every half hour or so we have to put in to the shade of the bank for a few minutes' rest.

It is past noon when we reach the bottom of the upper water – an ideal salmon pool, known as Duval, which ought to be, and is, full of fish. I say 'is' thus confidently, for the guides, shading their eyes, can spot fish lying in a pool with extraordinary accuracy. All I can see, even in that gin-clear water, is an occasional dark bar that might be a fish or might be a rock; but, as we skirt the edge of the pool, they exclaim continually, and by the time we reach its head they must have counted fully thirty.

Here we leave one boat; our water is still another half hour up-stream. But, by about 12.30, we are there, anchored at the head of Smith, another beautiful pool, and there begins what is to be perhaps the most remarkable day's fishing I shall ever have: remarkable for its series of historic disasters and for its ultimate happy ending.

I had determined to try out, during the week, a number of my obscurer flies of the right size, even some of those whose gut eyes were suspect – though I had soaked and tested every one. So I begin with a Benchill No. 1. He produces a fish within ten minutes, and another shortly after. This second fish takes with a violence amounting to fury; he is very lively, but after about five minutes' argument, the fly comes back to me. He has broken the barb short off. Casimir, one of my guides, who is a bigoted believer in double hooks, which I dislike except in very small sizes, mutters about the folly of fishing with only one hook when one can equally well fish with two.

Then I put on a Black Prince, and he accounts for a fish, but again a second fish lets go. This time the eye has pulled out. So I fall back on a Jock Scott, new, metal-eyed. Another fish takes with a bang that nearly pulls me out of the boat; one run, and again the fly comes back. This time he has bitten the fly clean in two, at an angle. I have never seen salmon take so violently as they are taking this morning.

Only two fish in the boat, and it is three o'clock and time for luncheon – the men have had a hard morning. But I put on another Jock and get one more fish. So to luncheon, which, it is understood, is a full hour. Personally, I lunch off sandwiches and cake, but Canadian guides expect as a right to be allowed to make a fire and cook eggs and bacon and tea. All this takes time, and it is past four when we start work again. The situation is not too good if I am to get

155

my limit. About a third of Smith remains, and to reach our other
pool, Deep Water, about half an hour's poling is necessary, and I still
have five fish to get.

The afternoon does not begin too well. I lose another fish, off a
Jock Scott, and Casimir almost blasphemes at single hooks. Both
guides remark, too, that my reel is running extremely light, and
when I come to adjust the check, I find that it is as tight as it will go. I
take the reel to pieces and find that one arm of the spring has
weakened dangerously. The guides shake their heads. Deep Water,
they say, always holds heavy fish, and they are very prone to go down
a long rapid at the bottom of the pool. I compromise by saying I will
finish Smith with the light rod and reel, and then put up the big rod
for Deep Water. A few minutes later another fish points their moral
very appositely; he is only a twelve-pounder, but a very lively one,
and I find that despite all efforts to brake the reel with my hand, he is
completely my master. He takes me nearly twenty minutes and half
way down a rapid at the end of the pool.

That makes four fish, and it is getting on for five o'clock. Apart
from the question of reaching my limit, I am anxious to see the top
pool; so, though an appreciable amount of Smith is still unfished, I
give the order to move up. We stop at the camp *en route* – three little
log-cabins perched on a bluff above the river – to unload our fish and
put up the big rod. I am glad to handle it again – I have not used it
since a notable day on the Thurso in an equinoctial gale in 1929 –
but, as I pull the line out, I have an uneasy feeling that this reel too is
not quite normal, though I overhauled and oiled it before leaving
Ottawa. However, time is getting on, so I stifle my misgivings and we
continue up the river.

Deep Water is certainly a magnificent pool, and the rapid at its
foot a particularly formidable one; I decide that I do not at all want
to be taken down it by a heavy fish. The stream runs like a mill-race;
it is pitted with very ugly-looking rocks, and, to my inexperienced
eye at any rate, there seems no point in its 400 yards of turbulent
waters where one could hope to hold a boat once it had started down
stream.

I stick to the No. 1 Jock Scott, for my reverses have made me
hungry for blood, and it is no time for fancy flies. Disaster continues –
I hook a good fish at the top of the pool, but he lets go. The reel makes
unwholesome noises, but does not actually default. Casimir makes
equally unwholesome noises about the comparative merits of single
and double hooks. Another fish lays hold, and, when he is coming
into the bank nicely, the reel definitely jams. I haul the line franti-

cally through the rings, but the fish is coming in too quick. He is gone. We examine the reel in gloomy silence. I establish definitely that the trouble arises not, thank God, when the fish is running, but only when I am reeling in. What causes it to jam, we cannot discover (and I may say that subsequent minute investigation has not revealed the cause). It might be worse; but after one or two experiments I find that I can overcome the jam by fierce pressure on the plate, and we start again.

There follows a long period of inactivity. I rise two fish, but they will not come again. At last, when the sun is almost behind the hills, I hook another. He does not give much trouble, and I say cheerfully to Casimir that he is ours. At that moment the reel falls off the rod into the bottom of the boat – I suppose I had failed to press the ring home hard enough. Casimir buries his head in his hands and groans, '*Il ne manqua que ça.*' But the fish is well hooked, and I pull the line in through the rings before it can slacken. We net him, and that makes five.

The reel is replaced, and, to avoid any repetition of such an accident, lashed on with adhesive plaster. Soon another fish takes, only a nine-pounder, and is despatched without trouble. Six. But it is getting dark, and we are nearly at the bottom of the pool. The guides declare they have seen several good fish as we came down, so we pole up sixty yards or so and I put on a 2/0 Wilson. It is taken almost at once by what I know is the heaviest fish I have seen throughout the day. As heavy fish do, he swims quietly but determinedly straight upstream as soon as he is hooked.

Then he turns, and goes for the head of the rapid like a shot out of a gun. I stop him once, and get him back on to a fairly short line. But he means to go, and does go, and nothing I can do will stop him. So we follow. If the rapid looked ugly when we coasted up its edges, it seems a perfect Niagara now. If I had to go down it in cold blood I should be extremely frightened, but now, with the fish crashing from one rock to another, and the reel jamming periodically whenever we gain on him and I try to recover a little of the eighty yards of line he has out, I have no time for fear. I can only recollect occasional glimpses of jagged reefs rearing themselves up under our bows in the gathering gloom, and a feeling of intense admiration for the way in which the men avoided such obstacles, and, still more, for the skill with which they instantly held the boat in the midst of the torrent whenever the fish paused for a second.

I remember, too, wondering vaguely what hope there was of our coming safely through to the smooth water glimmering in the far

157

distance, when suddenly, as by some miracle, we found ourselves in a little oasis of comparative calm under the far bank. It was not more than five-and-twenty yards in length, and the fish was already at the tail of it, evidently prepared to continue his journey towards the sea. But I had had enough of this Scylla and Charybdis business, and at the back of my head was a recollection of having been told that no French Canadian guide can swim (this is quite true – I verified it later). So I held on to that fish as I have never held any fish before, and damned the consequences and blessed my big rod.

It was deepish water, and both men were kept busy holding the boat; but then one embraced a tree overhanging the bank, which left the other free to manipulate the net; and, after a few minutes of desperate pull-devil-pull-baker, I got the fish into it. He was 25 lbs, which is big for the Bonaventure, and the best I have killed there yet.

Twilight had now definitely descended on us. The men had poled and paddled me a number of miles, and Deep Water was a good many yards of rapid behind us. But when I asked them if they felt like going back and getting the eighth fish, they did not hesitate for a moment. They took me back, while I marvelled at our ever having come down the middle of the river right-side-up. At five minutes to nine, the limit was reached – a twenty-pounder, whose attempts to go down-stream I was resolved to fight at all costs, and did.

So that made eight fish, weighing 103 lbs. I see that in my diary I have noted that I lost five; but on further consideration I think that, in one way or another, I must have said goodbye to at least eight. Whatever the statistics, it was a notable day.

The days that followed, though less spectacular, were also highly productive, and in all Tommy caught twenty-five salmon, with an average weight of 12 lbs 2 oz. After a discussion of the merits of using light tackle, such as he favoured, he concluded his marathon despatch with a report of the expedition which Lord Bessborough had just made to Anticosti.

The Governor-General, who had never fished before, relates one remarkable experience that deserves to be recorded, though frankly I do not believe it. He claims that he was fishing a pool; that he felt nothing whatever; that his guide said, 'A fish touched you then'; that at the end of the cast they examined the fly and found that it had been completely stripped – presumably by a fish – of what H.E. describes as 'its fur and feathers' – in fact that there was nothing on his line but a practically stark-naked hook.

I have a generous nature, and a high conception of a Secretary's duty towards his Chief, but nothing can make me believe that a salmon can thus make a meal of the wings and hackles of a normal fly without either hooking himself or communicating his presence to the angler. The story reminds me of the young lady from USA hailing the ghillie on a leased Scotch river with, 'Say, shepherd, the fish has bit the bug off the end of my string.'

Turning to less agreeable topics: I have recently discovered that my son's knowledge of French and Latin, after five terms at a Canadian school, is less than it was when he left England two years ago, and that he has no chance whatever of passing the entrance exam for Eton next summer without intensive private tuition. I am therefore contemplating getting some adequate young man to spend the first six months of next year out here, to teach him and his young cousin, Victor Gordon Ives (whose mother[1] is also a member of our Staff). I have written to John's future house-master, Sheepshanks, and to Jasper Ridley, asking them to put me on the track of a suitable tutor; and if by any chance you know of one, I wish you would communicate with either of them.

He must be an all-round man, capable of teaching the requisite amount of all subjects, but Latin and French are the *Hauptsachen* [key matters]. Life in the Dominions is not made easy for those who have young. Really, the standard of education out here is quite unbelievably low.   Yours ever, A. Lascelles.

This appeal soon led, through Jasper Ridley, to the appointment of Edward Ford, a young man just down from New College, Oxford, where he had held a scholarship and read Greats. Ridley summoned him to Coutts' bank and explained that he had had a *cri de coeur* from Ottawa, where the two boys had scored atrociously low marks in a mock-exam. Ford's long-term plan was to read for the Bar, but he had already taken tutoring jobs to earn pocket-money during his vacations, and now in the short term was attracted by the idea of six months in Canada. Although friends advised him against it, he ignored them and went – and, as things turned out, the visit dictated the course of his life, for in 1945 Tommy, who by then was Private Secretary to King George VI, brought him into the Royal Household, where he became Assistant Private Secretary first to the King and then to Queen Elizabeth II.

---

[1] Gwladys, known as Sally, was a first cousin of Joan's, and lady-in-waiting to Lady Bessborough.

159

Arriving in Ottawa early in the winter, Ford found himself admirably accommodated and looked after. He lodged with the family in Rideau Cottage: they gave him a large room on the ground floor as a bedroom, and Tommy surrendered his own study to make a class-room. They also threw a small cocktail party so that he could meet local people.

Ford, who had never seen Tommy before, found him 'marvellously spare and good-looking', and enjoyed long talks about Oxford and literature. Writing home to his mother on 25 November 1933, he reported:

I'm extremely well placed here – they've given me a delightful bedroom with green walls, plenty of room, a desk and all; it used to be the dining-room. Mr Lascelles has turned out of his room for us to work in. So I'm in great comfort, and we have excellent food, done in a refined way.

My host is a delightful man, well read, full of information on most things, and has been an athlete, hunting and shooting with the best. He was at Oxford (after Marlborough) with that incomparably brilliant lot of 1907 or so – Ronald Knox, Patrick Shaw-Stewart, Charles Lister, the Charteris and Grenfell clans etc., and has a tremendous affection for Oxford and Sligger [Urquhart] etc. He looks extremely young, though he is about forty-seven, with strongly-defined and very aristocratic features.

The family here consists of John (aged twelve), an extraordinarily good-looking boy, very tall, and with the slight indolence that goes with a fast growth. My other pupil is Victor Gordon Ives, a witty youth, who has to be curbed, where John has to be coaxed.

Soon Ford came to see that Tommy had made himself extremely popular in Ottawa. He had won many friends and did a first-class job as an ambassador: always very quick and amusing, and good at meeting people, he was also expert at escaping from mêlées and extricating himself from conversations that bored him. He used to say that sometimes he went round at cocktail parties reciting 'Mary Had a Little Lamb' out loud, because even if people could hear (which usually they could not), they paid no attention at all to what others were saying.

Meals in Government House tended to be extremely formal. Before dinner the Governor-General, accompanied by Lady Bessborough and preceded by the ADC on duty, would ceremonially descend the staircase from the first floor. In the drawing-room the men would bow to him, and the ladies, who wore white gloves, would curtsey. Even so, the atmosphere in the household was agreeably relaxed, and Ford greatly enjoyed working for Tommy, whom he described as 'always a pleasure to talk to.'

To Letty Benson

2 January 1934   *Government House*
Ottawa

My dear Letty, Late in time behold them come, *pom-pom, pom-pom, pom-pom, pom*; but here they are all right, and I was never in any real anxiety about them. If Christmas comes, can Letty's handkerchiefs be far behind? is what I say to myself; and anyhow, they were comfortably in time for Twelfth Night.

My elder daughter took to her room with whooping cough about the 18th December, and has been there ever since; otherwise, the festive season went off well enough, though we had the thermometer down in the thirties – below zero – for several days at a time. That sort of weather is just ridiculous nonsense – a childish survival; like meeting an ichthyosaurus in the woods of Belvoir.

I am quite convinced, by the way, that there *is* something in Loch Ness, aren't you? A well-known zoological expert, who happens to be a Roman Catholic, tried to prove to me yesterday that it was zoologically impossible. 'You have the face to tell me that,' I said, 'when you yourself believe in the Immaculate Conception?' He had nothing more to say.   Yours, Tommy.

Joan Lascelles to Helen Maclagan

16 January 1934   *Rideau Cottage*
Ottawa

Darling Helen, This house is a seething mass of children, with John at home and Victor living here all day. The tutor, Edward Ford, having only just come down from Oxford, is also more or less of a child, though he is most intelligent and nice and appears to be teaching the boys very well. There are moments, however, when Tommy and I hanker after an evening alone. Still, no doubt in a few years' time we shall be feeling equally upset if the children are never in!

161

To John Gore

29 December 1933   *Rideau Cottage*
                                                       Ottawa

My dear John, I have had a troublesome time acting as midwife at
the re-birth of the Canadian Honours List – endless pow-wows with
our agreeable but unbusinesslike Prime Minister (who, like all
extremely busy and extremely idle men, is a slave to *mañana*),
numerous cypher telegrams and transatlantic telephone talks with
Clive Wigram, the latter a very exhausting form of communication,
as, it seems to me, atmospherics invariably interrupt the most crucial
sentences.

By the time you get this, the list will be in print, and it will seem a
very trumpery mouse for the mountain of trouble in which it has
involved me. But it was really a very tricky business, reviving this
particular imperial tie after fourteen years in cold storage; the feeling
on the whole business is surprisingly acute out here, and, even now,
it is not beyond the bounds of possibility that it might cost Bennett
his job, for he has, in thus quietly resuming the *status quo ante*,
completely flouted his House of Commons, and indeed, quite a
sizeable section of his own party.

The list itself, insignificant as it may seem, is a work of genius, and
Bennett has lavished immense pains on going out into the highways
and byways to collect obscure but eminently deserving guests for his
marriage-feast. By the way, you might make a paragraph out of the
vulgar error, not confined to Canada, of talking of the 'Titles'
question. Even *The Times* cabled to its correspondent John Stevenson
today to ask if there was any truth in the rumour (which escaped in
Fleet Street but which has been absent here) that 'titles' were to be
revived in Canada at the New Year. Half the cause of the silly action
taken in this country fourteen years ago was due to the fact that they
will think only of 'titles' and not of 'honours', which, of course, are
the only things that matter. Nobody dreams of reviving hereditary
titles here, and there are never likely to be any more Canadian
knights. The only people for whom it is worth reviving the thing at all
are the long-service civilians, the doctors, literary men and social
service workers etc. We don't talk of the 'Birthday Titles List', and to
speak exclusively of the 'Titles' question, as nearly all Canadians do,
is entirely misleading.

Bennett, I am glad to say, says roundly that so long as the recom-
mendations are in his hands, the list will contain no politicians and

no profiteers; he is very strong on the Fountain of Honour regaining its pristine purity. There will, of course, be a recrudescence of the stories that he himself is hankering for a Peerage; I don't believe a word of it. I know the man pretty well now, and, though I don't say he would refuse a Peerage if personally offered one by HM, I don't see him lifting a finger to bring it nearer by any action of his own.[1]

Our tutor, Edward Ford, is a very nice young man, and a good guest. He hammers away at the boys in stern pedagogic fashion, but is the best of companions with them out of school. They both adore him, and I think are progressing. But they have a lot of leeway to make up in Latin, and I am not too hopeful of John flooring the examiners in March, though I think that with any luck he should be all right for June. Assuming he passes, Joan will bring him over and enter him at Eton in September.[2] I should much like to come too, but it seems certain that if I set foot in UK at all, I become liable to a whole year's income tax, which I can't afford.

If you do hear of anybody who will pay me £600 a year for coming up to London three or four days a week from Sutton, remember that, like Mr Bennett, I shouldn't say no. September would be the time, for a boy going home to a public school is always considered an adequate excuse for deserting such a post as mine.

Today, we awoke to find the thermometer at forty-two degrees below zero – an all-time low record for Ottawa, thank you very much. We have had about ten days of zero weather now, and this last straw makes the camel's back pretty fragile. It is wonderful how warm one can keep the house, but outdoor life becomes impossible, and the intensely electric state of the atmosphere is very trying to the nerves. Moreover, in such ultra-cold weather, the hot-water pipes make loud, frightening noises all night. I was woken at 1 a.m. this morning thinking I was in a dug-out with shells thudding dully above my head, and this went on almost till day-break, when for some obscure hydraulic reason the barrage lifted.

Love to Jenny, Yours, A.L.

[1] In fact Bennett did become a peer, being created first Viscount Bennett in 1941.
[2] Ford's efforts were well rewarded. In due course both boys passed into Eton at a creditable level. Later, when he became tutor to the future King Farouk of Egypt, they were greatly amused, and referred to him as 'Fordus' or 'The Pasha'.

To John Gore

7 June 1934   *Rideau Cottage*
                                                         Ottawa

My dear John, Your cousin, Lady Hambleden, has taken Sutton for a couple of months from the end of August. It is so long since I have seen her that I hesitate to write to her direct, but perhaps you could let her know that Joan, with John, will be staying with the Nixons [his sister Maud and her husband Fergus] early in September, and that she would much like to come over one day and poke about the garden, to report progress and confer with our gardener.

I hope Lady Hambleden will be happy there. I had the water-supply put right at vast expense last year, and it should give no trouble – provided the water is there.[1] Our spring has never shown any sign of failing, but you seem to have had such a prolonged drought that I suppose anything might happen.

I led my Government House cricket team to victory yesterday in the return of our two matches; we lost the first by sixty runs, but were thirty-five the right side this time. I only made seven, when, in attempting a leg-glide, I presented the edge of the bat to the ball, which went straight into the air and fell into the hands of the wicket-keeper; but, of my seven, four were from a late cut to the boundary which would have brought tears to the eyes of Lionel Palairet.[2]   Yours, Tommy.

To John Gore

15 December 1934   *Government House*
                                                         Ottawa

My dear John, [A batch of letters from Guendolen Osborne, recently re-read] seemed to me so good that I made a second copy, which I think ought to be preserved for my grandchildren. Will you read them, not too fast, as a series of letters should be read – i.e., consecutively, as a series, and not skipping on to those which look

---

[1] The supply came from a spring in a field beyond the churchyard. In the old days it had been pumped by a windmill – no wind, no water – but Tommy had replaced the mill with an electric pump.
[2] The celebrated batsman (1870–1933).

interesting? And will you forget that they were written by G.G.O. to A.F.L., and give me your frank opinion of their *literary* merit, and their value as an intimate scrapbook of glimpses into a decade which, I believe, will be as absorbing to 2034 as the Waterloo period is to us in 1934?

They are, of course, light, and made deliberately light to bring a laugh to a friend on active service. But, though I knew Guendolen very well at one time, I have been amazed to find how much wit and wisdom she put into her letters, and how individual a style – often suggestive of the great Jane herself – she had got. I have had to omit hardly anything; considering how fond she was of personalities, it is astonishing that she should never have been malicious. Of course, there are many allusions to allusions in my letters of which I haven't the faintest recollection now, and cannot elucidate. That is inevitable, I think, in any unilateral correspondence, but on the whole there seem to me comparatively few obscurities of this kind. Practically all the letters begin 'Dear Tommy', and are signed 'Yours, Guendolen', and that was the whole basis of our friendship – there was never any suggestion of a romantic colour to it, and, looking back, I feel we were much more intimate on paper than we ever were in conversation.

You needn't hurry over this, but I want you to be one hundred per cent honest. Yours, T.

23 December 1934 A multitude of unimportances has delayed the sending of this; but it has now enabled me to read the typescript through and correct a few of my many errors, and put in an occasional note. I do think they are damned good; but they leave me saying rather sadly, after Dean Swift, 'what a genius (for friendship) I must have had,' to be sent such letters – and how little I seem to have done to develop it in the post-war period, and how little, indeed, at any time, to deserve them. But you, please, will read them *im*personally, with never a thought for the writer or writee, save as legendary figures in a legendary age. A Happy Xmas to you all. A.L.

To Letty Benson

29 December 1934 *Government House*
Ottawa

Very many thanks, O Faithful Friend of All the Noses, and may you long be spared to carry on your work of Nasal Relief, and may your

165

last moments be blessed by a vision of all the Noses, great and small (not running, but standing in an attitude of prayer round your bed) which you have comforted over so many years. The best thing about this, the 1934 vintage of handkerchiefs, is the thought that, if God spares you and me, and the laundry-maid spares them, I may actually be able to flourish one under *your* nose before Christmas 1935 comes round. *D.V.*, we shall all be home again in the latter part of October, and if the D. don't V., He will hear some pretty straight home truths from me.

When the time comes, I shall be very sorry to go, because there are many people and many things in this country which I am fond of; on the other hand, I should simply hate to stay. That is life, all over, isn't it? I've no doubt I shall feel exactly the same when my time comes to die, and I've no doubt I felt exactly the same when they came and told me I'd got to go and get born; but I can't remember that with any certainty.

It rather looks as if I shall have to come back to London till my beastly children have got educated. What the hell shall I do there? Fifteen years and about fifteen days ago, you came to tea and offered me a nice cushy job; will you please come to tea a year hence and do the same? A job for a muffin, so to speak. I spent many evenings in the early winter typing out copies of the beloved baroness's letters to me, and sent them to Rene[1] for a Christmas card. Make her show them to you some day. They are, alas, a very faint recollection of her jewelled charm, but those of us who knew her can hear in them the rattle of the 'Ear' Trumpet and the crash of the Teapot. On the Day of Judgement my job will be not listening to the Last Trump, but finding Constance's lost trumpet, so that she may hear all the lovely things which the archangels have got written in their books about her. Only by then, please God, she will hear far better than any of us; as, indeed, in many ways she always did.

Love to Guy, and a happy New Year. I have been trying to calculate whether or no you have a son at Eton now, but the imagination boggles at the arithmetic involved. However, if anything does take you to Eton, throw a smile to my son at Sheepshanks'. I probably shan't see him again till August.

Love to Guy, and a happy New Year to all of you.

Yours, Tommy.

---

[1] Irene Forbes-Adam, Lady Wenlock's daughter.

PS I really do feel excited at the thought of seeing David and Martin grown up.[1] They will only say (I have done it so often myself), 'Some old boy who knew my father,' but still, it will give me a great kick to see them. And, let me put it on record, I've only a very few grey hairs, and they hardly visible.

To Helen Maclagan

January 1935   *Rideau Cottage*
                                                                          Ottawa

My dear Whelk, Thank you for yours of the 11th. I think I owe you for at least one other letter, and for an attractive bird on a Christmas card. You must have had a bad journey to Harewood – I was afraid you would when I read Press telegrams about the dense fog in the south of England at that time.

John seems to have enjoyed himself there and in London. I am glad he grew more conversational towards the end of the holidays; he has a cautious nature, and always takes careful stock of his surroundings before expanding in them – perhaps a good characteristic. His passion for detective stories is certainly disquieting, but as you say he is probably doing too much with his mind in other directions to have much spare energy yet for more solid literature. So far I have seen no sign at all of a liking for poetry in any form, but that may come later.

On the whole, he looks like being more of a realist than an idealist. There again, I am not altogether sorry – I'm inclined to think that pre-war generations tended to a rather sloppy and ineffectual idealism, which we should have been better without. Re-reading *Rupert of Hentzau*[2] the other day brought this home to me. I used to think Rudolf R[assendyl] the beau ideal of all that is wise and noble, and longed to know what decision he would have arrived at had not his final walk in the garden been so unfortunately cut short; now, I fear, I think he was an egregious mug to go into the garden at all, and, along with Sapt, cannot conceive why, when Fate had thrown all the cards into his lap, he ever thought twice about not picking them up

[1] David Charteris (born in 1912) later succeeded to his family title as the twelfth Earl of Wemyss, and Martin Charteris (born in 1913), after a distinguished career as Private Secretary to Princess Margaret and Queen Elizabeth II, was created Baron Charteris of Amisfield in 1978, when he also became Provost of Eton College.
[2] The sequel to *The Prisoner of Zenda*, by Anthony Hope, published in 1898.

and playing the hand to the best of his ability – a course that would obviously have made everybody happy and done nobody any harm. As it was, by his high-faluting indecision, he condemned a charming lady to celibacy, and landed all his friends in the devil of a mess.

We have just got through the heaviest week of the year, the festivities attendant on the Opening of Parliament. The latter was complicated this year by the Speaker of the House of Commons going barmy a few days before the House met, and as the Deputy Speaker is suffering from locomotorataxy, and as the presence of one or other of these officers is constitutionally necessary, a situation unparalleled in the history of representative government arose suddenly out of a clear sky.

As the Speaker was only mad nor' nor' west, so to speak, and stoutly refused to resign in his sou' sou' east moods, it all got very difficult, and it was only at the eleventh hour that his resignation was secured, and a new Speaker hurriedly elected. Apart from that, all went well; the annual controversy as to whether the Apostolic Delegate sits above or below the Cardinal of Quebec at the State Dinner (a dispute in which for four years I have resolutely refused to show either interest or partisanship) was happily shelved for another year owing to the deaths of both the Cardinal's parents; and the Drawing Room was attended by over 1,000 people, which meant that I had to announce their names for two hours and two minutes by the clock.

Politically, the air is electric, Bennett having come out at the last minute with a quasi 'New Deal' programme, which has got all the electorate guessing and left his opponents feeling rather naked. Personally, I think he is entirely sincere in his proposals; if the voters think so too, he will probably be returned to power again by a large majority whenever the general election comes off. The new Governor-General, though he may escape the black fog of depression that has clouded our skies throughout the last four years, will certainly have a much livelier time politically than we have had.[1]

There is, as a matter of fact, practically nothing in Bennett's programme that has not been in force in England since the days of Edward VII, but it is none the less hailed as startlingly bold and even revolutionary on this side of the Atlantic; and the plutocracy of the New World protests against it with even louder and fiercer cries than

---

[1] Tommy was not good at political prediction. R. B. Bennett lost the election in a landslide, defeated by the Liberal W. L. Mackenzie King, who became Prime Minister for the third time.

we heard used by the aristocracy in the Old, five-and-twenty years ago. Some of my millionaire friends in Montreal have been sobbing on my shoulder; but the only consolation I give them is that they had much better take their medicine from a doctor they know than from one they don't; for take it they must – that is quite certain. The days of plutocrats are, I believe, numbered; and, having been through the Twilight of the True Gods myself, I am fiercely delighted to see their false images overthrown.

We had Julian Huxley staying here for a night last week – a delightful creature, whom I'd not seen since Oxford days.[1] I wish we could have kept him longer – he is exceedingly good company. I look forward to finding him in the Zoo, where he has just succeeded Chalmers Mitchell. He left us to complete a lengthy lecture-tour, and has now, I fear, landed in Vancouver in the middle of the only serious snow-storm that usually temperate coast has known in the memory of man.

Here we have just read that at a place not very far to the west of us the thermometer went down to seventy-eight degrees below zero last night (i.e., 110 degrees of frost), and, as the cold usually travels eastwards, we expect weather that will make the zero conditions of the last fortnight seem comparatively mild.

I am in the throes of promoting an All-Canadian Cancer Fund, to mark the King's Silver Jubilee: not the most cheerful subject, perhaps, to associate with bells and bonfires; but it is amazing how difficult it is, in this land of many provinces (there is no such place as Canada save on the map), of internecine politics and fierce religious and racial passions, to find any one cause that has what the newspapers are pleased to call a 'Dominion-wide appeal'. I really believe this is the only one that cuts through all such dividing lines, and as my medical friends tell me that cancer is a Damoclean sword in practically every Canadian household, it should open their purses; and heaven knows, the money could not be better spent. They have an amazingly efficient anti-tuberculosis organisation here, but so far nothing has been done about cancer, from which they die like flies.

I hope John went back to Eton today in serenity, but I fear you have given him too good a time for him to leave without reluctance. It was good of you to write such full bulletins of his holidays, which we both very much enjoyed reading. Love T.

---

[1] The distinguished zoologist and author, 1887–1975. He had just been appointed Secretary of the Zoological Society of London.

To Helen

18 April 1935　　　　　　　　　　　　　　　*Government House*
　　　　　　　　　　　　　　　　　　　　　　　Ottawa

My dear Whelk, You are not, I am sure, pleased at J. Buchan's appointment; but spare your criticisms – which are probably very sound ones – because various circumstances, I feel certain, make him quite a good choice *relatively* – i.e. in relation to Canada as it is today. And after all, he was Canada's choice, with no prompting from any other quarter.[1]　　　　　　　　　　　　　　　　Love, T.

To Helen

12 May 1935　　　　　　　　　　　　　　　　*Rideau Cottage*
　　　　　　　　　　　　　　　　　　　　　　　Ottawa

My dear Whelk, Many thanks for yours of 3 May and for giving such a glowing account of John. It is very good of you all to entertain him so royally, and I am afraid he will have an exaggerated standard of holiday amusement when he has to rely only on his family circle.

Tomorrow I take Lavinia and our dog Toby down to Montreal, for the purpose of putting the latter on board a boat for Southampton, where he is to start his six months' quarantine against our return.

J. Buchan certainly writes delightful and pithy letters – and grateful ones too, for I've taken a lot of trouble for him. But I don't feel any urge not to break my resolution not to do any more secretarying.　　　　　　　　　　　　　　　　Yours, T.

To John Buchan

27 May 1935　　　　　　　　　　　　　　　*Rideau Cottage*
　　　　　　　　　　　　　　　　　　　　　　　Ottawa

Private

My dear John Buchan, Here is the 'Apochrypha' I spoke of. I have some hesitation in sending it, because it is very frank – it would be

---

[1] John Buchan, author and politician (1875–1940), had just been appointed Governor-General, and, to mark the appointment, he was created first Baron Tweedsmuir. Tommy had known him slightly for some years, and there is a hint in the next letter that Buchan asked him to stay on as Private Secretary; but it is no longer clear whether the memorandum of advice printed below was solicited by Buchan, or whether Tommy volunteered it.

useless were it not – and I would much rather have said most of it than written it. But it looks as if we should have little time for conversation before you sail. I know you will treat it as confidential. I could not let my clerk handle it, so you must forgive its slovenliness; also its incoherence, due to the fact that I have had to dash it off at odd moments, during a period of weeks.

I have put down just what came into my head, imagining myself talking to someone who has never been in Canada at all. That, I realise, is not your position at all, and much of this stuff will probably be stale news to you. Indeed, I do not pretend that there is anything in it of much value to an Empire-traveller and biographer of Minto.[1]

I have not said much about the Governor-General's lady, but nearly all I say about the G.G. applies, *mutatis mutandis*, to Her Excellency also. If to her it all sounds rather depressing, tell her that I set out to tell the worst; and that if my picture tends to be gloomy, the practical truth is that both my wife and I have had a very happy time here, and are resolved to come back to Canada whenever we get a chance to pay a visit. Neither of us has any regret that we embarked on the Canadian adventure: in spite of inevitable tediums and worries, it has been a most successful one for us.

With this letter I will send copies of the replies made to Addresses by the present Governor-General on his arrival. As he landed at Halifax, he had no need to speak in French, as you must do if you land in Quebec. The King will doubtless impress on you that the Governor-General should always speak in English first and in French second – even in Quebec.

A holograph letter you wrote in French to Judge Pouliot has been photostatically reproduced in one of the Quebec newspapers, with delighted commentary on the purity of its style. This will make a most favourable impression throughout that province.

Yours ever, A.L.

CONFIDENTIAL

The outward and visible function of a Governor-General of Canada is, of course, to represent the King in Canada. But he also has an inward function, supremely important in these days – to represent the English to the Canadians.

It is unnecessary to dwell on the former. Provided due attention is paid to the proper discharge of the formal ceremonies inherent in

---

[1] Buchan's life of Lord Minto, Viceroy of India, had been published in 1924.

Viceroyalty, the exercise of it is comparatively plain sailing. The most difficult thing is to know when it ends – to know when the Viceroy should become the man.

The second function is more complex, and to perform it successfully is no easy matter. Any man of education and imagination who is used to public life can adequately play the King on ceremonial occasions, or in official relationships; to win the sympathy and affection of a very diverse, self-conscious and politically restless people is more difficult. Yet this second task is today the more important of the two. Canadians, as a whole, are so deeply loyal to the present King that their loyalty needs little stimulus – it is a hardy plant that requires only a minimum of tending. So, too, their affection for 'The Old Country' is very strong.

What is not strong, and needs constant reinforcement, is their affection for Englishmen, in general and particular. The danger here is obvious: if Canadians do not like Englishmen in the flesh, sooner or later the spiritual British affiliation is bound to be weakened. The Governor-General is always the typical Englishman of the moment. As I said above, he, his lady, his family, his staff, 'represent the English' to the Canadians. Consequently, the *personal* popularity of all of them is, in varying degrees of importance, a major determinant in the success or non-success of any Governor-General's regime, which is ultimately gauged by the simple question, 'Has he weakened or strengthened the ties between Canada and the Mother Country?' – for, when all is said and done, it is as the chief guardian of those ties that he is sent out.

English people who come to live in Canada for the first time often experience a series of shocks in the early stages of their stay that warp their whole outlook. They become bewildered, bored or contemptuous, according to their individual temperaments. Whatever the cause, the effect is to make them appear aloof. To the Canadian mind, obsessed as it is by the national 'inferiority complex', aloofness is indistinguishable from a sense of superiority: the Englishman or Englishwoman is written off as one more 'high-hatted Britisher', and one more little rift is made in the imperial lute.

The first thing any such new arrival should do is to rid himself both of preconceptions of Canada (e.g., the 'great open spaces' legend; more of one's life here is spent in stuffy trains and houses than it is in England) and of standards of comparison with his English past. He should get into his head that he is going to live not in an outpost of the British Isles, but in a totally different country, and, what is more, in a social environment and in a social period that are

172

totally different from those to which he is accustomed. In a recent play, 'Berkeley Square', the hero is magically transplanted into the days of the Regency. It is not much of an exaggeration to say that a denizen of the modern West End of London must look on his journey to Canada as a transplantation to a provincial community of mid-Victorian times.

This parallel is not of course meant to apply to material things – the standard of material comfort, heating, lighting, transport etc. is probably higher in Ottawa today than in London; but it does apply not unfairly to the social and intellectual atmosphere – yes, and to the political atmosphere too. Canadian politics are in many respects still in the Eatanswill period.[1]

The one fatal attitude of mind for the newcomer is, 'We order this matter better in England.' Canadians, with that sense of inferiority I mentioned above – a normal symptom of adolescent nationalism – are always on look-out for it. They are uncannily quick to perceive it, even when no spoken word has betrayed it; and so sensitive are they on this point that they will sometimes plague one to the point of exasperation with such provocative questions as, 'You must find this very dull after London?', or with some self-depreciatory gambit such as, 'We Canadians are still only poor Colonials, after all.' So, I suppose, the British-born Romans in the England of the third century AD were wont to plague the new arrivals from Rome.

I have always found that the best riposte to this form of attack is to say simply – and in my case quite truthfully – 'It never enters my head to make comparisons of that kind. Of course, the two countries are bound to be different in many ways, but none the less I am very happy here.' If the inmates of Government House can school themselves into never looking at their new surroundings through English spectacles, and into eschewing the habit of comparison, they will automatically lessen one of the greatest dangers to a Government House – namely, the temptation to poke fun at Canadians and things Canadian in the home circle. Such jibes are inevitably repeated outside, sooner or later, and nothing is more disastrous than that the idea should become current that the Governor-General, his family or his Staff are critical of, or bored with, Canada. They are ill-mannered, too, for whatever shortcomings Canadians may have, they are the most spontaneously friendly people in the world, and thoroughly sincere in wanting to do everything they can to make the life of all at Government House as happy as possible.

[1] Scene of the parliamentary elections in Dickens's *Pickwick Papers*.

It is interesting to try and see the Governor-General through Canadian eyes – to get some idea of what the average Canadian wants his Governor-General to be. But a difficulty arises at the outset, in that there is really no such thing as an average Canadian. The Quebecer, the Maritimer, the man from the Prairie Provinces and the British Columbian are very different creatures in many respects, each with a distinctive outlook and habit of mind.

Of the people of Quebec it may be said, broadly speaking, that all they want is a Governor-General who shows respect for tradition and a sympathetic interest in their French ancestry, the French tongue and the Church of Rome. Any Governor-General with a certain amount of personal charm, a conversational knowledge of French and a store of patience can win the province of Quebec without much trouble. British Columbia is quite satisfied if it gets an English gentleman and sportsman, while the ideal of the Prairie Provinces is 'a regular fellow with no frills' and some understanding of agriculture.

Incidentally, in making contacts with this diverse population, a different technique is necessary according to the locality. In addressing a Quebec or Nova Scotian audience, for example, a speaker can make historical illusions that would have no appeal in Winnipeg or Regina. Even in mere externals this holds good: top hats are normal enough in the East, but should be worn as sparingly as possible in the Prairies – in fact only at formal functions in the large towns. So, too, although in Toronto the Governor-General regularly drives up the race-course in a four-horsed barouche with a mounted escort, this Ascot touch would astonish the natives considerably at, say, the Calgary Stampede, and would only bring ridicule on the occupants of the carriage. But, as the Governor-General spends far the greater part of his time in Eastern Canada, and as over sixty per cent of the whole English-speaking population of the Dominion is concentrated in the Maritimes and Ontario, it is the attitude of the inhabitants of these provinces that really signifies.

In general, then, Canadians expect that the Governor-General should play his part with due dignity, and with all the outward trappings of dignity on all public occasions – especially on those occasions that have a constitutional significance. The standard of pomp and circumstance at the Opening of Parliament, for example, or Their Excellencies' Drawing Room, is now very high, and it would be a great pity if it fell off. Both these ceremonies are really very fine shows, and in their small way compare not unfavourably with their

original models in England. Though individual journalists occasionally sneer at them, I have no hesitation in saying that the
majority of Canadians set great store by their maintenance. The
great moment in the life of the Bandar-log was when they were able
to say, 'Now we are like Bagheera.'[1] It is a great moment in the life of
Ottawa – and I use the comparison in no spirit of unkindness – when
it can say, 'Now we are like London.'

Some little time ago I had a lengthy correspondence (with Buckingham Palace, the Dominions Office etc), extant in the Secretary's
office, on the wrong-headedness of making the Governor-General of
Canada, should he pay an official visit to Washington, masquerade
as a private citizen the moment he crosses the frontier, simply
because the King, technically, has already got another representative in the USA – a technicality that is quite incomprehensible to the
average Canadian citizen. In that correspondence – which, I am
glad to say, had a happy ending – I emphasised that, to the
Canadians, the Governor-General is *their* Governor-General, the
personal representative of *their* Sovereign, the embodiment of
the imperial tie, their First Citizen, the Bull of their Herd – just as his
wife is the First Lady of the Land (a title habitually given her by
Canadian journalists).

It is this conception of the Governor-General's office that makes
them, on fitting occasions, delight in producing for him mounted
escorts, guards of honour or artillery salutes, and in handing
him formal Addresses of an Elizabethan pomposity. In return,
they expect him to receive such incense gracefully, and his Staff
to ensure that 'a good show' is put on. They delight no less in hearing their Governor-General's voice. They regard him, in fact,
as a valued public institution, the incarnation of their own
loyalty to the Throne, and of their sturdy and eminently healthy
Nationalism.

So much for the Canadian conception of the Governor-General as
an Officer of the Crown. What is even more important, as I have
already suggested, is their opinion of him as a man.

It seems to me that the two main things in a Governor-General
that appeal to individual Canadians are, first, that he should be able
to doff his Viceroyalty, so to speak, as he doffs his top hat – that off
parade they should find him approachable, human and sympathetic
– the three adjectives they continually apply to popular Governors-

---

[1] The Bandar-log were the monkeys, and Bagheera the black panther, friend of
Mowgli, in Kipling's *Jungle Book*.

General of the past such as Grey or Byng[1]; and second, that he should show himself interested in Canada, and happy to be in Canada.

There is no need to elaborate these two points at length, but here is a random example of the working of the first. Take an ordinary Government House dinner-party of about thirty people; at certain moments, set formalities have to be observed – the announcing of Their Excellencies, the presentation of their guests, the drinking of the King's health, the curtseys of the ladies as they leave the dining-room, the 'bringing-up' of different guests by the ADCs after dinner. All this is the regular routine of Government House, and must be carried out formally: but outside of this routine – no item in which takes more than a few minutes – the general atmosphere of the evening ought to be that of an ordinary dinner-party in London.

Without in any way diminishing the outward respect due to the King's representative, Government House ought never to be 'stiff'. The great success of the Devonshire regime was largely due to the pleasant family atmosphere they created in Rideau Hall.[2] Achieving it, of course, depends largely on the personalities of the individual occupants of the place – not only of Their Excellencies, but also of their Staff; but it can be encouraged artificially in various ways – for example, by going in regularly for a certain amount of minor informal entertaining – e.g. making a habit of getting a few people up to play lawn-tennis in the summer, or to skate or play covered tennis in the winter; by the Governor-General, if he is a golfer, playing golf with various members of the clubs he may frequent; by his occasionally lunching informally at the Rideau Club in Ottawa. Lord Byng used to make a point of fraternising with the younger men of Ottawa – getting them to small stag dinners (at which he would always wear a dinner-jacket and black tie), taking them for walks, and so on. In their middle age they still talk with reverence and affection of the impression his friendship made on them.

Lord Bessborough, via his interest in Community Drama, has not only got in touch with many Canadians who would otherwise never have seen the inside of Rideau Hall or even the outside of their Governor-General, but, as a result of the Dominion Drama Festival he instituted in Ottawa, has annually brought together people from all parts of the Dominion who hitherto had hardly exchanged greetings with any fellow-Canadians outside their own Provinces.

[1] The fourth Earl Grey was Governor-General 1904–11, and the first Viscount Byng 1921–26.
[2] The ninth Duke of Devonshire was Governor-General 1916–1921.

Such forcible mixing of the disparate elements in Canada is a function that practically nobody but the Governor-General can perform; it is extremely valuable, and is capable of infinite extension. Week-end parties at Government House, for example, offer great opportunities in this direction. They should not consist only of the monied magnates of Montreal or Toronto – charming people, in the main, but all resembling each other like a pack of beagles, and all representing one rigid point of view; a leaven of university dons, musicians, newspaper-proprietors, writers, clergy, social workers and so on should be introduced.

It is remarkable what iron barriers there are between the different social tribes in Canada, and they badly need breaching. But, it must be confessed, it is sadly uphill work trying to make such breaches in the dividing wall between French- and English-speaking Canada. The educated class in the Province of Quebec is limited; and within that class the number willing, or able, to mix is lamentably small, though there are a few shining exceptions. Yet, whether the mixing process be fruitful or not, anybody with any experience of Government House will agree that it must be pursued at all costs. It is fatal if Government House gets the reputation of seeking its guests only in one social, or professional, stratum. Its doors must be opened to all sorts and conditions of men.

So far, I have been trying to give some idea of how Government House should appear to Canadians. What would be no less instructive, if I could do it adequately, would be an indication of how Canada actually appears to a newly-arrived Governor-General. Fore-warned is fore-armoured; and, for English people to step into Canadian life with any degree of contentment, they ought to be fore-warned, that they may be armour-plated against the shocks that undoubtedly await them.

I must preface any such attempt by saying that, personally, I am now very fond of Canadians, and that any candour I may show in criticising them is the candour of a friend, and of one who has made many friends among them; also, that I exclude the travelled, cultured minority whom one habitually meets in London, and refer to the great mass of *echt*-Canadians, who have probably never crossed the Atlantic.

The national faults, common to all parts of the country, are, I should say, a naive parochialism; lack of general education; paucity of imagination (with its correlative, a rudimentary sense of humour), unbusinesslikeness, and – if this be a fault – the inferiority complex alluded to above, which makes them sometimes tediously, sometimes disarmingly, conscious of their failings. A few years ago, a certain smug complacency might have been added to the list; but the successive shocks of the Depression have largely corrected this.

Their outstanding virtues are their cheerfulness and their friendliness. They are a stout-hearted and a warm-hearted people; and, in criticising them, it must not be forgotten that they are essentially a *young* people, with little national and practically no family background. They have indeed the defects and qualities of Youth.

These qualities are obvious and soon discovered. I will try to analyse some of the failings I have ascribed to them. Their parochialism is abysmal. One is continually amazed at the lack of knowledge one Province has of the others, or the lack of interest shown by individuals, not only in the affairs of the outer world, but even in Canadian matters removed from their own parish pump. This is specially noticeable in the average member of Parliament; it is indeed hardly an exaggeration to say that in the present Cabinet only two men – Bennett and Perley[1] – could fairly be described as Pan-Canadians.

So, too, in the Press. There is no national newspaper, and will not be one for many years. But it is deplorable how little extra-provincial news appears even in the *soi-disant* great newspapers of Canada: if one has not time to skim six or seven provincial newspapers, it is a frequent experience to find in the ten-day-old London *Times* some quite important piece of Canadian news that has not been mentioned in, say, the Ottawa *Citizen*, the Montreal *Gazette* or the Toronto *Globe*. The foreign news service in all Canadian newspapers, with the possible exception of the Winnipeg *Free Press* and the Montreal *Star*, is puerile.

This parochialism colours the politics and the entire national life of the country. It also has a very narrowing effect on the conversational range of the individual. It cannot be gainsaid that, until one has learnt to take an interest in parochial matters, the conversation of neighbours at luncheon or dinner is apt to be boring or even to die a lingering death. That is what I meant by saying that English – or at any rate, London – standards must be discarded: one has got to learn to talk about simple, everyday things – as a general rule, be it understood, for there are many Canadians of both sexes who would be admirable company anywhere, though they take some finding.

[1] Sir George Halsey Perley, 1857–1938, was Minister without Portfolio in the Bennett administration, and often stood in for the Prime Minister.

But the average level of table-talk is certainly far lower than in England, particularly the talk of the ladies of Canada. The latter is essentially of the *Cranford* type, and often has the flavour (though rarely the charm) of the innocent prattling of Miss Matty or Miss Pole.[1] The question put to Lady Glenmire, on her first appearance in *Cranford* – 'Has your ladyship been to Court lately?' – might be an echo of many Canadian tea-fights. At the latter, however, it would be put not once but many times, for Canadian tea-fights are of gargantuan dimensions, and the new arrival must reconcile himself, or herself, to being asked the same conundrum by everybody in turn.

The wife of a new Governor-General will be asked, 'How do you like our Canadian winter?', followed instantly by the second barrel, 'How does His Excellency like our Canadian winter?', not fewer than five thousand times in the first few months of her residence. There is nothing to be done about it: it is a conventional conversational opening as unavoidable as the flowery platitudes of a polite Chinaman.

What is more depressing than these social trivialities is the second in my list of shortcomings – the almost universally low standard of education. There are few men in Canada, and hardly any women, to whom one can talk the ordinary language of 'cultured' England. They are essentially a literal-minded and un-literary-minded race. The most obvious figure of speech is apt to be taken *au pied de la lettre*, the most commonplace literary allusion is often not understood. People who are well-read, in the accepted English sense of the term, are so few and far between that a chance association with them stands out like a landmark. To a man, it comes as a shock to find that even legal luminaries can only rarely understand a simple Latin quotation, while to the ordinary citizen the Classics are esoteric mysteries.

One is often astonished, too, by evidences of complete ignorance of modern public affairs shown by men of undoubted mental ability; but such astonishment ceases to be felt by anybody who has sent his son to a Canadian school, and thus had practical experience of the childishly low standard of teaching throughout the country. Yet even here, beware of casting the first stone: the writer, after a long and expensive education, arrived in Canada for the first time, eleven years ago, firmly convinced that Newfoundland was part of the Dominion; and it is on record that Alfred Lyttelton, when Colonial

[1] Characters in Mrs Gaskell's novel, published in 1853.

Secretary, travelled down the Red Sea expecting to get his first glimpse of Aden on the starboard, or African, bow.[1]

To accuse the Canadians of being unbusinesslike might at first sight seem paradoxical: they are popularly supposed to have acquired that high standard of business acumen traditionally imputed to their southern neighbours. My own belief is that this transatlantic businesslikeness is a complete myth. I regard both Americans and Canadians as poor organisers, feckless planners and slovenly correspondents. Their reputation for being such super men of business is due far more to the bounty of Nature than to the wit of American man. The cold blasts of Depression have shown this reputation to be a very tender plant – witness the general state of affairs in the USA, and the appalling mess into which the Canadians have got their two great railways.

The haphazard manner in which Governmental and Parliamentary business is often conducted is startling to those educated in Whitehall or Westminster. There is a tendency to leave everything to the last moment, and then to attempt to evolve belated order out of chronic chaos by telephone or telegram. It is only fair to add, however, that in the past few years this tendency has been increased by the Prime Minister's inveterate habit of making himself the bottle-neck through which alone action can issue. In a less highly concentrated administration, both the Civil Service and the governmental machine generally would have a far better chance of running smoothly and efficiently. Moreover, it may well be that the very rapidity of the country's expansion during the past few generations, and the ease with which national and individual prosperity was achieved, are responsible for this happy-go-lucky neglect of mere details.

Canada has only recently been obliged to bother about ways and means; now that adversity has compelled her to study them more closely, a different habit of mind will very likely be acquired by the people at large before long. They certainly can organise if they try – the Royal Military College, the Mounted Police, the Winter Fair at Toronto – each of these widely-diverse national institutions is a model of efficient planning and administration.

Tommy concluded his memorandum with advice on the climate, particularly on how to deal with the winter. A few excerpts are given here.

---

[1] The Rt. Hon. Alfred Lyttelton (1857–1913), whom Tommy had known and greatly admired, was Secretary of State for the Colonies 1903–05.

In fine winter weather, skating or skiing, for those who like it, can be indulged in pleasantly enough out of doors. Lord Willingdon used to do a lot of snow-shoeing – an almost obsolete form of exercise. Otherwise, exercise must be taken indoors – on the Minto skating rink; on the covered tennis court at Government House, in one or other of the various curling clubs, or by playing squash or Badminton.

The winter, I have found, has a definite physical effect on those of riper years. The atmosphere becomes exasperatingly electric – everything and every person one touches gives one an electric shock. This is undoubtedly a trial to the nerves, which become increasingly taut as the winter months go on. Then, the afternoon exercise, whatever form it may take, produces a comatose condition, comparable to the effects of a drug, as soon as one gets back into the hot, steam-heated houses. The best method of treating this is that adopted by Badger in *The Wind in the Willows* – to seek seclusion for half an hour and have a brief nap after tea.

Towards the end of each winter a tendency to mild melancholia is apt to manifest itself. One wakes up feeling vaguely but unpleasantly depressed. This is due to the climatic vagaries I have mentioned, and to the hot houses. It is purely seasonal, and no notice should be taken of it.

As to clothes – I have had no special clothes whatever, except the Astrakhan wedge-hat worn by members of the Staff in winter in lieu of a top hat. Otherwise, I have got along very well on an ordinary English wardrobe. I have a fur coat, but only rarely wear it on formal occasions in an extra-cold spell. Ordinarily I wear a good, thick London overcoat when appearing in public, and, for everyday life, a solid coat of the British Warm type. I have never felt as cold as one does in a February north-easter in London. I wear thinner underclothes than I do in an English winter.

The great secret is always to get your outdoor clothes on – your overcoat, your scarf, gloves, snow-boots etc – before you show your nose outside the front door. Never leave a house, or a train, for a moment in winter without this precaution. You are probably leaving a temperature of seventy-five degrees above zero for one of twenty below. A change of ninety-five degrees in a few seconds cannot be trifled with.

One rarely, alas, has the opportunity in Government House life of wearing rough clothes. Country life, as we understand it, does not really exist in Canada. Sartorial conditions, therefore, are always those, if not of London, then of a weekend from London in somebody else's house. It is only on occasions of rare blessedness – in a fishing camp, for instance – that one gets a chance of wearing rough clothes.

For the long train journeys in the summer, on those days when there are no official duties I have found a coat and trousers of the Indian khaki drill known as 'Solario' most useful, as it is cool and can be washed. But a light grey flannel suit is just as good.

To amplify what I said about country life, it really comes to this: in Canada there is only the town, the villa and the Bush. In the Bush category I include the fishing or lakeside 'camps' of the well-to-do. These are often luxurious enough, but they are essentially temporary, and holiday, homes; and, in these days, the opportunities that a Governor-General or the senior members of his Staff have of getting away to them are all too rare. The golden age when Lord Lansdowne[1] could retire each summer to the Grand Cascapedia river for six or seven weeks of the best salmon fishing in the world is gone for ever.

None the less, the Governor-General, if he makes up his mind to it, can get away into the wilderness now and then, and it is an excellent thing that he should make such expeditions occasionally: any such tendency would be far from unpopular with Canadians generally.

To John Gore

20 June 1935   *Government House*
                                                                         Ottawa

You, Johnny, having been your own master all your life, and never a slave in a one-man office, cannot appreciate what I am going through this afternoon. It is 3.15 p.m. on 20 June; at 8.40 a.m. on 21 June I am scheduled ('ch' hard, as in school, on this continent) to leave Ottawa for Montreal. Thence, after spending the afternoon with the Melville Balfours, I take the Ocean Limited 9 p.m. to Montapedia; and, after a hurried luncheon, should be on my first pool in the Bonaventure River by 3 p.m. on 22 June, whence only horses so wild as to be practically negligible will drag me before noon that day sen'night. As my fly touches the water, my hand shaking so that the guides watch the top of my rod in wonder (these are annual symptoms which, I find, only increase with age) – at that moment,

[1] The fifth Marquess of Lansdowne (1845–1927) was Governor-General of Canada 1883–88.

now just forty-eight hours away, four months' agony will come to an end.

Somewhere about the middle of February, the river-fever began to stir my blood; with the snow still deep on the ground, I would sneak furtively to my fishing-tackle cupboard in the basement, and there, before going to bed, would stroke salmon-flies or give a few turns to a reel, till the cook, in *déshabille*, came out from her chamber to see why the light was burning.

Then, as time went on, clouds no bigger than a man's hand would float up into the clear sky of anticipation. The Raven, who never leaves us, knowing well that it is long odds against my ever seeing the Bonaventure again after 1935, lost no chance of croaking 'Nevermore' as each one crossed the horizon.

First, would there be an invitation? Surely that could not fail. And then came the news that my good host was faced with a major operation, which would, at best, incapacitate him as a fisherman all this summer. The Raven was jubilant; but he crowed untimely. Twenty-four hours before the operation, this good man rang me up from Montreal and told me what was in store for him. Then he went on, 'I have been going through all my affairs today' – he has very many – 'and putting them in order. I thought of you and the Bonaventure, and I have told the other members that I want you to go as usual. They all said they would be delighted.'

I heard afterwards that all his symptoms pointed to cancer of the stomach, and that before the operation he was convinced, with good reason, that he would not come through it alive. Don't you think that was the act of a great gentleman? If life be a boon, he has been repaid. For when they cut him open, though a tumour was there, sure enough, it was not malignant; and despite his nearly having caught pneumonia after the operation, he is now convalescent, and they tell me there is no reason why he should not have many more seasons' fishing.

Other clouds – many, no doubt, only the vapour of my fevered imagination – blew up thick and fast: our last summer – so many farewell tours; the looming general election; the precariousness of Bennett's health – would it precipitate a political crisis? Might not a royal visitor suddenly descend on us? My one assistant is over sixty and has but one kidney; what a slender thread is one kidney on which a man should hang his hopes! Then, with all the plans carefully mosaiced round the blank oasis of the coming week, the Governor-General's bronchial tubes gave out. He had to be put to bed, where he still is; plans for the summer had to be remodelled.

That was an ugly cloud. But it burst harmlessly; the Governor-General is even now only convalescent, and my absence or presence during the coming week can only be of the smallest import to affairs of State. Throughout, I have clung, as to a life-buoy, to the brave philosophy of Lady Nunburnholme: 'Whatever happens, the pheasants must be shot.'

Yet, even as I wrote those words, the orderly came in with a telegram, and (I give you my promise) my heart beat so I could scarcely read it. It must inevitably be in code, and its import could not be less than the death of King George or a declaration of war by Mr. Laval.[1]

But no: it is in clear. It is very short. It is only from Vice-Admiral the Hon. Sir Matthew Best, Commander-in-Chief of the America and West Indies Station, agreeing to my proposal that he should exchange courtesies with the Governor-General in Quebec on 2 August. Yet it was some minutes before my hand was steady enough to go on with this letter.

The Raven had his nearest approach to a triumph at the beginning of this week. On Saturday my daughter Caroline was sick as any dog, not once but again and again. On Sunday morning she had a temperature, on Sunday night she had a rash. (The Raven crowed like Peter's cock when he heard that dread word.) The doctor said it was German measles. 'German measles?' said I in a cracked, nervous falsetto. 'German measles! That's nothing to worry about, is it? You won't have to put me in quarantine, will you? Ha ha!' The doctor said, No, there was no reason why I should not go on with my daily business; but I had better avoid the company of children.

'Suffer little children to go right away from me,' said I, in that access of jovial blasphemy which is a symptom of nervous reaction from a really serious fright. The doctor was a little shocked, but the Raven crept back into his cage.

He came out with a rush and a cackle on Tuesday, though. Caroline's temperature went up suddenly to 104, and the rash spread like a flame. We called in George Campbell, who is one of the best children's specialists on this or any continent. He and the other doctor retired into the sickroom. When they came out, he said, 'Well, there is no doubt about it now: it's scarlet fever.'

I am a child in these matters. I never doubted but that word spelled doom and heavy quarantine. 'You can roll up the map of the

---

[1] Pierre Laval (1883–1945) was then Prime Minister of France.

Bonaventure,' I said bitterly to the Raven. 'It will not be needed for many a year.'

But I am a father first and a fisherman (I hope) second, and my very first questions were about my daughter's health. Only at the end of several minutes' talk did I nerve myself to ask casually (*num*, expecting the answer no), 'By the way, I was going away fishing on Friday. I suppose I can't do that now?' To my amazement they smiled and said in unison, 'Oh, there's no reason at all why you shouldn't go,' and one added, 'I'll just give you the Dick test to make sure.' The Dick test (long life to Dr. Dick, whoever he may be) is an immunisation test: they vaccinate you, and if, twenty-four hours later, your arm is not inflamed, you are immune from scarlet fever and cannot give it to others. They say it has never been known to fail. So the Dick test was applied to me, and the following day, my flesh was like that of Naaman when he emerged from Jordan, and so was Lavinia's (Joan was away in USA all through this crisis, and only got back last night).

So I am immune and free to travel. And now it's nearly five o'clock, and my afternoon mail has come, and there is nothing in it a man would hang in his WC, and my telephone has been as quiet as a sleeping child. So I shall just go to tell His Excellency he can kiss my -rse, and then, Johnny, I shall go home and PACK, taking care to leave the cast-box in my overnight grip, so that when I wake on Saturday morning, I can soak the two casts which will go, the one into action, the other into reserve, on Saturday afternoon. Yours, AL.

Even after such feverish anticipation, Tommy was not disappointed. In six days he caught twenty-four salmon, including one of thirty-four pounds – a record for him. As usual, he described the expedition at length in a letter to Maurice Headlam, but this time concentrated on the best day of all, 26 June.

To Maurice Headlam

11 August 1935   *Rideau Cottage*
                                                         Ottawa

My dear Maurice, Having contracted the habit of disgusting you with stories of Canadian fishing, I had better keep it up . . . [On the evening of 26 June] I started in at the top of the Rock Pool, and my good Samaritan [who had given over the water to him] was scarcely

185

out of sight before I rose what I knew was a notable fish. I gave him the requisite three minutes, and the second time he took it (a 3/0 Snipe Wing) faultlessly. He was a dignified and determined fish, who played as would an Archbishop hooked through the nose, but he condescended no vulgar violence and died decorously after not more than twenty minutes. When we got him in, the net brake, according to sound biblical precedent, and when we put him on the scales he revealed himself as 34 lbs – 4 lbs more than my previous best and, for the Bonaventure, an exceptionally heavy fish.

He had taken me all the length of the pool, but I went back to where I had hooked him and ten minutes later had hold of another fish. He led off by swimming steadily up-stream for several minutes, tactics which I have always been told denote a heavy fish; and having got to the top of Rock, he turned about, and for the next hour made slowly but resolutely for the sea, never showing so much as a fin, and paying not the slightest attention to any remonstrance on my part, though I had a heavy 15½-foot rod and stiff reel. He didn't hurry, and he didn't run: he merely towed the canoe majestically down-stream as if it, and I, had not been there.

He never paused in Rock, and went down the long but not dangerous rapid at its foot without a pause. In Malin, the long, quiet pool below, he rested at stated periods, without any sign of emotion or change of purpose; and eventually, in the gathering dusk, we found ourselves at the head of the Malin rapid. Now the Malin rapid is a formidable one, fierce and long, abounding in miniature Gibraltars, with their attendant Scyllas and Charybdises: a nasty rapid at all times, and no place to follow a fish with comfort in the twilight. Moreover, it is divided, half-way down, by Muskrat Island, on the eastern side of which the river is particularly violent.

I set my face against the passage of the Malin Rapid, and told myself that a triple-gut cast with a length of Japanese gut attached to a 3/0 fly were surely sufficient guarantees that I could have my own way. But my rod and tackle might have been built for dry-fly work on the Test, for all the good they did me: the fish simply brushed me aside, and when I stipulated that we should at least make our descent by the western channel, he steered remorselessly for the east.

He made the journey down the rapid – which is really quite a tricky one at any time – considerably more hazardous by suddenly turning in to rest behind some particularly large rock in mid-stream just when the canoe was crashing after him at about thirty miles per hour. He did this three times, and each time the guides had to throw aside their paddles, whip out their poles, and bring her to in a raging torrent, till he was ready to move on; even so, we got perilously far below him on each occasion.

However, at long last we came safely, and connectedly, into the still, deep reach that separates the rapid from Elbow, the next pool down. We had then had this fish on over an hour, had never had a glimpse of him, and the moon was up; yet it was not until then, after travelling three-quarters of a mile down-stream, that he started to run about. The guides stared into the gloom almost in awe. 'He is bigger than the other,' said Casimir, who is as cautious as a Scot. 'He is seexty-five pounds,' said Georges, who is both emotional and cocksure.

But he wasn't sixty-five pounds, and he wasn't even bigger than the other; when he had finished himself in the eddies at the edge of the slack water, he proved to be just twenty-seven and no more; but he had a jaw on him like Mussolini, and was much the same build – I have never seen a thicker fish.

Pundits say that, on normal salmon-tackle, no salmon ever born ought to take one more than fifteen minutes to land. I certainly think that if one habitually spent an hour and a quarter getting out a 27 lb fish, it would argue that there was something seriously wrong with one's methods; but in this particular case I can only say that I was, after the first ten minutes, very anxious to get home to dinner, equally anxious not to shoot any rapids, and a good deal harder on the fish than I usually am. Yet, for some reason which I cannot explain, he was completely my master.

We sail for home on 28 September. I shall be very sorry to leave Canada, very glad to get home, and still gladder to have done with Government House. Four and a half years is too long to be at this job at my time of life. I shall retire to Sutton Waldron and live on my capital till I can discover some way of increasing my income.

Yours, A. Lascelles.

In all, Tommy's four weeks on the river brought him a hundred fish, weighing 1,405 lbs. His average daily catch was five, and when he came to summarise his experiences on the Bonaventure he wrote, 'I doubt if any river in the world could offer a stray guest such wonderful and consistent sport.'

He did as he had promised: reaching England in October, he took the family to live in Dorset, but he had only a few weeks there before the Secretary bug once more claimed him. If he had any doubts about whether his time in Canada had been worthwhile, they must have been dispelled by this letter from the new Governor-General, who had heard of his impending return to Royal Service.

From John Buchan

6 December 1935   *Government House*
      Ottawa

My Dear Tommy, First let me congratulate you – or rather the Palace – on your appointment. I was always certain that if you could bring yourself to go there, you would be of incalculable value. In these days, when the Monarchy has such real power, a man like you, with your experience and abilities, is more needed than ever. I hope you will be happy; I am quite certain you will be successful.

You have left a mighty reputation here, and you are quoted as Roman lawyers quoted Justinian. Your 'Bible'[1] makes our official path smooth. I need not tell you how grateful I shall be if you can ever find time to send me a line. Any criticism of my doings will be especially welcome.

We all send our kindest regards and best Christmas wishes to you and yours.   Yours ever, John.

---

[1] Tommy had compiled a Green Book, which gave full details of protocol at Government House and on all formal occasions outside it.

RETURN TO THE FOLD

No sooner had he returned to England than Tommy found himself approached by Clive Wigram (who had recently been created a baron) and asked to re-join the royal staff. A vacancy had been created by the death, on 20 October, of Sir Frederick Ponsonby, first Lord Sysonby, who had been Treasurer to the King since 1920, and altogether had served the royal family for more than forty years. Wigram's suggestion was not that Tommy should replace Ponsonby directly, but that he should come in as Assistant Private Secretary to the King.

At first he refused, feeling on the one hand that he had been a secretary long enough, and on the other that he would be in a peculiar position if George V were to die, and he found himself once again working for the man from whom he had parted company, in such difficult circumstances, six years earlier. Wigram, however, assured him that the old King was in splendid health, and had several more years ahead of him. Tommy – without any other job in prospect, and clearly flattered by the warmth of the invitations emanating from the royal Household – gave in, and agreed to go back.[1]

On 11 November, in a note which he addressed to Helen from Sutton and marked 'Private', he confided:

Wigram has definitely asked me to go to Buckingham Palace, at a reasonable wage, but to work with him for the present. What HM means to do to fill Fritz Ponsonby's place *eventually*, I do not know, but I never thought they would offer it to me immediately. I have promised to give him a final reply this week, and I think it is going to be an affirmative. They are good enough to say they want me badly, and it means much, I think, to work with men one likes, at a job where one's presence is welcome. Moreover, it is no use going about

[1] Wigram deliberately concealed the extent of the King's debility, which he must have known.

the world singing 'God Save the King' if one isn't prepared to assist the Deity when called upon.

Later that day he wrote accepting the offer. On 13 November Wigram sent him an enthusiastic telegram from Buckingham Palace ('the King and Queen are delighted and you will receive a warm welcome'), and followed up the wire with a letter:

Lord Wigram to A.L.

13 November 1935   *Buckingham Palace*
Private

My dear Tommy, Thankyou so much for your letter of the 11th inst., which I was so glad to receive last night on my return from some days' shooting. I at once telephoned the good news to Sandringham, and I need hardly say how pleased the King and Queen are that you can join the Household Staff. I do not think that there will be any difficulty about your having a good holiday until the middle of January. When you are next in London, you might let me know and come and have a talk with me. In the meantime, I have asked Cromer [the Lord Chamberlain] to have you gazetted, as the appointments in the reorganised Household will probably appear in the next Gazette.

You will come in as Assistant Private Secretary to The King, and I understand that your consolidated pay will be £1,500 a year. If we can get a house for you, so much the better, but I cannot commit myself about this at present.

With all good wishes, and I am much looking forward to having you as a colleague.   Yours ever, Wigram.

Lord Cromer to A.L.

13 November 1935   *Office of the Lord Chamberlain*
                                                           St. James's Palace

Dear Tommy, Welcome to the King's household, where I know you will find the work interesting, and your experience will be of great service. I am sending the submissions for all the new appointments in the Household to the King at Sandringham today, so that, when approved, they may be published in the Gazette on Friday, 15 November, and appear in the papers next Saturday morning.

I am so very pleased you have decided to take this post.

                                                           Yours very sincerely, Cromer.

Alec Hardinge[1] to A.L.

14 November 1935   *Sandringham*

My dear Tommy, Just a line to say how very delighted I am that you will shortly become a colleague. I hope that the life will suit you – and I feel confident that it can be so arranged that you will have plenty of liberty – by which you, like me, set great store!

The King and Queen were extremely pleased when I went and told them, and I can assure you that everyone is delighted at the prospect of your coming.   Yours ever, Alec Hardinge.

Lord Cromer to A.L.

15 November 1935   *Office of the Lord Chamberlain*
St. James's Palace

My dear Tommy, This is just a line to let you know definitely that the King has approved the various Appointments to be made in the Royal Household, in consequence of Fritz Ponsonby's death, your own included, and these will be published in the Press tomorrow, Saturday.

As to the Uniform question, [Austin] Hertslet [the Chief Clerk] can give you the details, and I should imagine that the civil uniform you have been wearing in Canada can be adapted by changing the collar and cuffs to the red facings worn in the Household. If you have a Levée Dress Coat, I, personally, do not think you really need trouble about getting a Full Dress Coat, as you will hardly ever require this, and Assistant Private Secretaries do not, as a rule, get summoned for ceremonial duties such as Courts and Levées.

You probably already have white Knee Breeches, in case you require them for a Court or State Ball, but it would be as well for me to have a talk with you before giving any orders to your tailor.

Yours very sincerely, Cromer.

So Tommy returned to royal service; but, before he had had a chance to settle in, his worst fears were realised. In January 1936 he

---

[1] 1894–1960. Equerry and Assistant Private Secretary to George V 1920–36. He became Private Secretary to Edward VIII in 1936, and to George VI 1936–43. In 1944 he succeeded his father as second Baron Hardinge of Penshurst.

travelled down to Norfolk to take up his new job, but by the time he reached Sandringham the King had already lapsed into his final illness.

To Letty Benson

7 January 1936   *Sutton Waldron House*

My dear Letty, I think I shall have to give up being inoculated against colds. Since I took to it, six years ago, I have never (touching a whole forest) had colds; and if I had one now and then, I should think oftener of you – rheumily, perhaps, but gratefully. As things are, a handkerchief has almost come to be just a thing that lives in the pocket and doesn't come back from the wash. It has become prosaic; it has lost (pardon, My Lady) its rheumance.

Still, one can't do without them, can one? And you may be sure that your six white virgins have come to a happy home, and one where they are very welcome. Thank you.

I start my first spell of Sandringham in the middle of next week, not without some misgiving. What a wrench you gave to the wheel of my destiny that afternoon you came to tea in Savile Street in November 1920. I suppose it was all for the best. A happy new year to all of you.   Yours, Tommy.

To Joan

16 January 1936   *Sandringham*
                                                                      Norfolk

My darling, This is a rum place, all pitch-pine and trophies; it reminds me of Government House, Simla, as much as anywhere. Naturally I haven't seen much of it yet, and the outside not at all, but so far, there isn't anything to make one covet it as a home.

When I got to Liverpool Street, I found a first-class carriage reserved for me, which was highly embarrassing, as everybody stopped to read my name on the window, and stare at me like something new in the zoo, while all the guards hailed me as 'My Lord'. About half way down a young man appeared in the doorway of my carriage. I was about to tell him to go away when I recognised

192

him as the Duke of York.[1] He came in and sat with me for the rest of the journey, and was very amiable. I thought him much changed for the better since I last saw him eight years ago, but he put me in a bit of a hole by asking suddenly, 'What made you take this job?' – not an easy question to answer, to his father's son.

We arrived to find nearly an inch of snow on the ground. Claud[2] met us at the hall-door and I was set down to a belated tea with the Duke, the Queen presiding over us, while the rest of a large company resumed a game of 'Happy Families' with the York Children.

After tea I went off with Alec Hardinge to look at papers etc; dinner at 8.30 (Sandringham time[3]), all exactly like Government House. I had quite a cheerful meal between Lady Algy [Gordon-Lennox] and Claud; then a movie for the servants, which we all attended – quite a funny Tom Walls and Ralph Lynn film called 'Foreign Affairs', and bed at 11.30.

My bedroom, in the bachelors' wing, is a plain little room – I wouldn't give £15 for all its furniture: pitch-pine mantelpiece, ditto wardrobe and chest-of-drawers; black iron bedstead with brass knobs, one chintz arm-chair, but with a good fire and adequate writing-table. Engravings of naval battles, in maple frames, on a plain white paper.

The King – keep this strictly to yourself – is obviously not at all well; he has been in bed for two or three days, and not likely to leave it for some time. Luckily, Hewett[4] was staying in the house when he first felt bad; Dawson[5] is coming down tomorrow, by motor and a circuitous route, so as not to excite public alarm; so also is the Prince of Wales.

Hardinge says he has no temperature, and that if no congestion in the lungs appears in the next forty-eight hours, it may resolve itself into just a heavy cold. But they are obviously anxious about him, and say he is in a lower and more depressed state than they have ever seen him. I don't like the look of it at all. At his age, of course, and with his weakened constitution – apparently only half of each lung functions properly at the best of times – the machine might gradually run to a standstill at any time.

Meanwhile they are, wisely I think, going to put out a vague

[1] The future King George VI.
[2] Lord Claud Hamilton (1889–1975) was then Equerry to the King.
[3] At Sandringham all clocks were kept half an hour ahead of normal time to increase the amount of time available for shooting.
[4] Sir Stanley Hewett, 1880–1954, was Surgeon Apothecary to the King.
[5] Lord Dawson of Penn, the Royal Physician, 1864–1945.

communiqué to the Press tomorrow, to say that the strain of the Jubilee and of Princess Victoria's death[1] has told severely on him, and that he will not be able to make any public appearances for a long time.

Probably the guests who were due here next week will be put off, though I believe Princess Mary and the Duchess of York are coming anyway.

Now I must go to bed. Bless you, my darling.   Love T.

17 January 1936   *Sandringham*

My darling, On the whole, this is one of the least attractive places I have ever seen. House and demesne equally are unrelievedly grim. It is true that it has been a cheerless day, but in no circumstances can they be at all agreeable.

The whole place is suggestive of Iwerne[2] (without Iwerne's sur-roundings) on a large scale; moreover, a high road runs between the house and kitchen garden at a distance of about 200 yards, so that on that side at any rate there is little privacy. The shrubs, so far as I saw them in an hour's walk with Alec Hardinge this afternoon, are not exciting – just the ordinary things, berberis, myrtle, choysin, fancy hollies, variegated laurels etc. The country all round seems . . .

Midnight. I was interrupted by the Prince of Wales bursting in. Dawson of Penn came down with him. I fear it is very likely the King may die within the next few days. The machine is just running down, slowly but surely. He may hang on for some weeks; he may even make a comparative recovery; but at the moment everything points to the end coming before many days are out. His kidneys are hardly functioning at all, it seems, and he is very comatose; almost semi-conscious. The two doctors are excellent, and very calm; so is the Queen, though tonight at dinner she was obviously very strained, poor woman. After dinner we telephoned to various members of the family, and to the Press, the bulletin you will read in tomorrow's papers. I rang up Princess Mary and got her to come here tomorrow.

It has been a harrowing, anxious day, broken, as every death-bed and everything connected with the royal family seems to be, by occasional gleams of comedy. Anyhow, the Prince of Wales is far better prepared for a new life than he was seven years ago in

---

[1] The King's unmarried sister had died on 3 December 1935, to his great distress.
[2] Iwerne Park, belonging to the Ismay family, neighbours of the Lascelles' in Dorset.

Tanganyika! If the worst happens, I have no idea, of course, what my movements in the immediate future will be.

Goodnight, my darling. I wish you were here.   Love to all, T.

18 January 1936   *Sandringham*

Midnight

My darling, The King is no worse tonight – even, perhaps, a shade better. Princess Mary has arrived, looking very unwell, but, like them all, very cheerful outwardly. It has been a grim and monotonous day – doctors' bulletins to be given out and telegrams to be answered, and curious, unreal meals which convey no real hint of the fact that the King of England is dying in an upper room. We are all rather sad at the general demeanour of Edward VIII – especially myself, who had hoped for some alteration after eight years; but, *plus ça change* etc. However, I have put my hand to the plough – or walked into the cage – and I can't turn back now. If he asks me to stay on with him now, I feel I must do it, more than ever; for if the Crown is to survive the next reign, it will need honest men to hold it up, if ever it did.

The brightest spot in the day has been this delightful letter from old Lady Airlie, which touched me. I have answered her – I'm afraid there will be no Eastbourne now; it would have been fun if you could have come.

Goodnight, my darling. I miss you so much at these times, and wish you were nearer. Love to the children – I'll write to John at Eton. T.

Mabell, Countess of Airlie, to A.L.

17 January 1936   *Eastbourne*

My dear Mr. Lascelles, I cannot resist the pleasure of writing to tell you what a happiness it is to think that you have joined our *bande*. I was going to say *joyeuse*, but alas, I gather that it is not so at the moment.

It is wonderful to think that you are bringing your wide experience and many other even greater things into our midst. I do so look forward to seeing you soon. I wonder if you will come down here. My best love to your wife. I am here for about eight or nine weeks, *d.v.* God bless you.   Yours most sincerely, Mabell Airlie.

To Joan

18 January 1936   *Sandringham*

My darling, Not much more news this morning, but I think it looks pretty hopeless. Would you, as soon as possible, post me a pair of plain black morning trousers, which I am almost certain are in the bottom drawer in the big wardrobe in my dressing-room. If not there, they may be in that 'overflow' drawer of clothes which I dumped in the small spare bedroom wardrobe. They are of thickish black cloth with, I think, 'Anderson & Son' on the buttons.

    Poor Kipling – I am sorry he is dead.[1]   Love T.

PS Also send two of the white flannel shirts with a black stripe from left-hand small drawer in my big wardrobe, and two pairs of my dark woollen socks, top left drawer in the birchwood chest-of-drawers.

To Eric Mackenzie,
Comptroller to the Governor – General of Canada[2]

26 January 1936   *Buckingham Palace*

My dear Eric, I went down to Sandringham on the 16th for my first real contact since my appointment. Half-way down from Liverpool Street station the Duke of York, whom I had not seen for eight years, burst into my carriage and said, 'What's all this about the King not being well?' That was the first intimation I had that anything was amiss, and when the Duke went on to say that His Majesty's legs had swollen up the night before, I was full of misgivings, for dropsical symptoms are always the worst ones, I believe, in elderly people.

    When we got there, we found HM in bed; Stanley Hewett, luckily, was staying in the house as a guest. The swellings had gone down, and beyond a slight cold and catarrh, there was really nothing organically wrong; but both Stanley Hewett, professionally, and Alec

---

[1] Rudyard Kipling died on 18 January 1935.

[2] Colonel Eric Mackenzie (1891–1972): a close friend and former colleague in Ottawa, who stayed on when Tommy came home in October 1935. As Mackenzie had known George V and his family quite well, Tommy knew that he would be glad to have an account of the King's death and funeral; but this letter was intended to be strictly personal and private, and when Mackenzie had it duplicated, and sent to several leading Canadians in Ottawa, Tommy was not at all pleased.

Hardinge, as one who had observed him closely for years, were obviously very disquieted by the sudden 'going downhill' that had taken place and was still going on. Dawson of Penn arrived next day, and I may say I thought both these two doctors quite admirable in every way.

Within the next twenty-four hours, everybody, I think, had made up his or her mind that the King would never leave his bed, though naturally it was impossible to foresee how long it would be before the end came. He had no *illness* in the medical sense; the machine was just running down, slowly but surely – worn out by the after-effects of the Jubilee and Princess Victoria's death, which was a great shock to him.

The problem was, how to bring home to the world at large that he was really a very sick man without actually saying at any one moment that he was dying – for nobody can say that with certainty. This, I think, the bulletins did very skilfully, and the final ones, drawn up largely by Dawson of Penn, were admirably worded.[1] It was my task to extract these bulletins from the medicos, and to circulate them; my first call on the telephone was always to the Dominions Office, for a transmission to the Governors-General, so I hope you got yours ahead of the Press. Then began a flood of telegrams of enquiry, and we had not answered more than two-thirds of them before the enquiry became sympathy, and we had to begin all over again. Of the latter class, we had had over 10,000 by yesterday morning, and I should think one or two thousand more have come since then. At the Jubilee last year, I sometimes felt that Buckingham Palace ought to send all the overseas writers of such telegrams some direct acknowledgement from here; but now I am bound to admit this ideal is unrealisable.

At Sandringham, I scarcely left the house all the time I was there, so can tell you nothing about it, save that I am quite certain I should never want to live in that particular house, or in that particular corner of East Anglia. Here, I have been sleeping and eating in, and until today (Sunday) have hardly left my chair.

The story of HM's last words is, unlike most such tales, very nearly true. During the last few days, he was apparently in just the same state as a man coming out of an anaesthetic – a regular and peaceful coma, broken by rare intervals of semi-lucidity. During one such brief interval, during the last day, Wigram was in his room; the King recognised him, raised his head, and said the one word,

[1] The most famous bulletin was the last-but-one: 'The King's life is moving peacefully towards its close.'

'Empire?' – with a query in his voice that clearly meant, 'How goes the Empire?' Wigram assured him that all was very well with the Empire; the King smiled and fell back. This – I have it both from Wigram and from Sister Black, the King's faithful nurse – was his last attempt at conversation. He did actually speak again, for when the Privy Council, creating the Council of State, was held in his room, he did say, while he struggled to sign the order (his right arm was almost powerless by then), 'I am sorry to keep you waiting, you see I can't concentrate,' but that was only an almost instinctive and hardly conscious exhibition of courtesy that had been natural to him all his life. Sir John Simon,[1] who sat next to me at lunch twenty minutes later, told me that as they (Hailsham, Ramsay MacDonald, Archbishop of Canterbury and Simon himself) left the room, he nodded and smiled to them just as he always had at the close of an interview; his last words were really only an accompaniment of that gesture. So you can tell Canada quite truly that his last recorded thoughts were with his people overseas; and to me that proves how constantly his mind turned to them all through his latter years. For I am certain that when a man lies dying it is the cause, or the person, that has meant most to him in life, on which his failing mind fastens.

During his illness, I never saw him at all; but went up to his room after his death, and though, like all our generation, I have seen all too many dead men, none has ever had a more peaceful face. [The King died at 11.55 p.m. on 20 January.]

Next evening we took him over to the little Church at the end of the garden. A dark and windy evening, with flurries of rain; there were not more than a dozen of us, including the Queen and the family: the coffin was on a little wheeled bier, flanked by a few towering Grenadiers from the King's Company; somebody had an electric torch, which was our only light; Forsyte, the King's piper, led us playing a lament I did not know. As we came round the corner of the shrubbery that screens the Church, we saw the lych-gate brilliantly lit, with Fuller, the Sandringham rector, standing beneath it in his surplice and hood. There was nobody else in sight. The guardsmen, with scarcely a sound, slung the coffin on their shoulders and laid it before the altar; and there, after a very brief service, we left it, to be watched for thirty-six hours by the men of the Sandringham Estate.

I daresay that when the tumult and shouting dies, that little ceremony will remain in my mind as the most impressive of all.

---

[1] Sir John Simon was Home Secretary, Lord Hailsham Lord Chancellor, and Ramsay MacDonald Prime Minister. Cosmo Lang, Archbishop of Canterbury, became a central figure in the Abdication crisis later that year.

The departure from Sandringham was fine, too. The men – the Princes, Wigram, Claud Hamilton, Timmy Chichester, Harewood and I – walked across to the Church. The ladies – the Queen, Princess Royal, the three Duchesses, Lady Desborough, Lady Elizabeth Motion – drove, and we met them at the gate. After a short service the coffin was laid on a gun-carriage, and we, with the King's white shooting-pony, walked behind it to Wolferton station on a perfect winter's morning. The road was lined with people, six and seven deep, all the way. At the top of the hill leading down to the station, a single cock-pheasant rocketed across the road, very high, and immediately over the gun-carriage. All the way to London people were standing bare-headed by the track, on the roads and in the middle of the fields. At King's Cross I left them, and drove back here with the Queen and other ladies.

Tonight – Sunday – I took Joan and Lavinia to the lying-in-state, about 10 o'clock. Do not think we walked in the queue, for before dinner the end of the queue was reported by the police to be crossing Putney Bridge (about 2½ miles away). Billy Gore[1] had kindly fixed up that anyone with a Buckingham Palace Pass could get in at the back of Westminster Hall. This we did without any trouble, and stood on that raised balcony looking straight down the hall for about half an hour.

It was a very wonderful sight, the hall dimly lit and vaguely full of mist, with the two unending streams of people passing the crimson Catafalque, with its four guardsmen at each corner, four Yeomen below them and four Household Cavalry at the north end. But the thing that struck me most was that, all the time we were there, I heard no sound of a human voice, save an occasional whisper from one or other of the shepherding policemen. Silence as unbroken as that, from a London crowd, which had been many hours in the streets, is a very solemn thing.

Thursday will be an ordeal. I think we leave here about 8.45, and our walk from Westminster to Paddington takes two hours, in full uniform. We have another walk from Windsor Station to St. George's Chapel. The Earl Marshal and his heralds seem to have made a good job of the arrangements, which is to their credit, seeing that they have not had to organise a Sovereign's funeral for twenty-five years.

[1] William Ormsby Gore, 1885–1964, later fourth Baron Harlech, was then First Commissioner of Works.

PARTING OF THE WAYS

Tommy later saw 1936 as a nightmare; but in the turmoil of the new reign, he had no thought of resigning again. As he wrote later:

Looking back, I don't believe I could have done anything but what I did then – namely, to wait upon events. At such a time junior members of the Household cannot walk out on a new King because they happen to have disapproved of the Prince of Wales; moreover, I had to think of my colleagues: for months we were all working at high pressure with the business of a new reign.

Thus he worked for Edward VIII throughout his tenure of the throne, and in the summer sailed with the royal party aboard the yacht *Nahlin* on her voyage down the coast of Dalmatia. Although for months he and his colleagues had seen the Abdication crisis looming, when it finally burst upon them in November the shock was so great that he went out and walked round St. James's Park in the dark for more than an hour. Stanley Baldwin, the Prime Minister, told Tommy that he was so shattered by the news that he went straight to bed.

The official memoranda and reports which Tommy wrote during the year are not available for publication; but his own disillusionment comes out vividly in a letter home.

To Joan

23 November 1936   *Buckingham Palace*

My darling, He is going. He is unshakeable in his determination to go the whole hog, and having realised that it can't be done here, has definitely stated his intention of handing over. I understand he is impervious to any argument, and says quite frankly that the other thing comes first, and all the rest – and what a vast rest it is – nowhere.

It will happen quite soon, it seems – in a week or ten days; and at present only twelve people in the world know that it is imminent, so please be extra-careful of this letter. Although we have been thinking of the possibility all these weeks, it is a great shock to me now it has come. Apart from any personal feelings – inevitable after knowing him so long – I am ashamed that this thing should happen in England, and sad that such an immense store of affection and goodwill should be turned to ashes. Though I have little doubt that the change is ultimately for the best – I am inclined to think that as the years went on, the Hyde side would have predominated more and more over the Jekyll – the pity of it all is heart-rending – and, though probably the great majority of people will heave a sigh of relief the world over, there are obvious dangers in a sudden, sensational and utterly unprecedented change like this.

He will be the most tragic might-have-been in all history. Nothing but his own will could have saved him, and the will was not there; no human being, other than himself – and of course, herself – could have averted this dreadful thing. The future, naturally, is obscure. Indeed, we know few details beyond the bare fact that the decision is made and will be put into effect as soon as possible; the reason for it – there is only one – will be made clear in a public statement. 'I cannot have my cake and eat it – I chose to eat it,' in fact.

Our position here is very difficult. We have, with our right hands, to carry on as if nothing were happening, and at the same time prepare, as best we can (without, of course, stenographers or telephones, even) for what *is* going to happen. At such a time one can't raise questions of one's own future – nor, indeed, could anybody answer them yet. But I feel quite confident that the new man will want me to stay on, and I have, of course, no reason not to do so. I have never made any secret of the fact that Hyde's way of thinking was not mine, and can claim that I was one of the first to prophesy this ultimate disaster. Nor do I doubt that, once the transition period is over, life here will be far more satisfactory than it has been during this nightmare year.

No, I'm not worried about our ultimate future, but I am about the immediate future – about whether I can get away next week. If the bomb is going to burst then, I know you'll agree that I must be here – it will be as bad as the old King's death, and worse – because nobody will have the faintest idea what to do next! Such a thing hasn't happened since Richard II, and that is rather a long time ago.

I hate to think of your wrestling with the final clearance alone, and have been racking my brains to try and find some way of postponing the Marsdens' arrival, but without success.[1] On the other hand, it is very probable that the inevitable delays will crop up, and the final disclosure may be put off till after next week. If so, I could come, I hope, though I'm anxious about G. standing up – he is suffering great pain from his elbow, and is, naturally, terribly upset by this news. If he breaks down, I must stay here. Anyhow, unless the actual 'day' is 2 or 3 December, I trust I could get down for one day and drive up with you – not that that would be much help, I fear.[2]

Darling, this is a very woolly letter. I've been constantly interrupted, largely by people ringing up about arrangements for the Midlands tour, in which I have to pretend to be still interested; and tomorrow afternoon, I've got to spend at the People's Palace, planning a function which will never take place – not in this reign, anyhow. I do wish you were here, and it's no use telephoning because I can say nothing.   God bless you, my pretty. T.

Joan Lascelles to A.L.

24 November 1936   *Sutton Waldron*

My darling, It's almost impossible to visualise your news. Though as you say one had contemplated the possibility, it's very different to the reality. It makes one feel rather like the old Scotch lairds must have felt in '45, when they suddenly found a trusted relation or neighbour had turned traitor to the cause. It gives one a queer feeling in the pit of the stomach. However much one had suspected treachery, one would never want to believe it possible till faced with the facts. One also feels how wrong and undignified to have waited till now and not to have faced up to the issue earlier in the day. However – it's no good dwelling on all this, and better soon than wait for some almighty bloomer or scandal. But it's pretty trying for all of you at the moment.

Our possessions are now in manageable order, and I don't much mind where we dump them! Bless you, my darling, and don't worry

---

[1] They had let Sutton Waldron and were about to move back to London.

[2] In the event the Instrument of Abdication was signed, and the King's announcement read to the House of Commons, on 10 December.

about me or the future. I'm feeling quite fit and not at all tired. Must stop now.   All my love, Joan.

The Abdication finally severed Tommy's association with Edward; but, as he had hoped, he got on well with 'the new man', and served King George VI – first as Assistant Private Secretary, then as Private Secretary – throughout his reign.

The story of how the former King went into exile as the Duke of Windsor need not be repeated here. Yet there is one point that should be clearly established.

Over the years the Duke became increasingly embittered by the hostility of his family, the Court and the Government; he could neither understand nor forgive his brother's refusal to help him, or to grant the Duchess the title of Her Royal Highness, which he felt was her due. In his anger and frustration at being cold-shouldered, he persuaded himself that one of his principal enemies at Court was Tommy, who (he told friends) hated him, and whom he went so far as to describe as an 'evil snake'.

Tommy did not hate him at any stage of their ten-year association – and the Prince's own animosity was something entirely new. As Tommy himself wrote, even after the showdown of his resignation in 1929, Edward bore him no malice whatever:

While I was in Canada, he twice sent me messages to say that he would be glad to take me back whenever I wanted to come; and when I returned to England [in October 1935] talked away as if nothing had happened.

Later, Tommy added that although he had 'wasted the eight best years' of his own life in the Prince's service, he felt no bitterness towards him personally, 'for in all the years of our association he never said an unkind word to me.' What he could not stomach – any more than Edward's mother Queen Mary or his brother George VI could – was the former King's gross dereliction of duty in abandoning the throne of England.

This was the essential difference between the two men. Tommy was a stern moralist, impelled by an unbending sense of duty. Edward – in his view – had no sense of duty at all. So it was that Tommy wrote, of 'probably the most spectacular, the most discussed personality with whom I shall ever be in intimate association':

'If I am in any way inclined to judge him harshly, it is solely because he did great wrong to England, and to himself.'

INDEX

INDEX

Brown, Harry Atherton, amateur jockey, 12 and n.

Bruce, Hon. Randolph, Lieutenant-Governor of British Columbia, 66 and n., 69

Buchan, John, first Lord Tweedsmuir, Governor-General of Canada, 170 and n.; A.L.'s memorandum for him, xiv, 170–85; letter to A.L., 188

Burden, Mr and Mrs James A., 21n., 23, 144

Burke, T., English tenor, 52 and n.

Burkett, Dr, 84, 85

Byng of Vimy, Viscount, Governor-General of Canada, and Lady Byng, 33, 45 and n., 176 and n.

Cacouna, the Lascelles' summer cottage in Canada, 150

Cairo, 79, 81; Tutankhamen's trophies, 81

Calgary, 56, 57; Stampede, 174

Campbell, George, child specialist in Ottawa, 184

Canada:
Prince of Wales's visit (1924), 17, 32–46
his visit (1927), 49–73; Diamond Jubilee celebrations, 49
1931–35, 127–88; Honours List controversy, 162; political situation (1935), 168; A.L.'s memorandum for John Buchan xiv, 170–85

Canadian National Railway, 41, 46

Canadian Pacific Railway, 41, 53, 67, 68, 70

Carlyle, Thomas, 145

Carnarvon, fifth Earl of, and Tutankhamen's tomb, 83 and n.

Carter, Howard, archaeologist, 83n.

Cecil, Algernon, 147 and n.

Cecil, Lady Guendolen (née Osborne), 147 and n., 148; correspondence with A.L., 147–8; death, 147

Chadwyck-Healey, Chubby, 82 and n.

Charteris, David, twelfth Earl of Wemyss, 167 and n.

Charteris, Frances (née Tennant), 149n.

Charteris, Hon. Guy, 149 and n., 150

Charteris, Laura, 150

Charteris, Martin (Lord Charteris of Amisfield), 167 and n.

Chelmsford, first Viscount, father-in-law of A.L. Viceroy of India, xii, 1–2, 7, 38, 56n., 112; death, 129

Chelmsford, Viscountess, 111, 112, 129

Chicago, 33, 43

Child, Sir John, Bt., ADC in Canada, 130n.

Chilton, Sir Henry and Lady, 20 and n., 35

Churchill, Diana, 134

Churchill, Randolph, 132 and n.; causes resentment in Canada, 132–3

Churchill, (Sir) Winston, 52, 132n., 134 and n.

Clanricarde, second and last Marquess of, xii, 101

Clarke, Charles Cowden, 98n.

Collins, Dale, US novelist, 20n.

Coolidge, President Calvin, 21

Cooper, Lady Diana, 18 and n., 20 and n.; in *The Miracle*, 18n.

Cooper, Duff (Viscount Norwich), 18n.

Craig, Gordon, 78n., 79

Cranford (Mrs Gaskell), 179 and n.

Cromer, second Earl of, Lord Chamberlain, 190; letters to A.L., 190, 191

Cruikshank, Ronald, journalist, 142 and n.

Curzon, Lady Alexandra (Baba), 35n.

Dawes, Charles Gates, US Vice-President, 54, 55

Dawson of Penn, Lord, Royal Physician, 193 and n., 194, 197

Delamere, third Baron, 90 and n., 103

Delamere, Gladys, Lady, 90 and n.

Desart, Earl and Countess of, 8

Desborough, Lady, 199

Detroit, 33, 41; Ford Works, 41

Devonshire, ninth Duke of, Governor-General of Canada, 176 and n.

INDEX

Devonshire House, Piccadilly, gates in Long Island, 144

Dickens, Charles, 173

Dinesen, Izak, *see* Blixen, Karen

Dodoma, Tanganyika, 109, 110

Donaldson, Frances, 50

Duchess of Richmond, SS, 130

Dudley Ward, Mrs Freda, mistress of Prince of Wales, 99 and n., 100

Duncan, Isadora, and her children, 78 and n.

Durnford House, A.L.'s preparatory school, 142n.

East Africa:
Prince of Wales' visit (1928), 74–115; A.L.'s proposals for tour, 74–7; Egypt, 79–82; Kenya, 90–1, 96–104; Uganda, 90–6; Tanganyika, 104–9; safari, 104–9; tour halted at Dodoma by news of the King's illness, 109; Prince returns to England, 110

Edmonton, Alberta, 56

Edward VII, King, 168

Edward VIII, King, and Abdication crisis, 200–3; *See also* Wales, Edward, Prince of *and* Windsor, Duke of

Edward VIII (Donaldson), 50n.

Egypt, 79–82; the Pyramids and the Sphinx, 81, 82

Einstein, Albert, 90

Elcho, Lady, *see* Benson, Lady Letty

Elcho, Lord (d. 1916), xii n.

Eldoret, Kenya, 97

Elephant-hunting in Uganda, 92–5

Elizabeth II, Queen, 159, 167n.

Empress of Australia, SS, 51

Empress of Scotland, SS, 51, 71

Entebbe, Uganda, 90–1, 96

Enterprise, HMS, 110

Erskine, Tommy, ADC to Viscount Byng, 45

Escrick Park, York, 64, 66

Eton College, 7, 144, 159, 163, 166, 167n., 169

Fairs, 'Punch', real tennis champion, 24

Farouk, King of Egypt, 161n.

Finch-Hatton, Hon. Denys, pilot and hunter, 102 and n., 105–7, 107n.; killed in air crash, 107n.

Fishing in Canada, 40–1, 57–8, 104–5, 128, 135–8, 150–8, 182–3, 185–7

Fleischmann, Louis, 23

Forbes, Rosita, 83 and n.

Forbes-Adam, Irene, *see* Lawley, Hon. Irene

Ford, (Sir) Edward: tutors John Lascelles, 159–61, 163; and A.L., 160, 161; tutor to future King Farouk, 161n.; Assistant Private Secretary to George VI and Elizabeth II, 159

Fort Erie, dedication of Peace Bridge, 53–4

Fuad, King of Egypt, 80 and n.

Fuller, Rev. A. R., Rector of Sandringham, 198

Fuller, David, ADC in Canada, 130n.

Gandhi, Mahatma, 16

Gaskell, Mrs Elizabeth, 179n.

Geneva Conference (1927), 49, 54

Gentlemen Prefer Blondes (Anita Loos), 145 and n.

George V, King, xiii, 2, 8, 34n., 139n., 144, 163, 171, 184; and the Prince of Wales, 1; and the US Press, 17, 28n.; grave illness (1928), 109–14; convalescence, 120; Silver Jubilee (1935), 169, 194, 197: A.L. as Assistant Private Secretary, 188–96; illness and death, 192–8, 201; lying-in-state, 199; funeral, 199

George VI, King, 159, 203
see also York, Duke of

George, Prince (Duke of Kent), 73, 199; in Canada with Prince of Wales (1927), 49, 57, 58, 66, 68

Gilbert, Betty, 25

Gittings, Robert, 98n.

Gloucester, Alice, Duchess of, 199

Gloucester, Duke of, *see* Henry, Prince

Gordon, Jeanne, operatic singer, 52 and n.

Gordon Ives, Gwladys (Sally), lady in waiting to Lady Bessborough, 159 and n.

Gordon Ives, Victor, 159–61

206

INDEX

Gordon-Lennox, Lady Algy, 193
Gore, John, 5, 138, 139, 140n.; letters
from A.L., 128–33, 140–3, 145–9,
162–5, 182–5; references to A.L. in
Sphere, 140, 148–9
Goschen, David, 126n.
Goschen, Sir Edward, 20 and n.
Goschen, Gerard (Bunt), 20n., 34 and
n., 38, 123, 126, 149; marriage to
Vivienne de Watteville, 124–5
Gowers, Sir William, Governor of
Uganda Protectorate, 91 and n.,
92–4
Grand Cascapedia River, 152
Grant, Jos, 98n.
Grant, Nellie, 98 and n., 112
Grey, fourth Earl, Governor-General
of Canada, 176 and n.
Grigg, Lieutenant-Colonel (Sir)
Edward (Lord Altrincham):
Military Secretary to Prince of
Wales, 3, 74; Governor of Kenya,
74; and Prince of Wales' tour
(1928), 74, 84, 103, 106; letter from
A.L., 74–7
Grigg, Lady, 77, 97, 103

Hailsham, first Viscount, 198 and n.
Halsey, Admiral Sir Lionel, 2 and n.,
4, 14, 34n., 64, 70, 95, 104, 121,
138; with Prince of Wales in South
Africa, 47, 48; in Canada, 58; falls
out with Prince, 58, 64n., 69; and
A.L.'s resignation, 116–17, 119, 120;
letters to A.L. 117; views on the
Prince, 117
Hambleden, Lady, 164
Hamilton, Lord Claud, 193 and n.,
199
Hardinge, Alec (second Lord
Hardinge of Penshurst), 191 and
n., 193, 194, 196–7; letter to A.L.,
191
Harewood, fifth Earl of, xi, 4,
7 and n.
Harewood, Florence, Countess of, 8
and n.
Harewood, seventh Earl of, 7n.
Harewood, sixth Earl of, *see* Lascelles,
Viscount
Harewood House, 126, 144, 167

Hassanein Bey (Pasha), Sir Ahmed
Mohamed, 80 and n., 83–4; and
Rosita Forbes, 83; his travels, 83
Headlam, Maurice, 135 and n.; letters
from A.L., 135–9, 150–9, 185–7
Hearst, William Randolph and the
Hearst press, 32, 37 and n.
Henry, Prince (Duke of Gloucester),
15, 199; in East Africa (1928), 74–5
79, 81, 90; A.L.'s view of him, 90
Herbert, A. P., 137
Herridge, Canadian Minister in
Washington, 130
Hertslet, Austin, 191
Hewett, Sir Stanley, Surgeon
Apothecary to George V, 193 and n.,
196
History of Henry Esmond Esquire
(Thackeray), 69, 70 and n.
Hoare, Sir Reginald, 79 and n., 81
Holiday Fisherman, A (Headlam), 135n.
Hope, Anthony, 167n.
Hornby, Geoff, England polo player,
25
House of the Arrow, The (Mason), 20
Howard, Sir Esmé (Lord Howard of
Penrith), British Ambassador in
Washington, 17–18, 22 and n., 32;
and Lord Wimborne, 27, 28, 33,
35
Hurndall, Major, 30
Huxley, Aldous, 134n.
Huxley, Elspeth, 98 and n., 101n.,
107n.
Huxley, (Sir) Julian, 140, 169 and n.
Hyde Park Street, the Lascelles' home
in, 87, 101, 123

India, Prince of Wales's visit to
(1921–2), 1, 3–6
Irish-Americans, 36

Jasper Park, Alberta, 33, 40, 139
Jex-Blake, Dr and Mrs, 90
Johannesburg, 103
John Keats (Gittings), 98n.
Jungle Books (Kipling), 175n.
Jupiter River, Canada, fishing in, 128

Kaisar-I-Hind, SS, 77, 82
Keats, John, 98 and n., 144

INDEX

211

INDEX

Uganda, 90–6, 103; up-country, 91–5; elephant-hunting, 92–5

United States: Prince of Wales's visit (1924), 17–32; Wall Street crash and Depression, 133–4

United States Press and the Prince's visit, 17, 28, 31, 32, 36–7

Urquhart, F. F. (Sligger), 160

Vancouver, 33, 41, 42, 59, 64, 69, 78, 169

Victoria, British Columbia, 33, 42, 46, 53, 64–7, 70

Victoria, Princess, death of, 194 and n., 197

Victoria, Queen, and John Brown, 151

Voltaire, holograph letters of, 144

Wales, Edward, Prince of (King Edward VIII), (Duke of Windsor), xii–xiv; tours of the Empire, 1; in Australia and New Zealand (1920), 2; in India (1921–22), 1, 3–6; his Staff, 2–3; A.L.'s admiration for, 3; and Fruity Metcalfe, 4; riding risks, 10–13; letters to A.L., 14–15, 46–8, 73

visit to USA and Canada (1924), 17–46; and the US Press, 17, 28, 31, 32; and polo in USA, 27; in New York, 31–2; in Canada, 32–46; his ranch in Alberta, 32–5, 39, 40; in South Africa (1925), 47–8

visit to Canada (1927), 49–73; and Baldwin, 49–50; irresponsibility and immaturity, 50; the ranch, 53, 56–8; and the Peace Bridge, 54–5; Ottawa speech, 65, 69; A.L.'s disillusionment with him, 50, 69, 71

visit to East Africa (1928), 74, 115; names A.L. as executor of new will, 81–2; elephant-hunting in Uganda, 92–5; and Mrs Dudley Ward, 99 and n., 100; safari, 104–9; shoots lion, 107; behaviour on news of the King's illness, 109, 112, 195; hurried return to England, 110–12; further letters to A.L., 113, 121–2;

and A.L.'s resignation, 119, 120; interview with him, 119–20; and George V's last illness and death, 193–5, 199

See also Edward VIII, King *and* Windsor, Duke of

Washington, DC, 21, 22, 31

Watteville, Vivienne de, 124; letters from A.L., 124–5; marriage to Bunt Goschen, 124–5

Wenlock, Constance, Lady, aunt of A.L., 8 and n., 10, 64, 82–3; death, 139, 141–2

White Star Line, 41

Whitney, Harry, US polo player, 25

Wigram, Clive (Sir) (first Lord Wigram), Private Secretary to George V, 3 and n., 139n., 162, 189, 190, 197–9; letters to A.L., 120–1, 190

Willingdon, Marchioness of, 56 and n.

Willingdon, first Marquess of, Governor-General of Canada, 56 and n., 181

Wilson, Sir Matthew (Scatters), 9 and n.

Wilson, Pete, hunter in Uganda, 92–4

Wimborne, Ivor Guest, first Lord, uncle of Joan Lascelles, 23 and n.; and English polo team, 23 and n., 25–8, 34n.

Winnipeg, 33, 34, 71, 174

Winnipeg Free Press, 178

Windsor, Duchess of, 203

Windsor, Duke of: embitterment, 203; animosity towards A.L., 203

See also Wales, Edward, Prince of *and* Edward VIII, King

Winthrop, Mr and Mrs Roger, 23, 25, 31

Woods, Arthur, 37

Woodside, Long Island, 21 and n., 22–32

Woolf, Virginia, 110 and n.

York, Albert, Duke of (King George VI), 15, 90 and n., 193 and n., 196, 199

York, Duchess of (Queen Elizabeth the Queen Mother), 194, 199

York House, St James's, 2, 4, 87, 129

Zulfikar Pasha, 80